In the Theater of Love

Rediscovering the Exceptional Shakespeare

Thomas Brackshaw

Copyright © 2025 Thomas P. Brackshaw

All rights reserved.

No part of this book may be reproduced, scanned, or distributed in any printed or electronic form without permission. Please do not participate in or encourage piracy of copyrighted material in violation of the author's rights. Purchase only authorized versions.

Library of Congress Control Number: 2025908054

ISBN:
(Paperback)   978-1-7367522-8-9
(Hardbound)   978-1-7367522-9-6
(B&N)   979-8-9986663-0-8
(Kindle)   979-8-9986663-1-5

Author website and blog: https://ShakespeareByBrackshaw.com

To J. Arthur and Normand, the educators that sparked and encouraged my interest in Shakespeare, but most of all to my dearest wife, Maureen, for her patience and her support during the writing itself. Any wisdom within these chapters came through them to me.

Preface

Though teaching Shakespeare is itself a privilege, the initial rationale for this book was a simple desire to share more broadly my reasons for admiring his plays and the man who wrote them. Being a goal both too personal and too general for scholarly readers, the audience for such an endeavor defaulted to those intellectually confident individuals who, though curious about the plays, might very well be unschooled in the application of literary analysis. This crucial decision about audience carried several implications that couldn't be ignored. First, since familiarity with the plays could not be assumed, chapters on specific works would need a brief plot summary to provide context for the subsequent analysis. Second, an audience already anxious about Shakespeare's unfamiliar language and ideas would have no need for literary jargon and obscure historical or philosophical background. Clarifying the ideas conveyed by these works and the historical reasons they mattered to Shakespeare were the two guiding principles for each chapter. With those objectives in mind, the first chapter lays out the literary and sociopolitical trends that molded Shakespeare's assumptions about the world, the subjects that interested him, and how those ideas shape his art. Following that, close readings of each text illustrate how that worldview specifically affects his story. Relevant passages are always placed within the story's context and receive explanations that speak to common experience. The concluding chapter summarizes why the man and his work represent one of Western culture's important treasures.

Though the book's plan seemed quite logical, the final product has political implications not obvious to me at the beginning. While the motive and the intention for the project were both completely literary, my reading of the plays is difficult to reconcile with the political leanings of current scholarship which has little interest in determining

Shakespeare's message. The kind of literary analysis practiced in these chapters was abandoned and replaced by an effort to identify and expose textual evidence of Western biases still endured by various minorities. Liberals cheered the effort while conservative umbrage became increasingly strident. Because this book's arguments happen to align with culturally conservative ideas, they provide a convenient cudgel to use against dissenting viewpoints, an unfortunate and toxic byproduct of the current political divide. My non-political goal, to repeat myself, is simply to explain Shakespeare's relevance and defend the reputation he once enjoyed.

Though controversy may still be unavoidable, the risk of not making the argument is very real. I felt compelled to vigorously challenge prevailing opinions about Shakespeare's work because an *a priori* assumption about racial and gender attitudes consistently led to misreadings of characters and themes for what, rightly or wrongly, look like political ends. This is more than a simple disagreement about analytical methodologies or even politics. If Western culture, including its literature, needs re-evaluation, it's important for the process to be both honest and right. And what's happening to university English departments suggests scholarship is exhibiting neither of those traits.

The result of trends underway for at least five decades, the consequence of those prevailing critical viewpoints is examined in a 2023 *New Yorker* article by Nathan Heller grimly titled "The End of the English Major." Heller observes that the number of college humanities declarations has been falling at an alarming rate. Having spent a good portion of my education as a student of literature, I was both startled and curious at the same time. Statistics from a number of American universities detailed a steep decline in humanities majors. Several had already considered closing affected departments, a proposal eliciting woeful lamentations from the few remaining tenured faculty.

How did this happen? Very diligently, the author provided multiple reasons for this trend, including relentless tuition increases, the need to cater to prospective student interests, the lure of high salary careers in business and STEM occupations, the loss of federal and state funding, and the expansive goals of university administrators compelled to provide every possible educational and social experience the surrounding culture demanded. Briefly mentioned were the reported excesses of the New Historicism, self-inflicted by the same professors now protesting those evaporating majors and faculty positions. Firmly embedded in most humanities departments, this critical approach assumes Western literature, including Shakespeare, incorporates a variety of prejudices that deserve to be exposed, shamed, and eliminated.

My own tenure in graduate school occurred at the tail end of what was called the New Criticism, an analytical approach that correlated imagery and symbol to theme. The rigor of New Criticism's methodology produced many fine books about Shakespeare's plays, but its conclusions became too narrow and repetitive as a result of that rigor. Like all fashions, it eventually ran its course and was replaced by New Historicism, a term first used by Harvard's Stephen Greenblatt to describe an alternative approach to the evaluation of the Western canon. This school of critical thought operated with two basic premises. First, because an artifact's significance was a product of the historical milieu of both the artist and the critic, the text itself provided insufficient basis for analysis, a position that not only contradicted the methodology of my generation but justified historical inquiry as an essential element of textual study. Second, the significance of both the text and the analysis was relative to that historical context and therefore held no universally applicable value. This was a reaction against New Criticism's sweeping moral conclusions which, it was felt, needed to be replaced by a moral relativism championing acceptance and inclusion.

Since neither premise defined a rigorous methodology, however, the door was now open to every ideological breeze that blew through academic hallways. Feminism, Marxism, semiotics, anthropology and other ideological positions transformed literary criticism into the sociology and politics of existing power structures and their consequences. The movement's first salvos raised legitimate questions about how and why the literature commonly taught in universities had been written almost entirely by dead white men from western Europe, and what that implied about our cultural biases. The most obvious consequences of this examination have been twofold: first, it opened the canon to other English language authors, including women, people of color, and those with non-standard sexual orientations; second, it validated the conviction that authors of the older, accepted canon could and should be judged on their failure to recognize their underlying assumptions about imperialism, race, gender, and sexuality.

While the first of these consequences has certainly been worthwhile, the second has effectively served to discredit authors like Shakespeare for holding viewpoints for which their culture offered no alternatives. While New Historicism asserts that that is precisely the problem, their judgments have served as an indictment not only of that older, established canon of authors but of an entire history and culture that failed to identify and correct those biases. Everywhere these once heralded artifacts refused to be accepting or inclusive enough for modern tastes served as proof of Western culture's moral failures. Where those failures could be documented there was reason to devalue that artifact's worth. Nothing was sacred, not even Shakespeare.

Whatever a person thinks about their merits, those premises were implemented at a cost. "Contemporary critics pride themselves on their power to disenchant," one disgruntled student observed in a conversation with Heller. Given that atmosphere, the only significant interest an author like Shakespeare now inspires are the handful of characters supposedly corroborating the perception of Western culture's incipient biases. The death of English as a major should not have come as a surprise. After all, what possible logic could justify studying irrelevant artifacts where disenchantment is the prevailing message conveyed to still impressionable minds? Students cannot be expected to respect, let alone appreciate, subjects their teachers themselves see little reason to respect or love. This reduction of Shakespeare's power to inspire is the problem this book was written to address.

The hunger for something more than disenchantment is there, waiting for nourishment. Mr. Heller interviewed numerous students who, despite enrolling in business or STEM or pre-med disciplines, still seek out the occasional literature or history course. Though these classes are viewed as "easy" and lacking the discipline of quantitative measurements, such students acknowledge a hunger for a different kind of relevance than the one provided by subjects whose only promise is a lucrative salary or job security. One young man interviewed had eagerly read *Don Quixote* and hungered for other difficult texts; another young lady was drawn to *Pride and Prejudice*.

Even for these novitiates, the relevance of the old canon was still detectable and accessible. Doesn't this self-motivated searching imply that professional educators have failed utterly to explain the value of studying literature, new as well as old? When New Historicism's conclusions about Western prejudices predetermine what is historically relevant and what isn't, it appears very much like the cart is leading the horse. No one, not even a supremely gifted writer like Shakespeare, can communicate what they cannot possibly know. Instead of permitting contemporary ideology to determine what values should or should not be operative in an artifact, an examination of the historical context out of which a given text emerges seems far more honest and productive. Only then can the artistry and the relevance of those communicated values be accurately assessed. The best examples of New Historicism, like Jonathan Bate's two excellent books on the influence Latin classics exerted on Shakespearean drama, do exactly that.

Nor have the tenets of New Historicism been met with unanimous agreement, either. Harold Bloom's iconoclastic *Shakespeare and the Invention of the Human* took up residence on the *New York Times* Best Seller list despite his obvious displeasure with the ubiquitous premises of his academic colleagues. Though I disagree with Bloom's key assumptions about the plays, I greatly admire his unabashed love for Shakespeare's art. It's a refreshing change from a critical school that ended up glorifying an aggressive tolerance at the expense of a supposedly intolerant past. While *The Merchant of Venice*'s Shylock suggests Shakespeare may have shared some of the same antisemitic prejudices as his Elizabethan audience, his relevance, it seems to me, has very little to do with his racial, sexual, or religious biases, whatever those might actually have been. Since very little historically verifiable evidence about his life actually exists, the most reliable information we have about his beliefs must be gleaned from his plays and poems. Admittedly, facts about the milieu and the culture can provide some basis for understanding those texts, but what student are crying out for requires critics and teachers to engage in the hard work of finding relevance and the beauty of artistic cohesion. Whatever his shortcomings, that's the goal Bloom strives for, and it's what those few interested students hope to learn from their teachers.

Beauty and relevance are surely there in the relationship of Shakespeare's Romeo and Juliet, whose star-crossed love redeems a city at war with itself; in Hamlet who desperately searches for a way to turn revenge into something more like justice; in Desdemona, Cordelia, and Cleopatra who want nothing more than for the men in their lives to comprehend what love requires and promises. Throughout his career, Shakespeare struggled to accommodate every form of human desire into the moral framework of his faith, which considered desire the origin of most sins. Resolving the inherent moral contradictions of desire, which can lead to either good or bad consequences, became the driving force behind his major works. The effort to explain the nature and consequences of desire took Shakespeare on a very detailed journey into the conflict between good and evil. It's in that effort to accommodate desire that Shakespeare's lasting relevance can be found, for every age endures the same struggle to understand the causes of evil and what its presence says about human nature. And about those enduring verities that inspired individual lives as well as the great literature of the Western canon.

I'm well aware that part of art's magic is how it inspires us to think beyond the ordinary, that it fires off bright sparks of multiple, creative interpretations. New Historicism has had its successes. But like any other art, Shakespeare's plays deserve to be judged on what he tried to say through them, not on what we think he ought to have said. While there's certainly a place and a time for honest cultural self-evaluations, Shakespeare's plays, I would argue, incorporate a vision of human life that deserves admiration and respect precisely because they still have the power to enchant. A critical approach that loses sight of that is on a different mission entirely, one that is being harshly but properly evaluated by its prospective students.

Table of Contents

The Theater of Love 4

Romeo and Juliet 25

1 Henry 4 45

As You Like It 74

Hamlet 99

The Merchant of Venice 122

Twelfth Night 144

Othello 166

King Lear 187

Macbeth 221

Antony and Cleopatra 249

The Tempest 284

The Rarer Action 313

The Theater of Love

In the four hundred years since his death, Shakespeare's work has benefited from a wide variety of critical interpretations which, with very few exceptions, exhibit a shared respect and admiration for the plays and poems. But that exceptional Shakespeare has disappeared, buried under an avalanche of scholarly work inspired by Harvard's Stephen Greenblatt and collectively labeled New Historicism. In those past efforts to understand what his plays meant, generations of Shakespeare commentary examined character, plot, theme, and the moral significance of his plays. Greenblatt's army of academics, however, felt getting to his truth from a period and culture drastically different was basically impossible. Since textual meaning could never be understood in the same manner an Elizabethan would, scholars should not pretend they could see or explain that truth. Though the plays were Elizabethan, textual meaning belonged to the critic's period and place, and what New Historicism's scholars cared about was the way modern prejudices evolved out of economic, political, and social power structures, and those prejudices inevitably found their way into Western literature, including Shakespeare's.

This is the background to Farah Karim-Cooper's recently published *The Great White Bard*, which sets out to unravel the once idolatrous worship of Shakespeare's artistry. Though her stated goal is to make Shakespeare accessible to a culturally diverse audience, she describes a pre-modern Europe beginning to identify itself as separate and superior to populations inhabiting newly discovered continents. Many of the West's durable prejudices take root from this milieu, she postulates, and these affect Shakespeare's depictions of the Egyptian Cleopatra, of the Jewish villain, Shylock, and of the few non-white characters like Othello and Caliban, the uneducable primitive from *The Tempest*. Several pages of Karim-Cooper's book, for example, speculate how Globe actors may have constructed a prosthetic nose sufficiently Semitic to telegraph Shylock's villainy to a Christian audience eager for his religious comeuppance. Though such speculations show her intended audience is popular rather than scholarly, her conjectures draw from the same research her academic colleagues had developed and for the same reasons. If prejudice infects the Great White Shakespeare, this is sufficient proof bias and exclusion permeate every other area of Western culture as well. Eager to correct this cultural elitism, Karim-Cooper recommends casting excluded minorities in unexpected roles to break down unacknowledged racial, gender, and religious barriers. What's gained from this is a supremely talented Denzel Washington playing Macbeth. Noticeably infrequent in Karim-Cooper's book, however, are references from the play's text because Shakespeare's meaning is considered no longer accessible or very important. Because the only available significance now comes from a perception of history where inclusion and acceptance are greatly valued, her readers are left with a very diminished replica of a once exceptional Shakespeare.

Not only is this faded image dull and uninspiring, but, as the following chapters will show, it depends on misleading interpretations of many of the characters cited by Karim-Cooper and others with similar convictions. For a writer long considered crucial to any understanding of Western culture, a defense of Shakespeare's intellectual and moral relevance may therefore be overdue. Perhaps he did share his countrymen's antisemitic assumptions, but his consistent engagement with the complex morality of love and desire is far more prominent and deserves at least equal if not more attention. It is in that thematically rich nexus between desire and love, in fact, where a more inspiring perspective on his art can be found. Lamented by Ovid and vilified by Christian apologists, both important Elizabethan influences, the ambiguous nature of desire became the muse inspiring much of Shakespeare's dramatic art. While celebrated in the comedies, these topics eventually took him deep into the tragedy of evil and the fragile, wonderful discipline of mercy commended in the late romances. Though not the only concerns occupying his curious, intelligent mind, love and desire are never very far from his thoughts, and until a post-modern culture holding simplistic notions of beauty, sex, and romantic relationships understands the way his art is shaped by those forces, they will continue to find his most beloved plays obscure, difficult, and unworthy of much attention.

His body of work provides many reasons why the Globe deserves to be recognized as the theater of love. A quick overview of Shakespeare's literary output suggests the notable significance he gives to love and desire throughout his career. In his twenty-one years as poet and playwright, he wrote two minor epics, a collection of one hundred and fifty-four sonnets, and several other published poems. Popular enough to burnish his literary credentials, his poems address those two subjects extensively. The same attention to love is evident in the theatrical world where he is largely or entirely responsible for thirty-six, full-length dramas. Leaving aside several Roman plays, a few satires, his ten histories on the civil strife ushering in the Tudors, and a few late-career collaborations, the remaining dramas are primarily concerned with desire, romantic attraction, and the many other ways love and desire are manifested. That means almost twenty plays out of thirty-six are devoted to the subject.

In the annals of Elizabethan drama, this concentration on love is itself quite remarkable. By way of contrast, his main theatrical rivals, Christopher Marlowe and Ben Jonson, seem quite uninspired by the subject. Marlowe's reputation rests on his mellifluous rhetoric and an interest in the sin of pride while Jonson's main talent was satirizing human folly. Since so much of Shakespeare's work is focused on love and desire, the considerable number of plays devoted to these ideas is fertile ground for any number of interesting conclusions. Typically, however, individual plays are treated as unique, unrelated entities. While this has produced many first-rate books and articles, Shakespeare's very personal but evolving moral view of characters energized by attraction eludes this methodology. As history, biographical inference, as well as textual evidence begin to build out an understanding of this unique worldview, seemingly unrelated plays begin to show interesting thematic connections. Quite remarkably, what is discovered in one play supplements and clarifies the next one, each iteration bringing the author's guiding worldview into better focus. Particular plays, it turns out, gain additional clarity from an appreciation of their predecessors and contemporaries. The working critical assumption of these chapters, therefore, is that every play considered contributes to an understanding of each succeeding one.

Not enough is known about Shakespeare's personal life to explain why desire and love were such important topics for him, but several literary and cultural trends likely influenced his treatment of those subjects on stage. A story so important to an understanding of his drama, however, really begins with his poetry. When the plague temporarily closed London's theaters, Shakespeare supplemented his income with those minor epics and sonnets, some of which incorporated the conventions of Courtly Love. Established during the Middle Ages by French aristocrats, they developed a narrative for romance that codified an enduring set of mannerisms and assumptions about courtship. For poets, the literary posture known as Courtly Love provided a framework of easily recognizable romantic conventions that eventually became quite familiar to literate Elizabethans. The narrative emphasized the necessity of male humility and courtesy toward the object of his desire which, because the relationship involved an unattached man and a married woman, could never be consummated. To skirt the moral difficulties of illicit love, the resulting protracted courtship employed a vocabulary that turned love into a sort of ritualized religion. Conventionally, the woman remains cold and indifferent to her lover's fruitless pleas for satisfaction while the man, reduced to her humble and obedient servant, waits for her to satisfy his desire. Patiently enduring his sexual frustration, the man inevitably suffers alternating bouts of despair and hope (Lewis 2). Though French in origin, these conventions find their way into the Arthurian legend of Lancelot and Guinevere, into Chaucer's retelling of *Troilus and Cressida*, and into the popular Elizabethan sonnet sequences, including Shakespeare's. In Courtly Love's narrative, demure feminine chastity confronts male erotic passions that taint her ardent protestations with a coy blush of embarrassment. Though her virtue is unassailable, she is still flattered by his attentions which, sadly, win nothing but her affection and pity.

Though these poetic conventions carry over into Shakespeare's plays, their influence is often more subtle than obvious. Having reached the twilight of their appeal, Shakespeare works to refashion them into something fresh and remarkable. The early tragedy, *Romeo and Juliet*, is so delightful in large part because the entirely conventional language of his young lovers sets them apart from the angry voices dividing their respective families. But rather than a celebration of a love that is adulterous, illicit, and unrequited, as Courtly Love requires, his young lovers confirm their devotion through marriage and suicide. Tragically, a commitment forged in the heat of erotic desire inexplicably leads to death. The formula alters once again in *As You Like It*, where he gently mocks Courtly Love's absurdities as Orlando roams Arden Forest tacking fevered sonnets to his beloved Rosalind on every tree. To put their relationship on firmer ground, she schools her idealistic suitor with protracted and irreverent lessons about women. As she wittily replaces her man's naïve fervor with a more realistic assessment of the feminine, Rosalind reveals not only how deeply she loves Orlando but also how much she wants this relationship to last. She thus becomes the paradigm for Shakespeare's best heroines, all of whom teach their men the finer points of genuine love.

While the language of Courtly Love facilitates some of the emotional distinctions Shakespeare cares about, one other aspect of these conventions seems to have made a far more significant impression: the respect accorded a woman of virtue. The tension in Courtly Love between male passion and female chastity is never resolved in his favor, largely because feminine integrity did not allow her to violate her marriage vows to the unnamed husband. Though she is human enough to be flattered by his pleas, she maintains a position of moral superiority by resisting the temptation of male passion. Shakespeare, however, awards his most beloved female characters a different kind of moral superiority. Instead of unshakeable chastity, they are resolute for the relationship with the men whose passionate desire quite magically wins their hearts. Very often, these men struggle to fully comprehend the commitment they've miraculously inspired, but these are women who, like the Rosalind of *As You Like It*, know how to bring their men into a fuller, richer love. With women characters who are anything but helpless, Shakespeare replaces a commitment to virtuous chastity with a far more compelling commitment to relationship.

This paradigm of the strong, emotionally intelligent woman is repeated throughout the plays. In his last great tragedy, *Antony and Cleopatra*, the Roman Antony cannot decide where his loyalties belong until he is schooled in feminine constancy by a tawny Egyptian queen with a coquettish reputation. She proves her devotion by waiting patiently for his return from Rome where he has entered into a purely political marriage. That disintegrates with disastrous consequences when the sexual pleasure awaiting him in Egypt tempts the stoic Antony away from Roman responsibilities back into Cleopatra's arms. Though his return to Alexandria is entirely self-interested, the unwavering strength of Cleopatra's devotion eventually transforms his perception of her. Strikingly, rather than a moral impediment, the sexual nature of their relationship is an essential part of Cleopatra's love for Antony. Despite his suicide confirming his emotional bond to her, whether he ever fully understands either the strength or the value of her devotion is never very clear. For that reason, she alone reigns over the final act of this last, immensely moving tragedy.

Because Shakespeare's sexual morality is neither simplistic nor conventional, the Courtly Love battle between passion and chastity changes drastically. As his Cleopatra proves, Shakespeare's most admirable women characters do not fear and see no reason to resist being the object of male passion, welcoming the attention unreservedly. Nevertheless, his women are strong enough to insist love must still be experienced on their terms. Though male desire has transformed these women, strengthening their commitment to the men they trust will eventually acknowledge and value them, male emotional incompetence now represents the real impediment to relationships with the potential to enrich both. Precisely because of this brave acceptance of love's full complexity, however, his women earn what can only be described as reverence. Twice, that very special stature is given symbolic form on stage. It is there in *Romeo and Juliet* when a young girl, high up on her balcony, is wooed by a passionate young man standing below her in the dark. It is there a second time when Cleopatra draws a mortally wounded Antony up to her as she awaits his final kisses near the apex of her pyramid. In both scenes, the physical elevation of the women above their men is symbolic of their emotional stature, and until their men comprehend the miraculous constancy of feminine love, their unexamined erotic passions continue to deform how these women are perceived and, unfortunately, why they are misvalued.

As many critics have noted, Shakespeare's women resonate with audiences in ways his men never do. Though his male characters may rule empires or defend wealthy cities, they simplify desire to the erotic, a misreading that renders them emotionally stunted, indecisive, easily jealous or angry, and slow to understand what the beloved is offering. His women, on the other hand, know how to respond to desire. No longer beholden to an abstract, asexual purity, they have a warm, unmistakable vitality because each one fully embraces their desire for union with the men they love. Despite the risk of a dangerously powerful desire that all too easily deforms male judgment, they trust and embrace love fully, joyful for its promised blessings. When Juliet warmly reciprocates Romeo's ardor, he quickly forgets his unrequited love for the emotionally distant Rosalind. As each one of Shakespeare's most beloved women responds warmly to male expressions of love, they become far more honest and believable than the women of Courtly Love. And their steadfast constancy, which requires empathy, patience, and a resolute commitment to forgiveness, is precisely why they earn the author's reverence.

While Courtly Love provided the language and a familiar narrative for addressing love and romance, Shakespeare's thinking goes far beyond the merely erotic dimensions of love into the moral dynamics of temptation and evil, subconsciously instilled by his schoolboy exposure to the very influential Roman, Ovid. Hoping to improve the rough diction and syntax of native writers like Chaucer and Spenser, the Tudors promoted the elegant Latin of authors like Ovid whom the royals had come to admire. In this effort to improve English rhetoric, young Elizabethans translated selected passages of *The Metamorphoses* from Latin into English and then back again. During these rigorous, often tedious exercises, however, students inadvertently encountered stories about an unfortunate mortal's transformation into a lovely flower or star after an unwelcome sexual encounter with an amorous pagan god (*Shakespeare and Ovid* 21). In one fable, for example, the Roman god Jupiter assumes the guise of a gentle white bull to gain sexual access to the beautiful maiden, Europa. Having gained her trust, he carries her off to Crete where he rapes the unfortunate maiden. The name of a major continent commemorates her ordeal. *The Metamorphoses* repeats this story with different gods, different mortals, but always with the same outcome. More mature boys would also go on to translate Ovid's *Heroides*, stories of erotic passion's unpredictable power over women like Dido, eventually abandoned by her preoccupied lover, Aeneas, to a life of relentless sorrow and pain. Where Courtly Love recognizes feminine control over the romantic battlefield, Ovid is all about a sexual energy that obliterates every pretense of control, something that greatly complicates the emotional and moral dimensions of sexual relationships. As the plays will show, these mythological fables had an effect on Shakespeare that was deep, profound, but eventually quite troubling as well.

    Something about Ovid's style makes these fables seem playfully frivolous, but they are a serious effort to describe an inexplicably hostile world in which sexual desire inflicts great suffering on the helpless. Throughout Ovid's work, erotic desire is shown to be a force that has neither origin nor morality but simply exists, a mysterious force neither pagan gods nor ancient heroes could resist. Shakespeare's imagination seems to have been deeply struck by these stories of erotic desire's random, irrational, sometimes ludicrous, sometimes tragic power, a power manifested in two contradictory ways: on one hand, desire easily degrades both god and man into irresistible brutes who victimize the defenseless; on the other hand, the victims of this mysterious urgency are translated into lovely, poignant elements of the natural world. Over and over again in Ovid, erotic desire is both irresistible and transformative, ideas that reverberate throughout Shakespeare's work.

    For this and several other reasons, Shakespeare found his Roman mentor to be both an inspiration and a challenge: though they shared an interest in desire's effects, they differed in their moral and spiritual evaluation of its consequences. It is hardly an exaggeration, in fact, to suggest Shakespeare's artistic career at the Globe was a concerted effort to convey why the consequences of desire could be so disparate. Desire's capacity to degrade is evident in Shakespeare's very early minor epic *The Rape of Lucrece* where a despotic Tarquin stalks and violates the innocent Lucrece whose acute shame leads to suicide after she reveals the identity of her rapist. The intricate processes of desire's dark side are explored further in *Hamlet, Othello,* and *Macbeth*. But there's also another side to desire's transformative power which receives a far more encouraging treatment in *A Midsummer Night's Dream.* In this early comedy, an elf named Puck bewitches the fairy queen, Titania, who passionately woos Bottom, a rustic whose head now resembles an ass's after his own unfortunate encounter with the mischievous forest pixie. The delicate poignancy of a dainty but vigorously amorous Titania, blind to Bottom's abnormality, reveals the author's habitual sympathy for those afflicted by desire's arbitrary power. Similar to his very popular *Venus and Adonis*, the scene slyly reverses Ovid's dynamic, making the brutish Bottom the passive object of his female lover's furtive pleas for satisfaction. But the scene also demonstrates how passion's irresistible power easily deceives judgment into seeing beauty even in the grossest deformities. As Shakespeare's complex understanding of love begins to incorporate the inadequacies of language, vision, and reason, the magic in *Midsummer* becomes a prevalent Shakespearean metaphor for desire's disparate effects on the human imagination.

If a pagan from ancient Rome identifies the moral problem of desire for Shakespeare, it should not be too surprising that his answer develops out of the Christian faith that was such an integral part of Elizabethan life and culture. The way Christianity helped to resolve this issue, however, needs to be described from two different but interrelated perspectives, one historical and political which eventually had broad literary consequences, and a second inferred as unique and far more personal. The first of these, the historical and political environment of Elizabethan England, was succinctly described in a small, previously influential but now nearly forgotten book by E.M.W. Tillyard who documents just how influential orthodox Christianity remained in Shakespeare's lifetime. Many readers, Tillyard observed,

> . . . still think of the Age of Elizabeth as a secular period between two outbreaks of Protestantism: a period in which religious enthusiasm was sufficiently dormant to allow the new humanism to shape our literature. They admit that the quiet was precarious and that the Puritans were ever on the alert. . . . They do not tell us that Queen Elizabeth translated Boethius, that Raleigh was a theologian as well as a discoverer, and that sermons were as much a part of an ordinary Elizabethan's life as bear-baiting. (3)

In Elizabeth's pre-modern England, religion was indistinguishable from politics. Henry Tudor's break from a foreign pope unwilling to grant him a hoped-for divorce not only aligned England with the Protestant Reformation but simultaneously antagonized a Catholic alliance that included powerful countries like France and Spain. Even after the defeat of the Armada, a sense of imminent danger from Jesuit popery intensified Protestant zealotry which warned the queen her Anglican church was insufficiently vigilant for outbreaks of Roman idolatry and sin. Those tensions were greatly exacerbated by the shrill voice of Puritanism. S.T. Bindoff succinctly describes the troubled religious situation during her reign:

> Here was the real issue between Puritanism and Anglicanism, to which all else—sermons, sacraments, bishops, presbyters—was subordinate. The church of Puritan dreams would serve but one end, the greater glory of God, and live by one rule, the rule of the Scriptures. The Established Church appeared less concerned with seeking the kingdom of God than with supporting the Kingdom of England. It set uniformity before truth and conformity before conscience. (230)

This controversy between a politically established church and a growing minority of zealous believers gradually affected every aspect of Elizabethan life. Elizabeth attempted to accommodate the extremes by devising a middle way, the so-called Settlement of 1559, which formalized the religious split from Rome her father, Henry VIII, devised. In the end, though, this attempt to placate the Puritan elect stumbled over the issue of appointed bishops whose fealty to the queen looked uncomfortably like the fealty of Catholic bishops to a foreign pope hostile to the English crown. To question the bishops was to question the queen's authority to appoint them and, ultimately, the need for royal authority itself. Cromwell and the Puritan Revolution were not far off.

The effects of religious dissension were not only political, however. Similar fault lines appear in Tudor efforts to define an acceptable posture toward classical authors like Ovid whom they had purposely incorporated into educational practices to refine native literature and culture. While Chaucer and Spenser deserved recognition, neither measured up to the rhetorical elegance of classical writers. But in the volatile air of politicized religion, the pagan licentiousness of an author like Ovid became increasingly difficult to tolerate. Always useful and illuminating, Jonathan Bate observes that

> [t]he playful, polymorphous, polyamorous pagan gods were the

> very antithesis of Christianity's conception of the divine. In this respect, the iconoclasm of the Reformation was but a continuation and amplification of a process begun centuries before. Those painters and poets who located the source of their creativity in the gods and fables of classical antiquity inevitably found themselves at odds with that iconoclasm. . . .
> (*How the Classics* ch. 2)

Iconoclasm, the process of removing Catholic icons and murals from Protestant churches, represented an effort to cleanse that institution of what some considered temptations for idolatry. Urged on by prelates like Thomas Cranmer, parishioners removed statues from churches and whitewashed religious murals to appease the God of reformed theology.

Literature infected with classical licentiousness, the Puritans argued, needed to undergo a similar cleansing. If the humanists felt nothing could surpass the ideas and style of classical literature, the Puritans countered that Scripture contained truths the classics could never duplicate. The primary argument against the pagan writers was religious: where their gods are revealed to be "playful, polymorphous, polyamorous" beings, the Christian God was not only singular, unchangeable, and supreme but wholly concerned with nobler and worthier issues like justice, mercy, and redemption rather than gratuitous sexual gratification. This is the cultural context that explains why Milton, born within Shakespeare's lifetime, devotes his entire life and education to a Christian epic modeled on but meant to surpass Virgil; and it explains his vigorous support for a Puritan theocracy waging civil war against a king considered insufficiently zealous for the gospel. And it explains Shakespeare's increased attention to the moral as well as the spiritual implications of the desire that fascinated but saddened Ovid. The religious tensions within the Elizabethan political environment find their parallel in the tensions Shakespeare encountered as he tried to accommodate and resolve the moral problem Ovid raised. As the many Biblical references throughout the plays suggest, his resolution draws from the most familiar Christian source available.

Not everyone agrees, however. As brilliantly insightful and useful as his books are, Jonathan Bate holds a more typical view, seeing little evidence of Christian ideas in the plays. He positions Shakespeare squarely with the Renaissance humanists who found more inspiration in Ovid and Virgil than in scripture:

> Shakespeare's late plays, traditionally seen as his most spiritual works, take us to a number of temples, all of them ancient and pagan rather than Christian and modern: first those of Diana in *Pericles* and . . .Apollo in *The Winter's Tale*, then a trinity of shrines--to Venus, Mars, and Diana— in the final act of his final play, *The Two Noble Kinsman*. Add in the theophany of Jupiter in *Cymbeline* and the impersonation of Juno, Ceres, and Iris in *The Tempest*, and it becomes undeniable that Shakespeare's way of dramatizing divinity was more profoundly shaped by the humanist inheritance from ancient Rome than the modern contentions between Rome and Geneva. (*How the Classics* ch. 1)

While the classical allusions in Shakespeare are indeed obvious, the homage paid to Roman deities throughout the plays seems largely decorative compared to the subtler but far deeper influence Christian thought exercises. The mythology of *The Metamorphoses* is an effort to explain the relationship between the divine realm of the pagan gods and the natural world inhabited by mortals. But his depiction of the supernatural is not altogether praiseworthy and reflects an unrelenting pessimism about human existence. Aware of the possibility of salvation, of rescue from sinful desire, Shakespeare's depiction of the intersection between the human and divine remains far more hopeful and, strangely enough, far more tragic. In the face of divinity's sometimes terrible but always mysterious power, he somehow maintains a humble posture of wonderous awe, despite human suffering. That is the delicate balance that differentiates Shakespeare's tragedies from those of lesser dramatists.

Throughout the plays, Shakespeare's system of values remains profoundly and thoughtfully Christian. Yes, *King Lear*'s blind duke, Gloucester, ruefully observes that the indifferent gods of the universe playfully kill men for sport, but the expressed nihilism is countered by the very Christian kindness and mercy shown him by the son he had earlier rejected. As Alfred Harbage suggests in his reflections on Shakespeare's moral vision:

> If *King Lear* had meant to its audience what it is sometimes said to mean, there would have been panic at the Globe. The people there. . . did not want to hear that life is a tale told by an idiot or that clouds of glory trail in the Boar's Head Inn. They were not prepared for a two-hour operation in which old principles were cut away and new ones grafted in. They were too frugal to sacrifice to the day's entertainment the truths they lived by, and accept in exchange for sheer loneliness and fear. (*As They* 117)

Given the period's deep Christian roots and detectable evidence of a God who redeems in the plays, this seems eminently sane. Though modern, secularized man may promote the courage to confront a morally vacuous and meaningless universe, this was not how Elizabethans, including Shakespeare, saw man's place in the world. Harbage makes a far more compelling case because he accounts for the cultural assumptions of the period as well as the textual evidence. Shakespeare did not succeed artistically and financially by defying the moral and spiritual norms he shared with his audience. Quite the opposite, in fact. He succeeded by reminding them of the full implications of the truths that supposedly guided their daily lives. He used the stage to show them what they already accepted as right and good. Sure, the world was sullied by the consequences of undisciplined desires, but it also included brave men and women who lived differently, despite the risk and the cost. If there was dissension and despair, a fragile but visible good was cause for hope and joy. In the pervasively Christian Elizabethan environment, the Christian orthodoxies visible in the plays would not have been controversial in any way.

Even in the application of Christianity to his art, though, Shakespeare never seems restricted by the merely ordinary. Exploring why desire manifests in two morally disparate ways, one good, one evil, took his art past the conventional into the mysterious divine. What is it that differentiates one manifestation of desire from the other? Answering that question introduces the second way Christianity influenced Shakespeare's dramatic art. The parallels between the scriptural Fall and Ovid's fables where desire degrades and transforms are obvious. But Ovid and the pagans could only encourage stoic endurance to the inevitable pain of existence. Ovid's Roman mythology never addresses a purpose for suffering, never speaks of salvation, or of death as a transition into a different, perfected existence, all very basic and familiar Christian concepts. The faith Shakespeare lived and breathed described life much differently than a pagan Ovid could possibly have imagined. Providing a solution to suffering very different from Ovid's, the God of *Genesis* comforts Adam and Eve with a promise of eventual salvation from a life of sin, pain, and death, the grim consequences disobedience had earned. Part of Shakespeare's enduring appeal is not only his sympathy for human suffering and pain, which he shares with Ovid, but also a subtly expressed sense of another, more joyful dimension to life as well. That hope is most obvious in comedy's celebration of marriage and children, what Northrop Frye calls the mythos of spring regeneration. But it is also present, though less obvious, in Shakespeare's tragic art where death's ultimate metamorphosis conveys the spiritually rich meaning love and desire have for him. Limited only to the erotic, Ovid's work could never provide any comparable insight. Only Shakespeare's Christian faith could take him beyond Ovid's stoic endurance of the suffering inflicted by desire into the promise of love's joy, here in this world and incorporating even the erotic, which in essential ways reflects divine love. Though a conviction of a joy grounded in love and marriage is quite understandable in comedy, a similar conviction in his tragedies gives them a unique and incredibly poignant aura that no other literature, before or since, has duplicated.

In Christian literature, desire is treated with considerable ambivalence. In the Pauline epistles, for example, sexual desire is a temptation to be resisted, but if abstinence proves impossible then marriage is a tolerable second alternative. Other Old and New Testament passages demonstrate the danger of desire's temporary pleasures that easily distract from devotion to God and His commandments. Desire is the downfall of Samson, it causes David to murder the husband of his mistress, and it eventually brings a world-weary Solomon to his knees. As the *Genesis* story indicates, however, desire is also a gift from a loving God who understood Adam's need for companionship and comfort. Originally, it was pure and innocent and good. But the bite from the forbidden apple to acquire God's knowledge of good and evil is symbolic of all self-interested desires and initiates the irreversible expulsion from Eden and original innocence. The lesson from *Genesis* and other passages in scripture is clear: when desire is both self-indulgent and selfish, it becomes a dark, destructive force with devastating consequences. In Shakespeare's *The Rape of Lucrece*, Tarquin, the rapist, enjoys exercising his power, taking whatever pleasure is available for himself. His victim's welfare is of no consequence. Conversely, a habitual spirit of selfless generosity turns desire into love with all its attendant blessings. Exhibiting a generous heart, a worthy lover like the young Juliet wants her joy to be equally his. Repeatedly, Shakespeare asserts that generous selflessness is the only posture capable of transforming raw, selfish desire into love. This is so, thoughtful Christians like Shakespeare understand, because a loving God generously gave the world his son to reconcile his prodigal children to himself. This generous gift of love and mercy to the undeserving world is the model to be imitated, a proposition explored in *Measure for Measure*, a title derived from the seventh chapter of Matthew's gospel.

The promotion of generosity and the condemnation of selfishness is ubiquitous in Shakespeare. Though not a love story, *1Henry4* is an early assertion generosity is an essential moral obligation for right living. In this history, a self-indulgent Falstaff's insatiable, child-like appetite for pleasure threatens to derail Hal's royal destiny, one that requires sacrificing the pleasures Falstaff and others enjoy and take for granted. The argument is tied more directly to love in *As You Like It*, where the libidinous Touchstone pursues the innocent Audrey who will be discarded as soon as he has his way. His reductive desire deliberately contrasts with the romance unfolding between Rosalind and Orlando, which, though no less erotic, is guided by mutual interest and care. And then there's Malvolio, *Twelfth Night*'s puritanical steward who, having been tricked into believing his rich employer loves him, dreams of all the material and social advantages such a liaison would provide. Delusional and prideful, he of course fails in his quest for satisfaction. Repeatedly, a selfish desire to have what isn't currently possessed causes the tragic suffering of many of Shakespeare's male leads, including the Hamlet frantically plotting revenge, Othello desperate for assurance, the Lear hopeful for security and respect, and the Macbeth who wants Duncan's crown. The envisioned gratification is so seductive, these plays argue, that those unwilling or unable to exercise some moral self-awareness are doomed to inevitable and painful disappointment. Conversely, if selfishness is the root cause of sin, salvation must come in the form of generous selflessness, as seen in his most beloved women, Cordelia, Desdemona, and Cleopatra.

While the moral connection between love and generosity is important in both comic and tragic settings, tragedy's inevitable conclusion in death allows Shakespeare to suggest love's spiritual significance as well. Part of that significance is represented by the patient, admirable constancy of his revered women characters, attributes which Jesus celebrates in the familiar parable of the prodigal son from Matthew's gospel. There, a loving father graciously welcomes the son who left home and profligately squandered his inheritance. For the forgiving parent, the return home far outweighs the painful rejection of the son's leaving. This, Jesus is telling his followers, is what the Father's love looks like. It is patient, unwavering, forgiving, and unconditional. It is this kind of love, the New Testament argues, that distinguishes believers who model the Father's love from the rest of the world. And it is this kind of love that distinguishes Shakespeare's most endearing heroines from the men who are drawn into relationships by an overly simplistic understanding of desire. Shakespeare celebrates the emotional constancy of his loving heroines by suggesting their love not only reflects God's love but partakes of the same divine, eternal, loving, mysterious power that endures every tribulation, including death, and therefore has no bounds, no comprehensible limits. The most succinct and elegant statement this idea held for both his personal and professional life comes in his 116th sonnet, which celebrates God's love with the metaphor of a remote, unknowable but constant, guiding star whose light shines into the marriage of true minds. Without an acknowledgment of that love, the sonnet concludes, no man could write about love accurately or experience it in his life. For the tragedies, this notion begins as little more than a rhetorical flourish as Juliet's father's grief for a lost daughter finds expression in the metaphor of death as Juliet's lover. But the developing arc of this idea is worked out in each succeeding tragedy. It next appears negatively as the pearl that unites Claudius and Gertrude in death but appears again as the murdered

Desdemona's voice returning to protest her innocence. This dramatic metaphor is repeated a second time when Lear believes he hears the hanged Cordelia still softly calling him. It reaches its culmination in Cleopatra's dreamy reverie of her transformation into fire and air as death takes her to be Antony's loving wife. Often interpreted as strange and delusional, the repetition of this idea in each tragedy is evidence of the connection Shakespeare sees between human and divine love which Christians assert came into the world with the power to transcend death.

Despite the many classical references throughout the plays, Shakespeare holds his Christian beliefs with a light but very firm grip. Also evident in the epilogue to *The Tempest*, those shared beliefs and cultural values create an intimacy with his Anglican and Christian audience whose anticipated applause is seen as one final gift of mercy:

> . . . release me from my bands
> With the help of your good hands.
> Gentle breath of yours my sails
> Must fill, or else my project fails,
> Which was to please. Now I want
> Spirits to enforce, art to enchant,
> And my ending is despair,
> Unless I be reliev'd by prayer,
> Which pierces so, that it assaults
> Mercy itself, and frees all faults.
> As you from crimes would pardon'd be,
> Let your indulgence set me free.

Whatever Shakespeare may have been like in real life, his theatrical persona comes across as a completely humble, endearing, and gracious man of faith. Wrestling with the complex morality of love and desire took him deep into the causes and consequences of evil, but that journey also proved why generosity must transform desire into a love and mercy dimly reflecting God's much purer, completely unselfish versions.

So two very different views of Shakespeare's relevance coexist. In one view, the plays are pock-marked with multiple biases. As such, they are deemed less worthy of attention than more contemporary voices illuminating the painful consequence of those earlier injustices. This chapter has argued for another view. In the end, there's considerable irony in Karim-Cooper's effort to expose the incipient bigotry of a man who sees sin as the effort to obtain some desired advantage at someone else's expense, which is the very definition of bigotry. Even though the literary correction initiated by New Historicism may have been necessary, there's an unspoken but very real arrogance in the assumption the critic's view of the world is far more interesting and important than the one the author is trying to convey. The need for a more balanced critical assessment of Shakespeare's work should temper New Historicism's tone of indignant moral superiority. Hamlet was right: treat every man according to what he deserves and who shall avoid a whipping? If one idea deserves emphasis, it's that Shakespeare's complex worldview is cause for much pedagogical humility. That no one is without sin, biases included, is exactly why society is so desperately in need of rescue, why teachers and scholars can acknowledge Shakespeare's very human shortcomings without ever forgetting what also makes him extraordinary. When every facet of society is marked not only by bigotry but also by a tolerance for materialism, for a destructive sexual hedonism, for greed and amoral, cutthroat ambition, those bothered by such evils might actually find Shakespeare's antidote worthy of serious contemplation.

Romeo and Juliet

A year after the so-called Summer of Love, when sometimes violent protests erupted in opposition to America's military involvement in Vietnam, Franco Zeffirelli's gorgeous film version of *Romeo and Juliet* opened in theaters across the country. The timing was by no means coincidental. In the film's opening shot, dawn is breaking over a quaint Italian village still in deep shadow as a mellifluous voiceover recites the familiar prologue with exquisite diction. Set in Renaissance Verona, the story is a familiar tale of two feuding families, the Montagues and the Capulets, who fail to heal their differences until they have lost this "pair of star-crossed lovers" to their intransigent quarreling. Full of conflict, lyrical poetry, and passion, the story passes through hope into pathos, never failing to leave its audience moved by the tragic loss of what might have been. Capturing the detail as well as the spirit of the play, Zeffirelli's remake of this timeless story of love's triumph over violence perfectly captured the mood of the times,

Despite his fidelity to the original text of the play, however, what no one ever seems to notice is how unobtrusive the play's poetry seems to be. While credit belongs to both director and actors, that's the magic of a film so well done. Somehow, the rich visual and aural environment of Zeffirelli's film turns the play's poetic language into a seamless part of the experience. The difficult syntax, the imagery and metaphor, the repetition of phrases for rhetorical emphasis so bothersome on the page disappear into the rich tapestry of the cinematic fabric. It easily could have been different. Because the language, the characters, the events, even the way a scene like the balcony encounter is staged were all shaped by the poetic conventions of Courtly Love literature, *Romeo and*

Juliet's substantial debt to poetry is usually more obvious than in any other Shakespearean play. As C.S. Lewis's *The Allegory of Love* suggests, the literature of Courtly Love established a quasi-religious veneration of the virtuous and, therefore, physically unavailable lady who resists the tender overtures of a suitor too chivalrous to declare his desire explicitly (32). Conventionally, the lady is married, the wooing is tentative and secret, and consummation is impossible. In serving Arthur's wife, Guinevere, for example, Lancelot harbors a love both individuals recognize but which chivalric and marital obligations prevent them from ever enacting. In effect, Courtly Love ritualizes desire into courtship, and, as such, it constitutes the literary background for *Romeo and Juliet*.

Despite the poetic influences of Courtly Love, this early tragedy also owes a substantial thematic debt to Ovid whose fables depict the irresistible power of the erotic degrading both the gods and mortals into insatiable and brutish animals. But *Romeo and Juliet* changes the terms of both arguments substantially. Neither a conflict between Courtly Love's virtue and desire nor between irresistible erotic passions and their helpless victims, this early Shakespearean tragedy deliberately compares the benefits of young passions with the brutal, foolish and degrading violence of the juvenile feud. If hatred and violence degrade, diminish, and divide, love has a contrary capacity to enrich, unify and redeem. As an integral component of marriage, the play argues, sexual desire profoundly strengthens the bonds between the lovers, and it is their unshakeable commitment even unto death that shames the feuding families into a more neighborly peace. No longer virtue's antithesis but an extension of it, desire is sufficiently powerful to transform not only individual lives but society as well. This is an entirely different kind of metamorphosis.

Given that this is Shakespeare's second attempt at tragedy, *Romeo and Juliet* shows a remarkable advance over the earlier, very derivative *Titus Andronicus*, a far more difficult play to like. Instead of *Titus*'s bloody, vengeful protagonist, this play presents two young and innocent people, children, really, who refuse to take sides in their families' feud because they have fallen in love. In the play's moral and emotional opposition of civil strife and love, no one doubts that Romeo and Juliet have made the better choice, and because of their commitment to each other, as the chastened father of Juliet eventually acknowledges, they become "poor sacrifices [to] our enmity." Though the play alludes to the dangerous haste that results from passion, it mitigates that assessment of their culpability by laying most of the blame for their deaths on fate and the family feud. Motivated by wholesome and natural emotions rather than a morally repugnant desire for revenge, the play's two protagonists are effectively absolved of any wrongdoing and garner, therefore, a full measure of the audience's sympathy. Though the impulsive clash of teens on the streets of Verona does create exciting dramatic tension, the romance between these young innocents proves far more appealing than the play's violence. Absent any definable cause, the family quarreling makes no sense. Morally innocent love, which implies a possibility of healing and civic harmony, does.

    Besides the dramatic and lyrical presentation of pleasing subject matter, the play is also a structurally bold experiment that adapts a familiar comic formula for tragedy. The premise for many comedies is an authority figure who obstructs the desires of a young individual who somehow overcomes the hindrance by ingenuity or sheer persistence. Doing so releases everyone from unreasonable oppression so that joy and freedom are once again possible. Northrop Frye summarizes this structural principle of comedy as follows:

> What normally happens is that a young man wants a young woman, that his desire is resisted by some opposition, usually paternal, and that near the end of the play some

twist in the plot enables the hero to have his will. In this simple pattern, there are several complex elements. In the first place, the movement of comedy is usually a movement from one kind of society to another. At the beginning, the obstructing characters are in charge of the play's society. At the end, the device in the plot that brings hero and heroine together causes a new society to crystallize around the hero, and the moment when this crystallization occurs is the point of resolution in the action, the comic discovery. (*Anatomy* 163)

Here in *Romeo and Juliet*, youthful desire is hindered in several ways. First, the older generation's tolerance of the feud divides Montague from Capulet, Romeo from Juliet. In the famous balcony scene, both regret their surnames until Juliet resolves the dilemma by declaring that "a rose by any other word would smell as sweet" (2.2.44). Despite the lovers' optimism, however, the divide is not easily bridged.

The second obstruction is Capulet's effort to marry his daughter Juliet to the County Paris despite her resistance. The more she resists, the more belligerent he becomes. Both obstacles impede what everyone in the audience sees as the legitimacy of young, innocent but still secret love. That the lovers become sacrificial victims of these obstructions magnifies the pathos of their deaths. The moment of what could have been a comic resolution comes when, shamed by such a waste of youth, beauty, and love, the family elders recognize their fault and agree to reconcile. This adaptation of an essentially comic structure for a tragic purpose proved to be a brilliant and enduring modification. In only his second attempt at tragedy, Shakespeare is already moving beyond the Senecan formula that shaped *Titus* and trusting his instincts about what would please his audience.

Equally noteworthy, *Romeo and Juliet* very elegantly incorporates the language of Courtly Love, which entered the Elizabethan lexicon via the sonneteers. The assumptions and vocabulary of Courtly Love first appear in Sir Phillip

Sydney's very popular collection, *Astrophel and Stella,* but this sonnet sequence is widely imitated by Wyatt, Surrey, Sir Walter Raleigh, and by Shakespeare himself, an effort that had at least two consequences for this Courtly Love tragedy. First, the discipline of choosing words and metaphors concise enough to condense meaning into fourteen lines carries over into this exquisitely poetic play.

Second, Shakespeare gains a real appreciation for differentiating what is being emulated. Widely imitated, the overused tropes of the sonneteers eventually became stale and monotonous, and the challenge for Shakespeare, who explored the form some years after the fad had waned, was to inject it with fresh vitality. As a result, Shakespeare's sonnets will deliberately deviate from those conventions to revitalize the poetry. Where other poets address their verse to a coldly virtuous lady, Shakespeare addresses his to a charming but aloof man who refuses to get emotionally involved with women. Shakespeare complicates the picture further by introducing a dark lady who is anything but chaste and whose attractions create tension between the two men. But all these deviations from established poetic conventions only make sense because of the familiarity with the well-established rules of the courtly tradition. As Shakespeare had learned in grammar school, imitation and deviation need to work in concord. Both of these lessons have an effect on *Romeo and Juliet*.

That careful attention to language can be seen in the variety of rhetorical styles, particularly with Romeo, where it indicates his emotional development. Early in the play, before he sees Juliet and when he is still infatuated with Rosalind, he tries to define love to his friend, Benvolio, who wants to console him. Love, Romeo begins,

> . . . is a smoke made with the fume of sighs,
> Being purg'd, a fire sparkling in lovers' eyes,
> Being vex'd, a sea nourish'd with loving tears.

> What is it else? a madness most discreet,
> A choking gall, and a preserving sweet.... (1.1.190-194)

Because the artifice of Courtly Love takes the place of genuine emotion, a living, breathing Rosalind disappears from view. Little more than a construct of language, she is a figment of Romeo's fevered imagination. At this point, the speaker is young, emotionally infatuated, and knows nothing about the kind of self-sacrificing commitment that authentic love will eventually demand.

The language of love begins to change, however, when he first meets Juliet at the Capulet banquet. As the revelers dance, the lovers find a private moment. Now their exchange is poetry of an entirely different kind:

> Rom. If I profane with my unworthiest hand
> This holy shrine, the gentle sin is this,
> My lips, two blushing pilgrims, ready stand
> To smooth that rough touch with a tender kiss.
> Jul. Good pilgrim, you do wrong your hand too much,
> Which mannerly devotion shows in this:
> For saints have hands that pilgrims' hands do touch,
> And palm to palm is holy palmers' kiss.
> Rom. Have not saints lips, and holy palmers too?
> Jul. Ay, pilgrim, lips that they must use in pray'r.
> Rom. O then, dear saint, let lips do what hands do,
> They pray—grant thou, lest faith turn to despair.
> Jul. Saints do not move, though grant for prayers' sake.
> Rom. Then move not while my prayer's effect I take.
> [kissing her] (1.5.93-106)

Zeffirelli's movie, it must be said, captures the magic of this exquisite moment perfectly. Note that their dialogue is an embedded English sonnet, making the passage no less literary than Romeo's first definition of love, but it develops a religious metaphor of pilgrims and prayers that reflects the deeply felt reverence these two already have for each other. Romeo still assumes the Courtly Love role of the suitor humbled by all his mistress's many virtues, but the language has moved far beyond conventional infatuation. The emotions of awe and reverence and warmth evolve out of the anticipated relationship. Moreover, despite the artificiality of the language, it correlates seamlessly with the physical actions of the pair as they touch hands and take their first kiss. Language, action, and sentiment exquisitely combine to create emotional authenticity out of literary artifice. With complete assurance, Shakespeare uses Courtly Love conventions in two very different contexts to support dramatic intent. The contrast generates the meaning.

While *Romeo and Juliet*'s language derives from Courtly Love, it boldly deviates from other conventions, particularly the cold, unattainable lady. Although the feud and her father's desire to have Juliet marry the County Paris threaten to make her unattainable, as Courtly Love requires, the famous balcony scene demonstrates that Juliet is anything but reticent about her feelings for Romeo, who, standing below her balcony in the dark, has overheard what was intended to be a private profession of love. Her heart's secret revealed, she no longer has anything to hide. Translating the word "fain," which means "gladly" and the word "compliment," which means "customary behavior," will make the following passage clearer:

> Thou knowest the mask of night is on my face,
> Else would a maiden blush bepaint my cheek
> For that which thou hast heard me speak to-night.
> Fain would I dwell on form, fain, fain deny
> What I have spoke, but farewell compliment!
> Dost thou love me? I know thou wilt say, "Ay,"
> And I will take thy word. . . . O gentle Romeo
> If thou dost love, pronounce it faithfully;
> Or if thou thinkest I am too quickly won,
> I'll frown and be perverse, and say thee nay,

> So thou wilt woo, but else not for the world. (2.2.85-97)

Juliet is very different from the distant and unattainable Rosalind who frustrated Romeo earlier. Rather than resist, she is completely open to the prospect of being loved and giving love in return. The reluctant Rosalind contrasts with the eager Juliet who shares the innocent secrets of a young girl's heart, revealing a frank desire to be loved. Because of Rosalind's very conventional portrayal, Juliet's personality breathes with life and romantic enchantment. She is no cold, virtuous lady who spurns the advances of her lover. Romeo is her joy, and she is his.

Anyone who has loved deeply immediately recognizes the authenticity of this connection, but somehow Shakespeare makes room for their physical passion while very deftly maintaining their emotional innocence. He helps us appreciate their innocent sexuality by providing two additional, very bawdy perspectives on love. One comes from Romeo's friend, Mercutio, a relative of Verona's prince, and the second from Juliet's nurse, whose first speech quickly reveals her delightfully earthy personality. Lady Capulet, Juliet's mother, has entered her daughter's chambers where the nurse is attending her young charge. The nurse launches into a long speech where she recalls an incident from Juliet's early childhood when the girl could barely walk:

> . . . then she could stand high-lone; nay, by th' rood,
> She could have run and waddled all about;
> For even the day before, she broke her brow,
> And then my husband—God be with his soul!
> 'A was a merry man–took up the child.
> "Yea," quoth he, "dost thou fall upon thy face?
> Thou wilt fall backward when thou hast more wit,
> Wilt thou not, Jule?" and by my holidam,
> The pretty wretch left crying and said, "Ay."
> To see now how a jest shall come about!
> I warrant, and I should live a thousand years,

> I never should forget it. . . . (1.3.36-47)

Touching in its frank domesticity, the nurse clearly relishes her husband's earthy humor. Honest, good-hearted, and completely comfortable with things sexual, Juliet's nurse lacks any pretensions. Her mature, matronly humor provides one perspective on Juliet's innocent desire.

Similarly, Mercutio often spars verbally with Romeo, and, typical of young men, the humor is often about sex. After the encounter with Juliet at the party, Romeo eludes his friends to catch a glimpse of his new love. In the quiet darkness of the city streets, they call out his name in vain. Mercutio's voice is the loudest and most profane. He begins, of course, by mocking the conventions of Courtly Lovers:

> Romeo! humors! madman! passion! lover!
> Appear thou in the likeness of a sigh!
> Speak but one rhyme, and I am satisfied. . . .
> Speak to my gossip Venus one fair word,
> One nickname for her purblind son and heir,
> Young Abraham Cupid, he that shot so trim. . . .
> He heareth not, he stirreth not, he moveth not,
> The ape is dead, and I must conjure him.
> I conjure thee by Rosalind's bright eyes,
> By her high forehead and her scarlet lip,
> By her fine foot, straight leg, and quivering thigh,
> And the demesnes that there adjacent lie. . . .
> Ben. And if he hear thee, thou wilt anger him.
> Mer. This cannot anger him; 'twould anger him
> To raise a spirit in his mistress' circle,
> Of some strange nature, letting it there stand
> Till she had laid it and conjur'd it down.
> (2.1.7-26)

Like Juliet's nurse, such naughtiness offsets the purity of Romeo and Juliet's love. Following Mercutio's lewd humor, that distinction is sharpened by the balcony scene where the two young lovers, isolated from Verona's streets, meet very privately inside her garden walls. Quite appropriately for the mistress of a Courtly Lover, Juliet is elevated above him on her balcony.

By contrasting a noisy, bawdy street scene with a quiet, moonlit garden where two young lovers exchange vows, the setting itself becomes emblematic of Verona's two, very disparate views of romantic love. For the nurse and for Mercutio, love is either a matter of the flesh or, as the nurse's support shifts from Romeo to Paris, a pragmatic matter of availability. But the young lovers operate on a much different, far more elevated plane that is supported rhetorically as well as symbolically. The positioning of the lovers, he below, she up above, becomes a physical emblem of the relationship traditionally established by Courtly Love, which demands male reverence for his beloved. While physical longing is not denied, the emblematic setting gives their frank desire for union a patina of literary and moral legitimacy.

Quite subtly, the garden encounter implicates the limitations of Mercutio's purely sexual perspective on love. Just as their garden is worlds apart from the street, their love is not at all like Mercutio's or the nurse's. Reinforcing the imagery of pilgrims and prayers from their first exchange at the banquet, the garden setting and the language re-establish an atmosphere of reverence for this love that sets it apart from the bawdy, violent, all too normal world outside the garden walls. But the distinction between garden and street suggests a second, more dire implication. In a city beset by division and hatred, love's desire for union also isolates these innocents from the sinful world outside the garden. They are acolytes of a religion that, so far, boasts only two converts.

Just as Courtly Love acknowledges a tension between respect for feminine virtue and male desire, the reverent love of the balcony scene makes room, ever so lightly, for sexual passion. A bit frightened by her own boldness, Juliet gently tries to bring the encounter to a conclusion, but Romeo persists with just the slightest hint of sexual desire before they both retreat to emotionally safer quarters:

> Rom.   O, wilt thou leave me so unsatisfied?
> Jul.   What satisfaction canst thou have to-night?
> Rom.   Th' exchange of thy love's faithful vow for mine.
> Jul.   I gave thee mine before thou didst request it;
>   And yet I would it were to give again.
> Rom.   Wouldst thou withdraw it? for what purpose, love?
> Jul.   But to be frank and give it thee again,
>   And yet I wish but for the thing I have.
>   (2.2.125-132)

Though both seem aware of the physical implications of their love, they quickly turn away from that so they can first cement their commitment to each other. Whatever their emotional state, these young lovers never question that marriage provides the rationale for physical intimacy.

    In a garden sanctified by genuine love and separated from the world of the flesh, emotional bonding and marriage become the rightful premise for physical union. Unlike French, Italian and even most of the earlier English flavors of Courtly Love, where the woman's marriage to another justified her reluctance, Shakespeare's lovers accept marriage as proof of their devotion to each other. Breaking convention once again, Shakespeare's young lovers marry, exchanging the conventional pain of unrequited love for the joy of physical union.

    A bit later in the story, Shakespeare is quite frank about Juliet's sexual desire. Secretly married but before their wedding night, she eagerly awaits the arrival of her husband, whom the prince exiled for the revenge killing of Tybalt, Juliet's cousin and the murderer of Mercutio. Her anticipation of physical passion is unequivocal:

>   And Romeo
> Leap to these arms untalk'd of and unseen!

> Lovers can see to do their amorous rites
> By their own beauties. . . .
>   Come, civil night,
> Thou sober-suited matron all in black
> And learn me how to lose a winning match,
> Play'd for a pair of stainless maidenhoods.
> Hood my unmann'd blood, bating in my cheeks,
> With thy black mantle, till strange love grow bold,
> Think true love acted simple modesty. (3.2.6-16)

Shakespeare is very clear how important sexual desire and longing are in this love affair. In Juliet's reverie, the loss of virginity becomes a "winning match." Loss paradoxically leads to gain. Eagerly anticipating this rite of passage, she sees the wedding night's lovemaking as the actions of true love's "simple modesty." Based largely on the play's association of gunpowder with youthful passion, some have argued this overwhelming desire contributes to their deaths, but this does not seem to be what Shakespeare wants his audience to believe. As an integral part of nature's original design, desire is not something to suppress but, within the context of true love and marriage, actually enriches every dimension of love for both. No longer just a girlish, obedient daughter, Juliet has been transformed by Romeo's love which somehow increases her desire to share all she has and is with him. Emotionally overflowing, she wants to share the excess:

> My bounty is as boundless as the sea,
> My love as deep; the more I give to thee,
> The more I have, for both are infinite. (2.2.133-135)

In love's paradoxical reciprocity, the investments they make in each other multiply the benefits for both. Here as elsewhere in Shakespeare, abundance is the child of genuine love, which is a form of physical, emotional, and spiritual generosity. This is a theme that begins with his sonnets but appears in some form in multiple plays thereafter. Repeatedly, from these early plays through to his last effort, the paradoxical nature of love is that giving away everything constituting the self multiplies the many blessings that are showered upon the giver. Conversely, selfishness or an obsessive regard for self leads to crippling, spiritual poverty. This notion, a theme of Shakespeare's first eighteen so-called procreation sonnets, is only briefly alluded to here but gets much fuller treatment in *The Merchant of Venice*.

Having made his young protagonists largely innocent of any wrongdoing except, perhaps, undue haste, the sad demise of Romeo and Juliet could only be attributed to fate, as the prologue makes clear. Very succinctly, it establishes the play's tragic premise:

> Two households, both alike in dignity,
> In fair Verona, where we lay our scene,
> From ancient grudge break to new mutiny,
> Where civil blood makes civil hands unclean.
> From forth the fatal loins of these two foes,
> A pair of star-cross'd lovers take their life;
> Whose misadventur'd piteous overthrows
> Doth with their death bury their parents' strife. (1.1.1-8)

Anathema to New Testament Christianity, the revenge motif of a play like *Titus* was a dramatic vein that Shakespeare mined but quickly exhausted. Revenge and counter-revenge are the premises for the feud in this play too, and he would return to it one final time with *Hamlet* and for far sounder reasons. But *Romeo and Juliet* represents the beginning of his effort to find a more workable premise for tragedy than revenge. Here, the amorphous power of disaster victimizes the two young lovers, who remain largely innocent throughout. While this approach to the issues of tragic experience generates considerable pathos, *Romeo and Juliet* falls short, as the discussion of *King Lear* will show, of what is possible when suffering and death are more directly attributed to human culpability. In this play, Shakespeare seems content to wring as much pathos as possible from the opposition of a disruptive, evil feud with his innocent lovers.

As the prologue makes clear, a remote, nebulous fate is largely responsible for the play's tragic denouement. The hand of fate is evident when Capulet gives the guest list for his party to a servant who cannot read. By chance, he crosses paths with Romeo whose friends have just convinced him he should socialize more to get over the cold-hearted Rosalind. Perusing the guest list for Capulet's servant, Romeo decides to attend the banquet in disguise where he first sees the lovely and far more receptive Juliet. Fate steps in again when Juliet's cousin, Tybalt, kills Mercutio and is then killed by Romeo to avenge the murder of his friend. After the prince banishes Romeo, another mischance occurs when Friar Lawrence's letter explaining his plan to reunite the newly married couple never reaches Romeo who, based on his friend Benvolio's misinterpretation of events, believes Juliet is now dead. Resolute for death himself, he returns to Verona where the final misfortune occurs. Finding Juliet unconscious in the tomb, he drinks the poison he obtained just moments before Juliet awakens, and when she realizes what has happened she takes her own life as well. Except for the chance meeting at the banquet, which initiated their love, everything that could go wrong did go wrong. In the most uncomplicated but mysterious fashion, fate seems to have manipulated the outcome. Personal fault never sullies the two lovers.

Though later tragedies make irony and paradox far more prevalent than they are here, fate's numerous interventions in *Romeo and Juliet* still create ironic disparities between intention and consequence. After spending her wedding night with Romeo, for example, Juliet's refusal to marry Paris enrages her father, and he utters an ultimatum to her that, sadly enough, proves to be prophetic:

> . . . disobedient wretch!

> I tell thee what: get thee to church a' Thursday,
> Or never after look me in the face.
> Speak not, reply not, do not answer me!
> My fingers itch. Wife, we scarce thought us blest
> That God had lent us but this only child,
> But now I see this one is one too much,
> And that we have a curse in having her. (3.5.160-167)

Spoken out of the same kind of anger that fuels the warfare in Verona's streets, his words show the ugly, destructive side of human passion. If emotion propels the lovers toward disaster, at least those emotions contain the promise of abundance and joy. Though he dearly loves his daughter, Old Capulet's anger pushes Juliet toward Friar Lawrence's cell and the fateful plot that ends in death. The next time the father sees his daughter, she has consumed the friar's potion and, though still alive, appears to be cold, lifeless, and ready for the grave.

At this point, the play explains the coming catastrophe with a startling metaphorical association between love and death. At the discovery of her body on the morning of her wedding to Paris, old Capulet speaks to the prospective husband:

> O son, the night before thy wedding-day,
> Hath Death lain with thy wife. There she lies,
> Flower as she was, deflowered by him.
> Death is my son-in-law, Death is my heir,
> My daughter hath he wedded. I will die,
> And leave him all; life, living, all is Death's. (4.5.35-40)

Where the bridegroom Paris should have been one flesh with his newlywed Juliet, death is now personified as her lover. Death, not Paris, is his son-in-law and heir. But the association of love with death seems more than just an odd rhetorical flourish because it keeps appearing. After their wedding night, Romeo and Juliet indicate their reluctance to part with a beautiful Courtly Love *aubade*, a poetic set piece that announces the arrival of morning. Because any violation of Romeo's banishment is punishable by death, this tender and joyous moment is tainted with sadness. Juliet is divided between a desire for his company and her concern. Also reluctant to leave, Romeo bravely ignores any fears of death:

> Let me be ta'en, let me be put to death,
> I am content, so thou wilt have it so.
> I'll say yon grey is not the morning's eye. . .
> Nor that is not the lark whose notes do beat
> The vaulty heaven so high above our heads.
> I have more care to stay than will to go.
> Come, death, and welcome! Juliet wills it so.
> How is't, my soul? Let's talk, it is not day.
> Jul. It is, it is! Hie hence, be gone, away!
> It is the lark that sings so out of tune. . . .
> (3.5.17-27)

This strangely beautiful mixture of joy amidst the lurking presence of death foreshadows what is to come. Romeo does return to exile in Mantua, but like Old Capulet, the next time he sees Juliet, he will view what he assumes is her lifeless body, and the vision, though faulty, will lead directly to his suicide. His final words in the tomb continue to emphasize death as the amorous lover:

> Shall I believe
> That insubstantial Death is amorous,
> And that the lean abhorred monster keeps
> Thee here in the dark to be his paramour?
> For fear of that, I still will stay with thee
> And never from this palace of dim night
> Depart again. (5.3.102-108)

Upon waking and seeing Romeo's lifeless body, Juliet resolutely follows her husband. Kissing any unconsumed poison from his lips, then using his dagger to join him, she makes the metaphor of death as a loving paramour very real.

The physical union of their wedding night removes any fear of death and crystalizes the rhetorical into the actual. Marriage makes Romeo and his wife, Juliet, inseparable, a bond that lasts "even to the edge of doom." Catastrophe came as a result of fate, the stars, the feud, but also because a young boy and girl fell in love and, quite naturally, wanted to be together forever. Their hopes were fulfilled in a most unexpected and ironic way.

Though the death scene is absolute proof of the bond between the lovers, that commitment was by no means assured. For Romeo, banishment leads first to despair. Not until Friar Lawrence lists all the reasons for hope is he able to relinquish self-pity and comfort his wife:

> What, rouse thee, man! Thy Juliet is alive,
> For whose dear sake thou wast but lately dead;
> There art thou happy. Tybalt would kill thee,
> But thou slewest Tybalt; there art thou happy.
> The law that threat'ned death becomes thy friend,
> And turns it to exile: there thou art happy.
> A pack of blessings light upon thy back. . . .
> Get thee to thy love as was decreed,
> Ascend to her chamber, hence and comfort her.
> (3.3.135-147)

Convinced by the good friar's argument, he returns to her chambers for their wedding night where physical union confirms their emotional union. From that moment on, his commitment to her never wavers. Misinformed about Juliet's supposed demise, his response is swift and decisive: "Is it e'en so? Then I defy you, stars!" And a few lines later, he makes a grim but irrevocable vow with language newly available to him from their one night together: "Well, Juliet, I will lie with thee tonight."

Similarly, Juliet is tested when she hears that her cousin Tybalt has been killed by Romeo. Momentarily, her attachment to Romeo weakens. But when the nurse advises her to forget her husband and marry Paris, the prospect of such disloyalty to the man she has just slept with clarifies her resolve. After the nurse leaves, she vents her displeasure with the advice given. Though her words about the delightful nurse may seem overblown and harsh, they indicate her steely resolve to choose Romeo:

> Ancient damnation! O most wicked fiend!
> Is it more sin to wish me thus forsworn,
> Or to dispraise my lord with that same tongue
> Which she hath prais'd him with above compare
> So many thousand times? Go, counsellor,
> Thou and my bosom henceforth shall be twain.
> (3.5.235-240)

Later, alone in her chambers, she confronts and bravely overcomes a long list of her fears about taking Father Lawrence's sleeping potion. Thoughts of her husband steady her nerves. "Romeo, Romeo, Romeo! Here's drink—I drink to thee." And finally, like Romeo, her determination to join her husband in death beside his now lifeless body is unwavering, immediate, and absolute. In two short lines, the deed is done.

Both Romeo and Juliet pass from life into death as if death embodied their beloved spouse. Fear has been replaced by a longing for union that would have been unnatural and impossible before that fateful wedding night. Imagery, motivation, and action—like the kiss to find enough poison to die—all reinforce this association of death and love. Married, in love, and committed to each other body and soul, these two "star-cross'd lovers" in these circumstances could only end like this. As the play's prologue warned, their "death-mark'd love" was fated for a tragic end. With barely controlled anger, the prince has the final word:

> Where be these enemies? Capulet! Montague!
> See what a scourge is laid upon your hate,
> That heaven finds means to kill your joys with love.

>And I for winking at your discords too
>Have lost a brace of kinsmen. All are punish'd.
>(5.3.291-295)

A steep price has been paid for the sins of anger, pride, and negligence of what truly matters. The reconciliation between the families has come at the cost of two emotionally precocious children together with several of their kinsmen. As the families agree to erect golden statues of their dead son and daughter, the monuments are cold reminders of what has been lost and the pathetic futility of their commemoration.

Though an early play, *Romeo and Juliet* already exhibits several remarkable features that subsequent plays will develop further. Firmly rooted in the poetry and conventions of courtly love, *Romeo and Juliet* demonstrates the author's growing confidence in the potential of love as a subject fit for tragedy as well as comedy. It identifies multiple assumptions about love, from the reductively sexual, to the pragmatic, to the genuinely compelling, and these distinctions begin to shape his presentation of love going forward. And finally, that odd metaphor of death as Juliet's bridegroom becomes a fixture of later tragedies where the heroine's steadfast love becomes the power allowing her to transcend death into the divine realm of eternal life. Despite taking their final breath, Desdemona and Cordelia speak, and Cleopatra, imagining a final kiss from her dead lover, Antony, enters the realm of fire and air.

But within Ovid's fables, Shakespeare recognized that sexual passion functioned as love's driving force, a morally ambiguous power that fostered the blessings of romance and marriage or engendered the worst kind of irrational self-indulgence. While this play establishes a clear opposition between the sin of the feud's civil rancor and the healing power of romantic love, Shakespeare's plays will continue to explore the heavy penalty sin, rooted in self-indulgence, imposes on human relationships. And subsequent plays will also demonstrate a growing conviction that a love generously and freely given represents our only antidote to such evil. With increasing clarity and detail, he will explore the reasons and mechanisms for mankind's susceptibility to temptation, and why virtue is all too often the road less traveled.

Though the next play, *1Henry4,* explores a crucial period of English history, covetous desire largely determines the course of events. While morally complex circumstances tempt the aristocracy to take political authority that doesn't belong to them, a comic subplot indicts the selfish motives behind such ambitions. In that subplot, Sir John Falstaff's prodigious appetites impeach the aristocratic hunger for power. By showing how selfishness corrupts a culture where chivalric service had once provided social and political cohesion, *1Henry4* contrasts temptations of the flesh with the necessity for self-control, greed with generosity, and self-interest with a chivalry based on sacrificial service. Though a history play with no obvious connection to either erotic or romantic desire, these distinctions define a moral context for a conception of love that enriches, as Juliet proclaims, the more it is given away.

1 Henry 4

●●●●●●●●●

Refusing to chastise the young lovers for responding to erotic desire, *Romeo and Juliet* recognizes that the emotional impetus behind revenge degrades while a desire for union enhances life. But *Romeo and Juliet* never addresses the moral assumptions distinguishing the destructive from the affirmative manifestations of desire. Nor does it identify any culpability for the worse of the two possible outcomes. The audience simply witnesses how one set of behaviors leads to discord and death while the fragility of the other posture's brief moment of joy regenerates civic harmony.

While neither of those structural deficiencies detract from the pathos of this early tragedy, Shakespeare seems compelled to clarify the morality of human need in subsequent plays. Though it may seem incongruous to include a history play in a discussion of Shakespeare's evolving concern for the morality of desire and love, the Henriad, which includes *Richard II*, *1Henry4*, *2Henry4*, and *Henry5*, is very clear not only about what turns desire into sin but also what the consequences of that are and what is required to remedy such a choice. At the center of this moral problem is that delightfully funny character, Sir John Falstaff, who is the very definition of desire, need, and appetite.

While the entirely fictional character, Falstaff, is the personification of excessive appetite, the remedy for that sin is evident in the emerging authority of the Henriad's principle character, Prince Hal, who takes his father's place on England's throne and is responsible for reuniting England and France through military victory and marriage. The juxtaposition of the pleasure-seeking Falstaff and his erstwhile companion, Prince Hal, who lays aside his cherished friendships at the Boar's Head tavern and picks up his royal responsibilities when rebellion threatens, is a lesson in the personal sacrifices required of those who exercise political power. Though critics like Harold Bloom love Falstaff's childlike playfulness and decry Hal's eventual rejection of him as hard-hearted ingratitude, the prince's necessary self-discipline not only separates him from everyone else around him, including his father, the king, but establishes why the prince deserves to wear the crown his father stole from his morally weak predecessor, Richard II.

The connection between these histories and the other major plays about love is moral: the dynamic between a desire for power and the sacrificial self-discipline required to wield that power responsibly is identical to what Shakespeare considered the moral dynamics of genuine love. This accords with popular Elizabethan books like *The Mirror for Magistrates* which argue that personal virtue is the basis for political success. If Ovid teaches Shakespeare that human potential is deformed by undisciplined desire, the arc of Prince Hal's development argues that self-discipline and self-sacrifice are the necessary attributes of personal and political success. A form of generosity, self-discipline and self-sacrifice willingly surrender personal need for something greater than self, which is precisely what defines Shakespeare's most beloved heroines who remain steadfastly determined to transform a relationship crippled by male self-indulgence into something far richer. Like Hal, they refuse to accept what's merely pleasurable and transient in order to achieve a lasting good that benefits others. In these four history plays, then, Shakespeare begins to work out in greater detail the very moral worldview that affects every one of the remaining plays.

The Henriad describes the origins of the tumultuous War of the Roses during which the houses of York and Lancaster vied for the English throne. Lasting sixty-three years, it squandered treasure, lives, and political patience. As the conflict drew to a close, an exhausted England celebrated the Tudors for the order and stability they restored to the land. The protracted war profoundly changed England. Part of a national self-examination into the origins of that rebellion and its consequences, Shakespeare's Henriad acknowledges that England had gone through a significant transformation. As Alvin B. Kernan observed in his essay, "The Henriad: Shakespeare's Major History Plays":

> In the Henriad, the action is the passage from the England of Richard II to the England of Henry V. This dynastic shift serves as the supporting framework for a great many cultural and psychological transitions which run parallel to the main action, giving it body and meaning. In historical terms, the movement from the world of Richard II to that of Henry V is the passage from the Middle Ages to the Renaissance and the modern world. In political and social terms, it is a movement from feudalism and hierarchy to the national state and individualism. In psychological terms, it is the passage from a situation in which man knows with certainty who he is to an existential condition in which any identity is only a temporary role. (245-46)

These transformations in the way the world was viewed are the real subject of the four plays that comprise the Henriad. Each of the main characters, including Falstaff, provides a unique perspective on what those changes implied for Shakespeare's England. The pivotal moment in the transition from medieval to modern occurs in *Richard II*, the first play of the Henriad. Viewed from our democratic, secular perspective, the significance of that event is easy to miss, so it deserves careful attention.

As that play begins, Richard arbitrates a quarrel between Henry Bolingbroke, a Lancastrian, and the Duke of Mowbry, who had been implicated in the murder of Thomas of Woodstock, a distant relative of Bolingbroke's. Interrupting their medieval trial by combat, Richard banishes both men from England. His reason is unclear until later, when needing additional funds for his ill-conceived Irish wars, he rents out the lands of Bolingbroke's father without the banished duke's permission. To defend his inherited property rights, Henry returns from exile and is joined by other nobles who see Richard's actions as a threat to their own rights. Confronted by overwhelming opposition, Richard at first appeals to the medieval doctrine known as the divine right of kings in a feeble attempt to retain power. Basically, this was the conviction that kings, reigning supreme over their subjects, deserved the same absolute fealty God expected from His creation.

But religious principle provided meager refuge from aristocratic fear and outrage. Full of self-pity and long overdue introspection, Richard reluctantly relinquishes his throne to Henry and is taken off to prison where he is eventually murdered by one of Henry's supporters. Throughout, Henry is portrayed as a strong, decisive, authoritative figure, while Richard comes off as both weak and ineffectual. The next play in the Henriad, *1Henry 4*, picks up from this point, but Henry Bolingbroke's usurpation of Richard's throne spawns a series of unintended consequences that bring England out of its feudal past into the modern world. Not altogether sanguine, in Shakespeare's estimation, that process and its consequences are the subjects of *1 Henry4*.

Implicit in Shakespeare's complex treatment of these events are the feudal traditions of chivalry, an important part of the story's background. Though familiar to anyone who has read *Sir Gawain* or the tales of King Arthur and his knights, these stories provide a highly romanticized impression of the medieval aristocracy. Shakespeare's view of the matter is, as always, more nuanced, for he seems aware of chivalry's moral value as well as the reasons men defy them. As Johan Huizinga suggests in *The Waning of the Middle Ages*, this system of manners and morals emerged from an aristocratic warrior class that sought to obscure its sometimes less than savory actions with rituals, pageantry, and customs that idealized their lives (81).

Eventually documented in ballads and stories, these romanticized knights crisscross through English literature, promulgating an admirable standard for aristocratic conduct. According to chivalric rules, adherents are honor-bound to God and king by sacred oath; they should speak only truth to a lady-love; and each knight was obliged to rescue any victim under duress, but particularly ladies vulnerable to the unscrupulous. Honor meant following such rules of conduct, which had a foundation in Christian principles of obedience, service, and honesty. Though a central concept addressed by several of the play's characters, only Prince Hal, the wayward son of Henry Bolingbroke, actually embraces the true meaning of honor. While everyone else betrays the high standards of chivalry, Shakespeare seems interested not just in the failures but in the cause of those failures. An ahistorical fiction of Shakespeare's imagination, Falstaff's purpose is to demonstrate the origin and consequences of those departures from established moral norms.

The failures begin with Richard, who cannot resist the temptation to fund his Irish war with money confiscated from lands that the exiled Bolingbroke would eventually inherit. Richard's theft proves to be his undoing because it strikes at the very lifeblood of aristocratic power: land and rents. But the rebellion he invites has far wider implications than any of the participants envision. When Richard very dramatically hands his crown to Bolingbroke, not only does this dilute the royal claim to divine rights but the duke's assertion of individual rights very publicly circumscribes state authority. The balance of power between the crown and the aristocrats is profoundly altered; the political and psychological divide between the English populace and their governing class is diminished; and the general understanding of rights as well as duties to the state begins to evolve. Though the *Magna Carta* signed by King John several centuries before these events had planted English democracy, those seeds took firm root in this very crucial moment. Henry's motivation for returning to defend his income and land rights may very well have been without undue malice or ambition, as he claims, but Shakespeare rightly saw Bolingbroke's assertion of his rights against the crown as one of the most significant events in recent English history.

The first unintended consequence of this crucial event was the disruption of loyalties, which was the glue that held the hierarchical feudal system together. Unlike modern political structures which incorporate power into impersonal administrative institutions, feudal royal power required a cooperative nobility willing to pledge fealty to the crown in exchange for generational wealth and privilege. These benefits come to define the aristocracy's social strata, cementing that class's relationship to the king. Functioning a bit like American governors, the aristocracy was responsible for the mundane tasks of local administration and for gathering conscripts from their tenants to support the king's military campaigns. Where divine rights gave royal power a patina of spiritual and moral legitimacy, the system depended far more on those chivalric virtues of obedience, loyalty, integrity, and honor. Though it seemed perfectly justified at the time, Bolingbroke's decision to return from France to challenge Richard's authority violated all of these personal virtues. And when every other aristocrat joined his cause, their defiance effectively violated much of what held that structure together.

The second effect, closely related to the first, was perhaps even more consequential. Bolingbroke's actions began the process of validating the concept of individual rights, which from this point on, existed in constant tension with state authority. On the positive side, this process eventually led to English democracy and the great American experiment, which defends each person's right to pursue life, liberty, and happiness. But, viewed through the same moral lens with which Shakespeare viewed English history, including Henry's pivotal decision, rights are inextricably entwined with needs and desires. This unavoidable intrusion of desire into every motivation is the original sin documented in *Genesis,* the story of our collective fall from pristine innocence, and whether our age accepts it as literally true or rejects it as unscientific, the Elizabethans would have clearly recognized it in Henry's decisive resolution to the dilemma.

On a very personal level, Bolingbroke needed his rental income to retain his status and power; the desire to keep all of that brought him back from exile to demand what every other noble considered his rightful due. Yet he somehow failed to grasp that a justifiable assertion of customary rights would undermine royal power, that a weakened and humiliated Richard would have no choice but to relinquish his scepter to a stronger Henry, a man who could not resist the temptation to take by force what did not belong to him. Ironically, therefore, Henry ends up duplicating Richard's avariciousness. Near the end of his reign, a chastened Henry seeks spiritual forgiveness by promising to lead a crusade to free Jerusalem, but at his advanced age, his hope for political expiation is really grounded in his son, Prince Hal.

Though Richard precipitates this crisis by impounding Bolingbroke's rents, Henry and every noble who supports his cause are likewise guilty of putting self-interest before loyalty, and that self-interest is used to justify taking what did not belong to them. This is precisely the moral hazard that Falstaff, whose only occupation is petty thievery, embodies. Though his size is a frequent butt of Hal's jokes, Falstaff's prodigious waistline is a visual reminder of an insatiable appetite symbolic of aristocratic cupidity.

> Hal. How now, my sweet creature of bombast, how long is't ago, Jack, since thou sawest thine own knee?
> Fal. My own knee? When I was about thy years, Hal, I was not an eagle's talent in the waist, I could have crept into an alderman's thumb-ring. (2.4.326-331)

Funny as these exchanges are, they serve to remind us that unrestrained appetites are responsible for England's departure from chivalrous virtue.

Thematically, the Henriad seeks to present an alternative to such egocentric behavior, and, not surprisingly, that alternative is both moral and Christian, requiring every politically responsible person to willingly relinquish what pleases, what feeds a perceived need, for a future, worthier purpose. It's what the gospels call dying to the self, exemplified in Christian thinking by Jesus's willing sacrifice for the redemption of humankind. It is an attitude of habitual, instinctive generosity that, as Shakespeare understood, needs to govern every human relationship, from those large social and political relationships between king and subjects to those very personal relationships between men and women. In every sphere, the choice is between self-interest and self-sacrifice, between rebellion and obedience, between sin and righteousness, between habitual consumption and generous giving, between perpetual youth and responsible adulthood. When Henry takes Richard's crown, the reason to choose the better of those numerous opposites is no longer obvious. And when the nobles choose to join his cause, order dissolves, chaos threatens, harmony is untuned, and only the virtuous can discern the proper way forward. What once was clear is now fraught with confusion.

Very quickly in *Richard II,* that confusion appears when the good Duke of Lancaster, who describes his beloved England as "this other Eden, demi-paradise," can no longer discern where his loyalties belong after Henry seizes the throne. Did fealty belong with Richard, the anointed king? Or with Henry, the more effective and decisive man? With tradition or with pragmatic power? Weakened loyalties made perpetual turmoil far more likely because ambitious men, using Bolingbroke's own logic, could justify armed opposition whenever royal prerogatives encroached on their perceived rights. Once Richard's crown is removed by force, everyone's property and rights are under similar threat, and protecting those becomes every man's paramount concern. Until those protections can be negotiated and clarified into law, political stability would remain imperiled by self-interest. These consequences form the moral and political background that explains Sir John Falstaff's large, loveable, and quite unforgettable presence in *1Henry 4*.

On stage, he is indeed irresistible. Falstaff multiplies the vitality already seen in Juliet's nurse and Mercutio. He is a force unto himself, a figure that Bloom rightly identifies as a supreme achievement in characterization. He makes his first appearance in *1Henry 4*, where Bolingbroke, enthroned as Henry4, struggles to quash a rebellion that threatens his reign. Meanwhile, his son, Prince Hal, has been distracted by this fat, witty, playful companion, Sir John, who inhabits the local tavern and subsists on the prince's generosity. Boldly asserting that Falstaff "teaches us not to moralize," Bloom continues:

> ...Falstaff wants childlike (not childish) play, which exists in another order than that of morality. ... he is neither immoral nor amoral but of another realm, the order of play. Hal entered that order as Falstaff's disciple. . . . Hal struggles all through *Henry IV, Part One*, against the fascination exercised by the great wit. It seems just to observe that Falstaff charms the tough and resistant prince for many of the same reasons that Falstaff, properly played, dominates any audience. (298)

And dominate an audience he does. Queen Elizabeth, it is said, requested a sequel to *1Henry 4*, which had been performed for her at court, just so she could see more of the fat rogue, Jack Falstaff. Shakespeare complied, featuring Falstaff in *2Henry 4*, *Henry 5*, and the comedy, *The Merry Wives of Windsor*.

Appealing to our own childish inclinations, Falstaff's incessant playfulness is all but irresistible, so we are naturally predisposed to approve of Bloom's glowing admiration. But the dynamics between Falstaff, Hal, and Hal's father, Henry Bolingbroke, carry moral implications that deserve careful attention. Bloom's emphasis on Shakespeare's gift for creating vibrant personalities like Falstaff is certainly true, but it is far from the whole truth, or even the most interesting truth. Any such unqualified admiration ignores Falstaff's motives for this friendship with Hal who, once he becomes king, is expected to favor his tavern friends with royal largesse. That expectation is eventually verbalized at the prince's coronation but is soundly rejected by the new king who strikes many, including Bloom, as ungrateful after his tenure with his witty, playful companion.

Much of the plot conforms closely to Shakespeare's sources, Holinshed and North. Sir John Falstaff, however, is Shakespeare's own creation. But no prose description does him adequate justice. Falstaff has to be experienced on stage, where he comes dangerously close to subverting the main political themes altogether and making the play entirely about himself. Fat, perpetually hungry, addicted to sack and capons, Falstaff has endeared himself to Henry Bolingbroke's son, Prince Hal, and together with other assorted ne'er-do-wells, they haunt the Boar's Head Inn and play at being petty thieves. With child-like delight, he is forever playing with both words and truth; he puts on mock plays where he pretends to be Hal's royal father evaluating—favorably, of course–his influence on the young prince; when challenged, he will improvise an explanation for his many failures and lapses with virtuoso creativity. But throughout his escapades, one thing is certain: Falstaff is never serious. As Bloom says, he is perpetually in the mode of play. It begins the moment he sets foot on stage:

Fal. Now, Hal, what time of day is it, lad?
Hal. Thou art so fat-witted with drinking of old sack, and

        unbuttoning thee after supper, and sleeping upon benches after noon, that thou hast forgotten to demand that truly which thou would'st truly know. What a devil hast thou to do with the time of day? Unless hours were cups of sack, and minutes capons, and clocks the tongues of bawds, and dials the signs of leaping-houses, and the blessed sun himself a fair hot wench in flame-colored taffeta; I see no reason why thou shouldst be so superfluous to demand the time of the day.

Fal. Indeed, you come near me now, Hal, for we that take purses go by the moon and the seven stars, and not by Phoebus, he, "that wand'ring knight so fair." And I prithee, sweet wag, when thou art a king, as God save thy Grace—Majesty I should say, for grace thou wilt have none—

Hal. What, none?

Fal. No, by my troth, not so much as will serve to be prologue to an egg and butter. (1.2.1-21)

From beginning to end, this is the Falstaffian octave. He refuses to be disheartened by Hal's catalog of bad behavior. In the familiar spirit of male friendship, Falstaff transforms Hal's good-natured insults into opportunities to display his wit. The effortless pun on grace, the royal title or the prayer before a meal, is part of his natural, agile, perpetual playfulness that proves both irresistible and lovable. Infinitely inventive, Falstaff is always at play, exercising his imagination to feed his insatiable appetite for fun.

    But the witty banter about time also implies two distinct perspectives on the passing hours, a fundamental topic of concern in a history play. For Falstaff, time is a limitless playground providing abundant opportunity for amusement. He obeys only one, very simple rule: life exists to satisfy that child-like appetite for pleasure. The addictive impulse to satisfy every appetite, however, ignores another, more Christian perspective of time which sees life's passing hours as the theater wherein God works out His plan for the world, where each individual has a responsible role to play in the outcome. Each person, in fact, has been provided with gifts that, to be a responsible party to God's plan, he must employ for the benefit of others. Success, both in worldly as well as in moral and spiritual terms, means accepting that divinely appointed purpose. The purpose for Hal's life was set when his father was anointed king. Falstaff's purpose, though, is much different: "I am not only witty in myself," he confesses in *2Henry 4*, but am "the cause of wit in others." Bloom is right about Falstaff: he is play personified. But, like most children, he remains oblivious to the inevitable consequences of advancing time, something both Hal and the Lord Chief Justice attempt to rectify at different times in the action.

Falstaff's imaginative stories and witty dialogue mask one very relentless truth: everything mortal is subject to time. Time passes, age increases, and mortality awaits. Falstaff's unwillingness to admit his rightful age in *2Henry 4* greatly offends the Lord Chief Justice, who represents the law that Fat Jack was born to violate:

> Do you set down your name in the scroll of youth, that are written down old with all the characters of age? Have you not a moist eye, a dry hand, a yellow cheek, a white beard, a decreasing leg, an increasing belly? Is not your voice broken, your wind short, your chin double, your wit single, and every part about you blasted with antiquity? and will you yet call yourself young? Fie, fie, fie, Sir John. (*2H4* 1.2.181-189)

Hal's first question to Falstaff, then, turns out to be altogether rhetorical: "What a devil hast thou to do with the time of day?" The devil's answer, of course, is "nothing" because the inevitability of judgment cannot be allowed to distract from the pleasures of the moment. Unless it is ignored, the passing of time brings everyone to an end that has the very unfortunate effect of diminishing pleasure, something that doesn't sit well with anyone still clinging tightly to childhood. But time is a reality that not even Falstaff can evade, try as he might. His physical decline as the Henriad progresses is a reminder of what awaits every sinner. And time is something that Hal, as heir apparent, cannot afford to ignore.

Like the Chief Justice, Hal can be quite direct in his critique of Falstaff's character. Absent any indication of Jack's reformation, Hal will occasionally resort to denunciations that may be intended for humor but contain sufficient truth to be shocking. While play-acting Hal's impending confrontation with his father, the king, Falstaff generously describes himself as "a good, portly man. . ., of a cheerful look, a pleasing eye, and a most noble carriage" (2.4.422-424). Contradicting Falstaff's favorable opinion of his own virtues, however, the prince offers a much different opinion that presages the eventual rejection of his lovable companion. Pretending to be his own father meeting a prodigal son, he undams a torrent of royal displeasure:

> Thou art violently carried away from grace, there is a devil haunts thee in the likeness of an old fat man. . . . Why dost thou converse with that trunk of humors, that bolting-hutch of beastliness, that huge bombard of sack. . . that reverent Vice, that grey Iniquity, that father ruffian, that vanity in years? Wherein is he good, but to taste sack and drink it? Wherein neat and cleanly, but to carve a capon and eat it? Wherein cunning but in craft? Wherein crafty, but in villainy? Wherein villainous, but in all things? Wherein worthy, but in nothing? (2.4.446-459)

As long as Falstaff's spell remains unbroken, this diatribe will seem either incongruous, given Hal's willing association with Jack, or cruel and unwarranted. But the devil, as the Bible cautions, is well versed in making sin look far more appealing than virtue. Harsh as it may be, Hal's language implies an awareness of a virtuous state that he could choose but which will remain forever foreign to Falstaff and the others. Despite any intended humor in this little vignette of the prodigal son's return home, it heralds the prince's separation from his very funny but wayward companion.

    Such moments carefully foreshadow the eventual rejection of Falstaff, which, the play reminds us in multiple ways, is a choice Hal must face. It's there in the odd little scene where Hal and Poins keep calling Francis, the Boar's Head server, from different rooms until he doesn't know who deserves his attention. It's there in Falstaff's playful vignette of the prodigal son returning to his disappointed and angry royal father. From the very beginning of the play, in fact, Hal knows that this choice is inevitable. When his fun-loving companions exit the stage after the discussion of time, Hal reveals what lies hidden beneath his dissolute appearance:

> I . . .will a while uphold
> The unyok'd humor of your idleness,
> Yet herein will I imitate the sun,
> Who doth permit the base contagious clouds
> To smother up his beauty from the world,
> That when he please again to be himself,
> Being wanted, he may be more wond'red at. . . .
> If all the year were playing holidays,
> To sport would be as tedious as to work. . . .
> So when this loose behavior I throw off
> And pay the debt I never promised. . .
> My reformation. . .
> Shall show more goodly and attract more eyes. (1.2.195-214)

The contrasts between moon and sun, darkness and light, capriciousness and steadfastness, are deliberate preparation for the moral distinctions that the play is developing between the values of Falstaff and Hal. Many critics, including Bloom, are bothered by Hal's deliberate manipulation of public perceptions and the apparent shallowness of his connection to the loveable Falstaff, whose "loose behavior" the prince knows he must eventually "throw off." But the play makes very clear why this must be so. Because Henry Bolingbroke dethroned Richard with aristocratic support, his son, Prince Hal must "pay the debt I never promised," a phrase that undoubtedly reminded the Elizabethans of the debt Jesus obediently paid for their spiritual salvation. The language reinforces the notion that Hal represents the promise of England's salvation from the turmoil following the usurpation of Richard's throne.

As the personification of unbridled human desire, Falstaff's eventual rejection as the governing force in Hal's life is a necessary step toward the duty and honor enshrined in chivalric lore. Hal's tenure at the Boar's Head with Falstaff is a lesson in the nature and consequences of sin, and the obvious pleasures available there are temptations that he is required to give up if he is to govern differently than his father. Good governance, it turns out, involves real and very personal sacrifice. Hal's rejection of Falstaff actually proves he is sufficiently worthy to rule. To read that any other way is to misunderstand the sacrifices and responsibilities of power.

But Hal must bide his time patiently even though the self-interest behind the overthrow of Richard and embodied in Falstaff continues to dissolve the last vestiges of divine rights and chivalry. As Huizinga implies, those stories of aristocratic valor were as much myth as reality. The hollowness of that chivalric posture was exposed in the aftermath of a stolen crown. In his essay, "The Economy of the Closed Heart," Edward Hubler suggests that, all along, many in the English nobility failed to live up to the expectations defined by chivalry. Chief among them was Northumberland, father of Henry Percy, affectionately known as Hotspur.

> The purest instance is Northumberland . . . who is motivated by "advised respects" throughout *Richard II* and remains unchanged throughout the two parts of *Henry IV*. He sends his son to death in a vain attempt to secure his own position and later, when still another rebellion is failing, he writes to his

fellow rebels letters of "cold intent" announcing his retirement to Scotland. It is his whole character. (473-74)

But, except for Hal, this brand of self-interest infects everyone, including Northumberland's charming but choleric son, Hotspur, whose bravery on the battlefield stirs the king, Hal's father, to lament his own son's dissolute behavior. Bolingbroke is discussing the two young men with Westmoreland, who is praising Hotspur's bravery in battle:

> West. In faith,
> It is a conquest for a prince to boast of.
> King. Yea, there thou mak'st me sad, and mak'st me sin
> In envy that my Lord Northumberland
> Should be father to so blest a son—
> A son who is the theme of honor's tongue. . .
> Whilst I, by looking on the praise of him,
> See riot and dishonor stain the brow
> Of my young Harry. (1.1.76-86)

Though he envies Northumberland for fathering so valiant a son as Hotspur, Henry is wrong about both young men. As events unfold, Hotspur emerges as one of the rebel leaders to oppose Henry's reign, while his own son will defeat Hotspur in battle and allow his disreputable companion, Falstaff, to take the credit. It will be his son, Prince Hal, who will actually become "the theme of honor's tongue."

Though considered the very emblem of chivalry, Hotspur eventually disproves the lore. As his nickname indicates, his commitment to the virtues that once sustained the feudal way of life is subject to a volatile temper that is accompanied by a wit as sharp as Falstaff's. As the rebels plot to overthrow Bolingbroke, the Welshman Owen Glendower brags that he 'can call spirits from the vasty deep," to which Hotspur replies, "Why, so can I, or so can any man, But will they come when you do call them" (3.1.52-55)? He can be incredibly charming, even self-aware at times, as shown by the sweet way he parts from his wife as he heads off to battle. Playfully, she asks:

> Lady. Do you not love me? Do you not indeed? Well,
>   do not, then, for since you love me not, I will not love myself.
>   Do you not love me? Nay, tell me if you speak in jest or no.
> Hot. Come, wilt thou see me ride?
>   And when I'm a' horseback, I will swear I love thee infinitely.
> (2.3.96-102)

In this intimate encounter, surprisingly, the battle-hardened Hotspur can be quite tender and loving. But when honor and duty call him to mount his war horse, his priorities are clear enough. He is a warrior first.

But the actions belie the words, for Hotspur's implementation of those traditional aristocratic virtues evaporates whenever he feels slighted. Hotspur's quarrel with Henry begins when all the nobles come to Henry's aid as he returns from France to protect his rights. The coalition of nobles quickly disintegrates, however, when Henry and Hotspur disagree over which of them should hold prisoners of war for ransom, a common and lucrative practice at the time. Pride wounded, Hotspur continues to fret over that decision and other perceived slights to the honor of the disaffected aristocrats. In his eyes, Henry has forgotten the debt owed to the nobles for their support. That wounded sense of justice rationalizes his participation in the rebellion against "this canker, Bullingbrook."

Though Hotspur's choleric personality may explain his unsteady grasp of concepts like loyalty, obedience, and honor, his reputation for those virtues, which Henry so admired, is a pretense. And that pretense, also evident in Hotspur's father, Northumberland, is widespread. In the lead-up to the attempted coup, Hotspur receives a letter from an unnamed associate who is backing out of the plot. Alone, Hotspur comes onstage reading from that letter:

> "But, for mine own part, my lord, I could be well contented to be there, in respect of the love I bear your house." He could be contented: why is he not then? In the respect of the love he bears our house: he shows in this, he loves his own barn better than he loves our house. Let me see some more. "The purpose you undertake is dangerous." --why, that's certain. 'Tis dangerous to take a cold, to sleep, to drink, but I tell you, my lord fool, out of this nettle, danger, we pluck the flower safety. "The purpose you undertake is dangerous, the friends you have nam'd uncertain, the time itself unsorted, and your whole plot too light for the counterpoise of so great an opposition." Say you so, say you so? I say unto you again, you are a shallow, cowardly hind, and you lie. . . . Why, my Lord of York commends the plot and the general course of the action. 'Zounds, and I were now by this rascal, I could brain him with my lady's fan. (2.3.1-23)

Like Falstaff, Hotspur's unforgettable personality buzzes with authenticity. But the letter he reads from shows that, in this newly transformed England, loyalty and courage are no longer absolute values. They are mutable and subject to circumstance, which seems to confound Hotspur, despite his suspect reputation for honor and chivalry.

Any belief that England ever really adhered to those values disappears when both Richard and Henry Bolingbroke take what doesn't belong to them. Those robberies exact a price on a nation's moral structure, and every subject throughout the land must pay for that rapacity. Once again, Falstaff reflects that moral decay. Looking to line his pockets illegally, Jack's preparations for war against the forces of Hotspur savage the very same self-regard of the aristocrats. Asked to recruit soldiers for the fight against the rebels, he accepts bribes from rich citizens looking to escape the general conscription, filling the ranks of his battalion with the desperate and unfortunate military castoffs who lack money to buy their way out of service:

> If I be not asham'd of my soldiers, I am a sous'd gurnet. I have misus'd the King's press damnably. I have got, in exchange of a hundred and fifty soldiers, three hundred and odd pounds. I press me none but good householders, yeomen's sons... such a commodity of warm slaves, as had as lieve hear the devil as a drum.... I press'd me none but such toasts-and-butter, with hearts in their bellies no bigger than pins' heads, and they have bought out their services; and now my whole charge consists of ancients, corporals, lieutenants... slaves as ragged as Lazarus in the painted cloth... such as indeed were never soldiers but discarded servingmen,.. the cankers of a calm world and a long peace, ten times more dishonorable ragged than an old feaz'd ancient... A mad fellow met me on the way and told me I had unloaded all the gibbets and press'd the dead bodies. No eye hath seen such scarecrows. (4.2.11-38)

Like Falstaff, the cowardly rich manage to avoid the king's press by paying their way out of duty into safety. This is the fallen state of the nation's honor. The rot is widespread. And when Prince Hal questions the appearance of Falstaff's men, Jack callously acknowledges that they are but "food for powder; they'll fit a pit as well as better." With this unsavory disregard for his conscripts and a deep concern for his own purse, Falstaff is no different than the cautiously self-interested Northumberland, the choleric Hotspur, or any of their followers who now take up arms against Henry. Every rebel joins this cause for what they might gain for themselves.

That chivalry and all its associated virtues are in fact dead and ready for burial should be absolutely clear when Falstaff addresses the matter of honor directly. His friend, Prince Hal, meets him briefly before the battle against the rebels commences:

> Hal. ... Say thy prayers and farewell.
> Fal. I would it were bed-time, Hal, and all well.
> Hal. Why, thou owest God a death.   [Exit]
> Fal 'Tis not due yet, I would be loath to pay him before his day. What need I be so forward with him that calls not

on me? Well, 'tis no matter, honor pricks me on. Yea, but how if honor prick me off when I come on? How then? Can honor set to a leg? No, or an arm? No. Or take away the grief of a wound? No. Honor hath no skill in surgery then? No. What is honor? A word. What is in that word honor? What is that honor? Air. A trim reckoning! Who hath it? He that died a' Wednesday. Doth he feel it? No. Doth he hear it? No. 'Tis insensible then? Yea, to the dead. But will't not live with the living? No. Why? Detraction will not suffer it. Therefore, I'll none of it, honor is a mere scutcheon. And so ends my catechism. (5.1.124-141)

Though partly a rationalization of the same cowardice Falstaff displayed when fleeing a disguised Hal and Poins during the Gadshill robbery, his final catechism on honor also incriminates aristocratic idealizations of their own behavior. Repeatedly, the lie has been exposed, and Falstaff is its indictment by word and by example. Ever the playful child, even during the battle against the rebels, he draws a bottle of sack out of his holster, then takes credit for defeating Hotspur, whose lifeless body he wounds so his dagger won't appear unused. With Falstaff standing over the body of a fallen Hotspur, the incident is emblematic of the sad, fallen state of England's honor. The moment might also suggest why Shakespeare named this character Falstaff.

Bolingbroke's seizure of a crown that didn't belong to him required an equally flawed justification of honor. Falstaff's catechism merely reflects the moral decline of which honor's debasement is but one measure. As the rebellion indicates, Falstaff and Henry Bolingbroke both struggle in the same moral quagmire in different ways, and both men rationalize decisions that have been based largely on satisfying personal need. That sin has corrupted every aspect of Henry's reign. Everyone, not just Falstaff, has lost sight of what honor really means. The chivalric staff of English honor has indeed fallen.

For the future of England, Hal has to think and act differently. Relinquishing the pleasures of the Boar's Head Tavern is the price he must pay for the responsibilities his father incurred by deposing Richard, what Hal terms "the debt I never owed." When Hal magnanimously pays Falstaff's debt at the inn and to the travelers Falstaff robs at Gadshill, his generous spirit in small things indicates that he will also make good on the moral and political debt his father incurred. That generosity of life and spirit distinguishes Hal from the fat companion who lives to satisfy his appetites. The self-centered Falstaff takes while the generous Hal gives. The distinction is both moral and spiritual. That generosity—evident a second time by his willingness to let Falstaff take credit for subduing Hotspur in battle–stands in stark contrast to both Northumberland's self-concern and Falstaff's self-indulgence. Both of these characters embrace self-interest at the expense of significant moral, political, or social values that operate for the greater good.

Hal's perspective on honor is firmly grounded in the generous spirit of service he shows throughout, whether he is in the Boar's Head Tavern paying Falstaff's tab, in his father's presence at court, or on the battlefield. At court, for example, he humbly apologizes for the faults of his youth and tries to allay the anxiety of a distraught father who fears his errant son might even "fight against me under Percy's pay." Hal's response to this is forthright and apologetic:

> . . . God forgive them that so much have sway'd
> Your Majesty's good thoughts away from me!
> I will redeem all this on Percy's head,
> And in the closing of some glorious day
> Be bold to tell you that I am your son. . . .
> And that shall be the day, when e'er it lights,
> That this same child of honor and renown,
> This gallant Hotspur. . .
> And your unthought-of Harry chance to meet.
> (3.2.130-141)

Hal's pledge to redeem himself on the battlefield by defeating Hotspur very dramatically ties his fate to the outcome of that confrontation. At this point, his words must be proven by actions, but Hal has seen his father's fear and sorrow and has responded, not with Falstaff's irreverent wit or Hotspur's angry self-defense, but with a respectful and gracious promise to reform. Earlier, he had promised to emerge from the dark clouds that hid his noble intentions for the future. Now that his time has finally come, he is prepared to honor both his royal father and his earlier promise. As his actions align with his words, he is reviving the true meaning of honor.

Before the opposed sides join in battle, the same grace and respect he showed to his father are extended to Hotspur. While the leaders of both armies confer, Hal tries to prevent the confrontation where "many a soul shall pay dearly for this encounter."

> The Prince of Wales doth join with all the world
> In praise of Henry Percy. By my hopes,
> This present enterprise set off his head,
> I do not think a braver gentleman . . . is now alive
> To grace this latter age with noble deeds. (5.1.86-92)

Admitting that he has "a truant been to chivalry," an indication of his humility, the prince follows this gracious tribute to an enemy with a challenge to fight Hotspur in single combat so no soldiers would have to die. Though the rebels mistrust this and reject the challenge, Hal's willingness to risk his life for the good of others reflects the same generous heart that paid those debts in the tavern. And it is this generosity of spirit that reasserts the kind of honor that will inspire his nation. Unlike Falstaff or Hotspur or even his father, Henry IV, King of England, Prince Hal does not give his personal needs and desires primacy. This is what distinguishes him and what will make him the one able "to pay the debt I never promised." In *Henry V*, Shakespeare's play about Hal's reign as king, he becomes the inspiring battlefield leader that reunites England and France and brings peace to the two nations.

At the end of *1Henry 4,* however, Hal not only defeats Hotspur but performs one additional act of respect. The prince comes upon Falstaff, who has feigned death to avoid a fight with one of the rebels, and he is moved to offer what he thinks is a final tribute to his friend:

> What, old acquaintance! Could not all this flesh
> Keep in a little life? Poor Jack, farewell!
> I could have better spar'd a better man.
> O, I should have a heavy miss of thee
> If I were much in love with vanity! (5.4.102-106)

Hal has no illusions about his friend, whose sin was vanity, the overindulgence of self. Yet even though he is well aware of the temptations that Falstaff embodies, his brief but heartfelt homage indicates an appreciation for Jack's playful spirit. Though, when the time comes, he will forsake his once-loveable companion, he was never immune to that vitality and wit. But Hotspur's rebellion and his father's fears require his attention, and he redeems those misused hours with a demonstration of his devotion to duty and honor. Not only has he been generous with his praise and his effort to prevent the needless deaths of his subjects, who are not, as Falstaff quipped, merely fodder for the pit, but he has been gracious and tolerant of the very man whose inventive playfulness tempted him away from his duties.

Throughout Falstaff's appearances in all three plays of the Henriad, he retains a similar though evolving moral and thematic purpose. Falstaff, of course, is not dead when Prince Hal leaves him at the end of *1Henry 4*, but when he reappears in *2Henry 4* he is portrayed as an older and a very different man in essential ways. He retains his irreverent and inventive wit, but as he enters the stage with his servant, his first words are a question about the health of his urine:

> Fal. . . . what says the doctor to my water?
> Page. He said, sir, the water itself was a good healthy
> Water, but for the party that ow'd it, he might have
> more diseases than he knew for. (1.2.1-5)

After *1Henry 4*, age and disease plague Fat Jack, and his declining physical condition reflects a world where honor has now fallen even further from what was once understood to be genuine virtue. When mutineers again raise their swords against the king, Prince Hal's brother, John, tricks them into surrendering, after which they are arrested and sent to prison for "present execution," a sharp contrast with Hal's chivalrous behavior before the battle with Hotspur. The now feeble Henry Bolingbroke, King of England, promises to sponsor a crusade as penance for the acts that initiated this moral decline. But as that second play about the reign of Henry IV draws to a close, the expectation is raised that Hal, now King Henry V, is the only one able to reverse England's political and moral decline.

The first step in that direction is the very painful but necessary rejection of Falstaff. As Hal's coronation procession passes nearby, Fat Jack calls out in delirious joy that his patron from the Boar's Head will now accommodate every desire. "God save thy Grace, King Hal! My royal Hal!" But when Hal recognizes his old friend, his pronouncement is stern:

> I know thee not, old man, fall to thy prayers,
> How ill white hairs becomes a fool and jester!
> I have long dreamt of such a kind of man,
> So surfeit-swell'd, so old, so profane;
> But being awak'd, I do despise my dream.
> Make less thy body (hence) and more thy grace,
> Leave gormandizing, know the grave doth gape
> For thee thrice wider than for other men.
> Reply not to me with a fool-born jest,
> Presume not that I am the thing I was,

> For God doth know, so shall the world perceive,
> That I have turn'd away my former self.... (5.5.47-58)

Harsh as Bloom finds this, any conscientious parent knows love's compassion must be mixed with correction. The fault is Falstaff's. Always ignorant of the way time changes circumstances, Falstaff assumes his Hal will be the same man he was at the inn. He cannot be, of course, and Hal's rejection is meant to educate this recalcitrant child about the inescapable realities of time. His rejection is unmistakably moral and spiritual, his speech imbued with the language of the pulpit. The reference to white hairs and graves is a pointed reminder to Falstaff that, with his time nearing an end, he has few hours left to reform his life before eternal judgment comes upon him.

    The theme of time began with Falstaff's first words to Hal, and the new king's rejection of Falstaff brings it to its recognizably Christian conclusion. Shakespeare has prepared us for this moment with multiple references to the Biblical story of the rich man and the beggar Lazarus from Luke 16:19-26. In this parable, the rich man, known to the Elizabethans through Chaucer as Dives, will only share the crumbs from his table with the poor leper, Lazarus. But when both men have left this world, Lazarus resides in heaven with Abraham while Dives suffers the fires of eternal damnation, begging a single drop of water from Lazarus to relieve his parched tongue. But the divide between heaven and hell is too great and his suffering is both inescapable and eternal. Falstaff himself makes such a reference when he insults his red-faced friend, Bardolph, in *1Henry 4*. "I never see thy face," he says, "but I think upon hell-fire and Dives that lived in purple" (3.3.30-33). He refers to Lazarus a second time when describing those scarecrow-like military recruits drafted into service in place of men rich enough to bribe their way out of Falstaff's impress. Each time, the reference is applied to those who are victimized by Falstaff's indifference to anything but his own welfare.

Falstaff knows the story of Lazarus but ignores its lesson about generosity, the opposite of his habitual self-regard. Judgment can be a necessary form of love, and so Hal drives that lesson home.

In his stern rejection, Hal reminds Falstaff that there is a penalty for ignoring time. Hal understood that lesson when he realized his wasted hours almost cost him his father's respect and his kingdom. Since the story of Lazarus emphasizes the importance of time in the face of impending judgment, it makes one more appearance in the Henriad. It comes in *Henry V*, a play that recounts Henry's glorious victory over the French, where we learn of the death of Falstaff. The hostess of the Boar's Head Tavern recounts the fateful last minutes of his passing, and it is there that we return one final time to the parable from Luke's gospel of Dives in hell, looking up at Lazarus, resting in Abraham's bosom. His tavern friends discuss whether Falstaff is bound for heaven or for hell:

> Bard. Would I were with him, wheresome'er he is, either in heaven or in hell!
> Host. Nay sure, he's not in hell; he's in Arthur's bosom, if ever man went to Arthur's bosom. 'A made a finer end, and went away and it had been any christom child. 'A parted ev'n just between twelve and one, ev'n at the turning o' the tide; for after I saw him fumble with the sheets, and play with the flowers, and smile upon his finger's end, I knew there was but one way; for his nose was a sharp as a pen, and 'a babbl'd of green fields. "How now, Sir John?" quoth I, "what, man? Be a' good cheer." So 'a cried out, "God, God, God!" three or four times. Now I, to comfort him, bid him 'a should not think of God; I hop'd there was no need to trouble himself with any such thoughts yet. So 'a bade me lay more clothes on his feet. I put my hand into the bed and felt them, and they were as cold as any stone; then I felt to his knees, and so up'ard and up'ard and all was as cold as any stone. (*H5*, 2.3.6-26)

Although the hostess's reference to Arthur's bosom is wrong, that very merry and loveable rogue, Falstaff, may very well reside in the bosom of Arthur's England. As a literary character, he has endeared himself across the ensuing four centuries. But, despite its many virtues, the England of the legendary Arthur has fallen, in these plays, a long way from paradise, and the hostess's allusion to the Lazarus story, where the leper, now in Abraham's bosom, looks down from heaven on the very ungenerous Dives in hell, implicates the pleasure-seeking self-absorption of Fat Jack. Never repenting of his greed before death, Dives suffers eternal damnation. Though she knows the reference, its meaning seems to be lost on the good proprietor of the Boar's Head, for in her mind, Falstaff must surely be in heaven. Like all of us, she has shared in his playful good humor and has willingly overlooked his many sins. But when she recounts how Falstaff babbled about the green fields of Psalm 23, it seems he may very well have been looking for spiritual comfort on his deathbed. This fond recounting of Falstaff's death suggests that his thoughts have finally turned to his spiritual and moral condition, but there is no textual evidence to suggest, as his loving friends do, that he has repented in time to avoid the fate of Dives.

Because Falstaff embodies the seductive nature of sin, his admirers easily get caught up in the pleasure of his company. With him, duty, responsibility, and the passage of time are easy to ignore. But the fear lurking within Falstaff's last words helps to identify the risks of never growing up, of avoiding responsibility. Except for Hal, no one else in the play ever accepts full responsibility for their shortcomings, and no one else ever reforms their behavior. Falstaff's witty vitality may be entertaining, but by clinging to youth and ignoring the passage of time, he forsakes any ability to evolve into his better self.

As appealing as Falstaff certainly is, his presence in the Henriad is a reminder that self-indulgence spawned discord and rebellion in England. Satisfying that hunger for pleasure is so deeply engrained in human nature that resistance, when circumstances call for it, can seem both futile and pointless. For better or for worse, that is the way the world and its inhabitants ended up. It is why the gospels speak of the need to die to self, to model the Christian savior's commitment to serving a cause greater than self. Leadership, the play argues, is more about duty and sacrifice than it is about privilege. A father's decision to depose the reigning king obligates Hal to a life of service to country. That obligation requires the rejection of Falstaff and all his addictions to pleasure as a prerequisite to the coronation.

If the human desire for pleasure and comfort spawns the world's evil, these four histories also confirm a second aspect of experience that will influence his tragedies: while the consequences of sin may intrude into peoples' lives, inflicting disorder, conflict, even death, the passage of time unveils a mysterious, countervailing power that brings retributive justice to the unrepentant. Despite individual sin and its consequences, the Henriad suggests Prince Hal's emerging leadership was proof of the world's orderly and benevolent design. Neither Falstaff nor Hotspur are psychopathically evil, but their imaginative and energetic willfulness disrupt normal familial, social, and political expectations. Only after Hal's coronation and the rejection of Falstaff will sin's discord, embodied in Jack's pleasure-seeking and Hotspur's rebellion, come to an end.

Shakespeare's involvement in historical drama was crucial to the evolution of his art. That effort led to an appreciation of the human origins of evil and the evidence of a providential force working within time. As a result, an entirely different type of tragic drama becomes possible, beginning with *Hamlet*. Aspects of the Henriad also affect Shakespearean comedy, where the folly of unregulated human desire which, in other hands often turned into sharp, sometimes bitter satire, is mitigated by a more benevolent and ennobling desire for love. Perhaps the allure of Falstaff's delightful personality mitigates Shakespeare's distrust of human desire, but whatever the cause, his view of human nature gains nuance and balance, giving his comedies a softer, gentler edge that appeals to those willing to admit to their own folly. In his most optimistic comedy, *As You Like It*, for example, sin may dominate the hearts of several characters, but the love between a young man and an iridescently charming woman makes the redemption of flawed human nature possible. Rosalind, the play's heroine, is the canon's purest, extended example of the Shakespearean female teaching her suitor about love's essential truths. In the histories and the tragedies, the hand of providence is visible in decisions and events. In comedy, it is visible in a loving woman's commitment to relationship. As such, Rosalind becomes the paradigm for Shakespeare's most compelling female characters.

As You Like It

An example of pastoral comedy, *As You Like It* incorporates that genre's traditional distinction between urban corruption and the simple moral purity available in the country. Like much of western literature, the conventions of this genre found their way into English poetry and drama from Greek and Latin predecessors. Essentially a literature of wish-fulfillment, the pastoral genre originated sometime around 300 B.C. with the Sicilian poet, Theocritus, and developed deeper roots in the western canon as a result of Vergil's *Bucolics*. As Gilbert Highet puts it, pastoral writers characterize rural life by its

> ... simple love-making, folk-music (especially singing and piping), purity of morals, simplicity of manners, healthy diet, plain clothing, and an unspoilt way of living, in strong contrast to the anxiety and corruption of existence in great cities and royal courts. The coarseness of country life is neither emphasized nor concealed, but is offset by its essential purity. (162)

By juxtaposing civilization's corruption with the regenerative powers of rural life, the pastoral genre gives the very human longing for simplicity and lost innocence an appealing geographical location.

Like many other pastorals, much is said in *As You Like It* but not much really happens. Naturally enough, therefore, conversation quickly turns to the nature of love, perhaps the most significant factor of human happiness. The play provides multiple perspectives on the topic. As several minor characters implement their inadequate assumptions about love, the words and actions of the play's charming main character quickly establish a far more compelling definition.

Notable for her emotional strength and maturity, Rosalind earns high praise from Bloom:

> Rosalind is unique in Shakespeare, perhaps indeed in Western drama, because it is so difficult to achieve a perspective upon her that she herself does not anticipate and share. A stage play is virtually impossible without some degree of irony, that is the audience's privilege. We enjoy such an irony in regard to Touchstone, Jaques, and every other character in *As You Like It*, except for Rosalind. We forgive her for knowing what matters more than we do, because she has no will to power over us, except to exercise our most humane faculties in appreciation of her performance. (204)

Self-awareness, Bloom correctly asserts, is Rosalind's special gift. From her very first lines until the final syllables of the epilogue where she politely asks for applause, Rosalind remains a unique character because she sees herself and the world around her with disarming objectivity. That capacity is evident, for example, when she makes fun of her own habitual loquaciousness: "Do you not know I am a woman?" she coyly asks her cousin and closest friend, Celia, "When I think, I must speak" (3.2.249). This good-natured honesty, Bloom observes, frees her from the dramatic irony of characters who only see themselves partially. With exquisite wit and charm, she demonstrates that a person is most lovable when she herself is transparently loving, one consequence of her capacity for objective self-assessment. This, Shakespeare seems to be saying through his remarkable heroine, is what genuine love looks like. Every other perspective on love expressed by the play's other characters pales in comparison to what Rosalind lives out with wit, charm, humor, self-awareness, and unmistakably genuine emotion. The play delights because she herself is so delightful.

    Even more noteworthy than her charming personality, however, is Rosalind's role as the play's tutor in the art of romantic love. While her lessons are designed to engage emotionally with her admirer, Orlando, she quickly grasps the sincerity of his ardor, despite his reliance on the conventional tropes of Courtly Love. Though he expresses his desire for her in words authored by other men for other women, Rosalind, like Juliet, delights in rather than fears the power of his longing. Unafraid of his emotions and undeterred by what his language inadequately conveys, she welcomes rather than resists the love that moves him. Like Juliet, Rosalind is incapable of playing the chaste, cold-hearted object of her suitor's affection.

That acceptance of everything Orlando is dovetails neatly with the pastoral's incorporation of the erotic as an essential component of life, what Highet calls pastoral's "simple lovemaking," amplified further by pastoral literature's emphasis on nature's fecundity. Ovid may have fixated on the unfortunate consequences of sexual desire, but Shakespeare came to understand the obligation, not to avoid the erotic, but to bravely respond to its allure with a moral discipline that enhances rather than detracts from life.

Though the erotic is never a major component of the play's discussion, it threads its way into the play's fabric not only because of the pastoral setting but also because Shakespeare's brave heroines live out his axiom that love's promised transformation can only be realized through a complete acceptance of the other. John Russel Brown makes the following observation about the transformative power of a fully realized love:

> Both Falstaff [*1Henry 4*] and Benedick [*Much Ado About Nothing*] remember Jove's transformation into a bull; the difference between these two lovers lies not in the presence or absence of bestiality, but in the use—the order or disorder–to which that 'simplicity' is put. In the very conclusion of his comedies, Shakespeare did not care to celebrate 'platonic' love which ignores or supersedes man's 'hearkening after the flesh'; the love which triumphs is a full one, established at the

risk of disorder and compounded of beast, man, and spirit. (136)

As the play very carefully differentiates those value assumptions that foster a joy that endures, the secret of Rosalind's allure, what Bloom calls her vitality, becomes clearer. In contrast to the conventional lady of Courtly Love, *As You Like It*'s charming female protagonist captivates because she sees male desire not as a problem but as an opportunity to foster emotional and spiritual growth. Her optimism is infectious, and that joyful anticipation of every aspect of love inevitably enchants and fascinates. Where the play's other perspectives on love may be the unfortunate reality, her version of love remains a universal hope.

Yet there is more to her than unalloyed joy, too, for Rosalind is unwilling to leave Orlando mired in his unqualified romantic expectations. She wants more for herself and for him, so she spends considerable time and energy qualifying his unrealistic ideas about women. What's truly remarkable about this exercise of educating her lover is the complete absence of any meanness, superiority, or self-pride. Because she is so self-aware, Rosalind seems to be sharing her insights into the female heart rather than correcting male ignorance. And not just sharing her best self but her whole self, the good, the bad, and the ugly. Throughout, the process exudes the same joy and charming wit that she exhibits everywhere else. This is caring and love of a completely different order. Rosalind may be the first in a lengthy catalog of Shakespearean women who reprise this pedagogical function within their relationships, but all the remaining major plays pay homage to women who administer similarly to love's miraculous transformations.

Unlike the women of Courtly Love, who simply inhabit an eminence men give them, Rosalind earns her elevated status by embracing every dimension of her relationship to Orlando. Though the audience never doubts his love for her, her ownership of their relationship and her level-headed investment in its health differentiate her from her suitor who seems all but incapable of seeing beyond his desire. Characters like Juliet and Rosalind exhibit a very special awareness of the human emotions inside and around them which separates them from their men. It's as if a woman's unique ability to create, birth, and nurture new life, what Shakespeare seems to consider her nature, distinguishes her not only physically from Orlando but emotionally and spiritually as well. This position may irritate feminist sensibilities, but it explains why Lady Macbeth only partially succeeds in expunging any maternal instincts that might interfere with murder. By way of contrast, Rosalind is iridescent with these feminine qualities, and it is why she flourishes in Arden, far from the sophistications of court and closer to procreative nature.

Where the forest is a world of simple virtues, the city and court are masculine environments where the assertion of rights and power establishes an appearance of order that ultimately proves untenable. For much of the first two acts, that world is beset by conflict and teeters on the verge of disruption. There, brother contests with brother. Enduring inadequate educational and financial support from his miserly older brother, Oliver, Orlando chafes under his sibling's guardianship. The origin of this fraternal conflict remains vague. Though Oliver privately acknowledges that Orlando is "gentle, never school'd and yet learned, full of noble device [and] enchantingly belov'd," he dislikes the young man intensely. He admits he doesn't know why his very soul "hates nothing more" than this younger sibling (1.1.165-66). Nevertheless, the simmering conflict takes a savage turn when Oliver proposes a match between Orlando and Charles the wrestler who has been hired to eliminate the troublemaker once and for all. Ignorant of this evil plot against his life, the unsuspecting Orlando is now in mortal danger.

But Charles also provides the first glimpse of another, far different world, free of intrigue, conflict, and moral hazard. When Oliver asks for news from the court, the wrestler recounts how its current ruler, Duke Frederick, had deposed his older brother, Duke Senior, who now lives as an exile in Arden Forest. Though Oliver hears this as a warning of a younger brother's dangerous ambition, it is also a second example of how brotherly discord disrupts and divides the corrupt court from an ancient and far more innocent garden:

> Oli. Where will the old Duke live?
> Cha. They say he is already in the forest of Arden, and a many merry men with him; and there they live like the old Robin Hood of England. They say many young gentlemen flock to him every day, and fleet the time carelessly, as they did in the golden world.
> (1.1.113-119)

Here, the golden world of primal innocence and ease is conflated with the very English forest of Robin Hood, known for his generosity to the poor. The description is meant to invoke a mythical time of innocence and virtue, very much like the Biblical Eden. In stark contrast to the discord of the present moment, this golden age invokes a time when people lived peacefully and gave generously. That young nobles gravitate toward Arden suggests something in man makes simple goodness preferable to intrigue and corruption. This "something" is the essential human nature the play seeks to define through events in Arden. Because that goodness is a natural extension of mankind's ability to love well, the women feel much more at home in Arden than they do in Duke Frederick's court.

The vulnerability of the powerless is exposed a second time with the introduction of the play's two female characters: Rosalind, the daughter of the deposed Duke Senior, and his niece, Celia, the daughter of his wicked younger brother, Duke Frederick, who usurped civil authority from his elder brother.

In contrast to the play's feuding sets of brothers, the two female cousins share a deep, unshakeable friendship. And because of their emotional maturity, falling in love happens easily. When they witness the match between Charles and Orlando, who not only survives but defeats his opponent, Rosalind tells the young gallant "you have wrestled well and overthrown more than your enemies (1.2.253ff). Though she has fallen quickly herself, Duke Frederick learns that Orlando is the son of Sir Rowland de Boys, who "the world esteem'd . . . honorable," but whom Frederick "did find. . . still mine enemy" (1.2.225ff). As a result, Orlando is forced to flee the court, leaving his beloved Rosalind behind. Clearly, he too has been deeply smitten, referring to her as he exits the scene as the "heavenly Rosalind."

Having now banished the victorious but unfortunate young wrestler, Frederick's ignoble jealousy and distrust threaten to poison the close relationship between the two female cousins, Celia and Rosalind. He worries that Rosalind could further inflame his subjects, who already dislike the pain inflicted upon the exiled duke's family. "Her very silence, and her patience," he fears, "speak to the people, and they pity her" (1.3.78-79). For the incipient danger posed by her obvious virtue, Rosalind too must leave. Intrigue and suspicion have now divided children from parents as well as young lovers, and the castaways are sent off on separate journeys into the forest. Despite an appearance of order, the so-called civilized world rejects anything of real value.

Rejection, which tests the character of the evicted, begins to differentiate Orlando and the two female cousins from everyone who remains behind in the deceptively civilized court. For the girls, banishment could easily have severed their relationship, but the love between these very vulnerable women remains steadfast. Facing a potentially hostile world by herself, Rosalind's normally cheerful disposition momentarily evaporates and, with her thoughts racing, she responds to Celia's sympathy in short, clipped phrases that reveal her fear:

> Cel. O my poor Rosalind, whither wilt thou go? Wilt thou
> change fathers? I will give thee mine. I charge thee be
> not thou more griev'd than I am.
> Ros.   I have more cause.
> Cel. Thou hast not, cousin,
> Prithee be cheerful. Know'st thou not the Duke
> Hath banished me, his daughter?
> Ros.   That he hath not.
> Cel. No, hath not? Rosalind lacks then the love
> Which teacheth thee that thou and I am one.
> Shall we be sund'red? Shall we part, sweet girl?
> No, let my father seek another heir. (1.3.90 – 99)

Where the masculine world of self-assertion divides, Celia reminds her disconsolate cousin "that thou and I [are] one." Devotion and love are what qualifies them for the forest.

    Celia's unwavering commitment to her cousin goes far beyond mere words, too, and they flee the court into the forest. For their protection, the two women disguise themselves as brother and sister. Rosalind assumes the identity of the young man, Ganymede; Celia will take the name Aliena, indicating her estrangement from an unworthy father. For these intrepid women, the forest brings a sense of freedom, of new possibility, something the cheerful Celia recognizes. As they prepare to leave the court, she remarks, "Now go we in content to liberty, and not to banishment" (1.3.137-38). Escaping the palace intrigues and the masculine jockeying for power and advantage, the forest represents an opportunity for these women to define the love they desire for themselves.

    Similarly, once Orlando's escapes from Frederick's court, he is no longer defined by those masculine traits of assertiveness, courage, and strength, necessary where the weak, the powerless, and the vulnerable are all subject to the stronger. The prickly self-assertion exhibited when he challenged Oliver's neglect is replaced by kind concern for the family's elderly servant, Adam, who generously offers his life saving for the arduous journey ahead of them. Drawing on the wisdom of Matthew 10:29, Adam confidently expresses his belief that all will be well. Providence, which graciously feeds the birds of the air, will supply whatever they need. He epitomizes, therefore, the trust and generosity that Arden fosters:

> ... He that doth the ravens feed,
> Yea, providently caters for the sparrow,
> Be comfort to my age! Here is the gold,
> All this I give to you, let me be your servant....
> Let me go with you,
> I'll do the service of a younger man.... (2.3.43-54)

Where distrust and animosity unleash division, now kindness begets kindness. When the old man falters on their journey, Orlando makes his companion comfortable and sets off in search of food. Encountering the deposed Duke Senior at his supper, Orlando instinctively resorts to the male belligerence that operates at court, but his good-natured host reminds the intruder that "your gentleness shall force, more than your force move us to gentleness" (2.7.102-03). Here, the aggressive self-assertion so normal in Duke Frederick's world is unnecessary, and its absence is precisely what makes fear unnecessary and Arden a safer haven for the vulnerable. In contrast to the court, Arden is a place where true nobility is independent of birth, wealth, power, or authority. Kindness and generosity are the traits that matter here, and, like the two women, escaping from court encourages Orlando to be more himself.

But nature does not participate in the bifurcated morality of human nature. As the first lines of one of the play's mournful songs remind us, nature is not altogether benign: "Blow, blow, thou winter wind, thou art not so unkind as man's ingratitude" (2.7.174ff). Both nature and human nature have been corrupted by original sin. But sadness is not pessimism: Duke Senior elaborates Adam's view of a providential nature benevolently answering every human need with additional moral nuance:

> Are not these woods
> More free from peril than the envious court?
> Here feel we not the penalty of Adam,
> The season's difference, as the icy fang
> And churlish chiding of the winter's wind,
> Which when it bites and blows upon my body
> Even till I shrink with cold, I smile and say,
> "This is no flattery: these are counsellors
> That feelingly persuade me what I am."
> Sweet are the uses of adversity. . . .
> And this our life, exempt from public haunt,
> Finds tongues in trees, books in the running brooks,
> Sermons in stones, and good in every thing. (2.1.3-17)

The first man's sin ruined the unblemished benevolence of the original world, introducing adversity, suffering, and death. As several of the play's songs remind us, Arden is no Eden. Forced to endure banishment and exile, the duke has accommodated himself to a nature that has been changed by "the penalty of Adam." His distinction between court and forest might initially seem naïvely romanticized, but that misses the point of his speech. He admits, for example, that nature has "feelingly persuade[d] me what I am." Enduring nature's "icy fang" and the "churlish chiding of the winter's wind" brings a recognition of his own helplessness and the need for sympathy and generosity toward others. Here, even suffering has a purpose, encouraging sympathy and kindness for the less fortunate. Though this is nature unadorned, it also remains unencumbered by the self-centered misconceptions of a corrupt civilization. Here, nature's simple pleasures and freedoms as well as its "icy fang" cultivate an appreciation for life's sometimes bitter sweetness. Despite its origins in pastoral literature, Shakespeare refuses to simply duplicate that genre's romanticized nature.

Within that very Christian perspective of sinful man's place in a world that all too easily distracts him from the possibility of virtue, *As You Like It* begins to delineate what values and behaviors insure human well-being within its lightly handled but complex view of nature. Beset on one side by a morally indifferent nature and, on the other side, by human evil, the implicit answer to both assaults on a peaceful existence, of course, is love, and the play provides four sets of characters to define what human nature needs in that regard: the self-indulgent, sex-obsessed Touchstone; the cynical Jaques; those mismatched lovers, Silvius and Phebe; and, of course, Rosalind and Orlando. Taken together, these four views of love help define what love isn't and what, by contrast, it actually should look like.

Like the wicked Oliver and Duke Frederick, Touchstone, the court jester Rosalind and Celia bring along with them into the forest, is largely driven by selfish desire. Once in Arden, he quickly finds and pursues Audrey, a country wench who is completely guileless. Unfortunately for her, Touchstone's view of love is mired in the physical, and, employing courtly wit and cynical attention, he tries to seduce the gullible young lady. She is little more than food for his sexual appetite. Ironically named after the stone used to distinguish real gold from dross, Touchstone's courtly wit and bawdy insinuations remain largely incomprehensible to this innocent young girl.

> Touch. Truly, I would the gods had made thee poetical.
> Aud. I do not know what "poetical" is. Is it honest in deed and word? Is it a true thing?
> Touch. No, truly; for the truest poetry is the most feigning, and lovers are given to poetry; and what they swear in poetry may be said as lovers they do feign.
> Aud. And would you not have me honest?
> Touch. No, truly, unless thou wert hard-favor'd; for

	honesty coupled to beauty is to have honey a sauce to sugar....
Aud.	Well, I am not fair, and therefore I pray the gods make me honest.
Touch.	Truly, and to cast away honesty upon a foul slut were to put good meat into an unclean dish.
Aud.	I am not a slut, though I thank the gods I am foul.
Touch.	Well, prais'd be the gods for thy foulness! Sluttishness may come hereafter. But be it as it may, I will marry thee.... (3.3.16-42)

Even his marriage proposal is sinister, for he engages a minister of dubious reputation, Sir Oliver Martext, whose name proclaims his spiritual and legal insufficiency. In an aside to the audience, Touchstone makes his intentions clear:

> ...I were better married of him than of another, for he is not like to marry me well; and not being well married, it will be a good excuse for me hereafter to leave my wife. (3.3.90-94)

Oblivious to her simple goodness, Touchstone abuses her trust and innocence to satisfy his sexual appetites. Ovid's dangerously sexual beasts are visible in this unattractive picture of male desire. It is concerned only with its own satisfaction.

But simplicity and honesty expose the duplicity of Touchstone's witty rhetoric. In another exchange with the shepherd Corin, Touchstone's sophistication is deflated by the young man's honesty about the simple demands and pleasures of his life:

Touch.	.... Wast ever in court, shepherd?
Cor.	No, truly.
Touch.	Then thou art damn'd.
Cor.	Nay, I hope [not].
Touch.	Truly, thou art damn'd, like an ill-roasted egg, all on one side.
Cor.	For not being at court? Your reason.
Touch.	Why, if thou never wast at court, thou never

	saw good manners, then thy manners must be wicked, and wickedness is a sin, and sin is damnation. Thou art in parlous state, shepherd.
Cor.	Not a whit, Touchstone. Those that are good manners at court are as ridiculous in the country as the behavior of the country is most mockable at the court....
Touch.	Shallow, shallow. A better instance, I say; come....
Cor.	You have too courtly a wit for me. I'll rest.
Touch.	Wilt thou rest damn'd? God help thee, shallow man!....
Cor.	Sir, I am a true laborer: I earn that I eat, get that I wear, owe no man hate, envy no man's happiness, glad of other men's good, content with my harm, and the greatest of my pride is to see my ewes graze and my lambs suck. (3.2.32-77)

Measured against the values Corin lives by, values like hard work, promoting peace between neighbors, cultivating gratitude, tolerant endurance, and appreciation for nature's abundant gifts, Touchstone's civilized manners and wit end up looking exceedingly shallow and disingenuous. Though not being gold itself, the fabled touchstone was used to identify pure gold from its imposters. Similarly, this courtly wit provides a baseline by which all the other lovers can be measured. In a sense, he represents the lowest common denominator: the erotic is unarguably part of romantic love, but it can't be the only part.

    The second perspective on love comes from Jaques, the play's melancholic commentator, who reveals his natural disposition in a reported encounter with Touchstone. After witnessing Touchstone railing against fortune and time, Jaques desires the "liberty" of a court fool so that he too can "speak my mind...[to] cleanse the foul body of the infected world" (2.7.51ff). What Jaques sees, however, is as limited a perspective as Touchstone's. In his famous seven ages of man speech, he concludes that man's "strange eventful history [ends in] second childishness, and mere oblivion, sans teeth, sans eyes, sans taste, sans every thing" (2.7.164ff). Despite any joy in the previous six stages of life, the sad end of human endeavors, according to Jaques, is a pointless stupor devoid of all sensibility and pleasure.

    Like Touchstone, Jaques is a reductionist, a person who simplifies the complex for his own purposes. If the court jester's only purpose is to satisfy the desires of the flesh, the melancholic reduces the complex to expose whatever he considers human folly. Love does not escape his ire. The lover in his seven ages speech is diminished to an absurd and irrational foolishness, men driven mad by desire and tacking poems "to [their] mistress' eyebrow" on every tree. Little wonder, then, that his encounter with the love-struck Orlando does not go well:

> Jaq.   I pray you mar no more trees with writing love-songs in their barks.
> Orl.   I pray you mar no moe of my verses with reading them ill-favoredly.
> Jaq.   Rosalind is your love's name?
> Orl.   Yes, just.
> Jaq.   I do not like her name.
> Orl.   There was no thought of pleasing you when she was christen'd. . . .
> Jaq.   You have a nimble wit. . . . Will you sit down with me? And we two will rail against our mistress the world and all our misery.
> Orl.   I will chide no breather in the world but myself, against whom I know most faults.
> Jaq.   The worst fault you have is to be in love.
>   (3.2.259-282)

By oversimplifying love, Jaques removes every possible joy from the world and slips into a melancholy that colors his view of human motives and experiences.

If Touchstone somehow embodies an essential force of nature, Jacques has his virtues too. Ever sensitive to human foibles, the cynic quickly identifies Touchstone's nefarious intention to desert Audrey as soon as he beds her. Jacques intercedes, dismissing the fake minister, Oliver Martext, and insists the couple engage a legitimate churchman to be properly married. Whatever his shortcomings as pleasant company, Jacques has a gift for preserving virtue. In these short, seemingly unconnected encounters, then, the play presents three perspectives on love: undiluted erotic desire, a reductive conviction of love as the essence of human folly, and, through Orlando, the romanticized love of the poets. Eventually, all three will be shown to be inadequate.

Love needs to be properly appreciated, *As You Like It* argues, because cruel pride all too easily wastes youth and beauty, which constitute love's precious and fleeting moment. This is the purpose for those mismatched lovers, Silvius and Phebe. Like Orlando, Silvius is completely overwhelmed by his feelings for Phebe, who, unlike Rosalind, can barely tolerate her lover's adoring presence. "Now I do frown on thee with all my heart," she begins, "and if mine eyes can wound, now let them kill thee" (3.5.15-16). When Rosalind, still disguised as Ganymede, witnesses the cruelty of Phebe's words, she interjects herself into this exchange to remind the shepherdess of her hard heart and the fleeting opportunity for love:

> Ros. . . . Who might be your mother,
> That you insult, exult, and all at once,
> Over the wretched? What though you have no
>   beauty—
> As, by my faith, I see no more in you
> Than without candle may go dark to bed—
> Must you be therefore proud and pitiless?

Being anything but "proud and pitiless" with her Orlando, she tries mightily to correct Silvius' thinking:

> You foolish shepherd, wherefore do you follow her,
> Like foggy south, puffing with wind and rain?
> You are a thousand times a properer man
> Than she a woman. 'Tis such fools as you
> That make the world full of ill-favor'd children.
> 'Tis not her glass, but you that flatters her.

And she concludes by reminding Phebe how fortunate she is to have someone who loves her so unequivocally:

> But, mistress, know yourself, down on your knees,
> And thank heaven, fasting, for a good man's love;
> For I must tell you friendly in your ear,'
> Sell when you can, you are not for all markets. . ..
> (3.5.35-60)

The warning is fraught with comic irony, however, because Phebe has instantaneously fallen in love with Rosalind-Ganymede, who must now treat the suddenly smitten shepherdess with the same cruel honesty that she has just censured. Even for the glorious Rosalind, love has a way of humbling every shred of human pride. While the complete irrationality of love has become obvious to all, Rosalind's empathy for Silvius increases her appreciation of Orlando's unshakeable devotion to her and, therefore, the gratitude she owes him for that love. This initiates the movement away from deceptive disguise and toward the revelation of every hidden truth.

If Touchstone's acquiescence to the flesh, and Jaques's displeasure with all forms of worldly corruption ,and Orlando's romantic illusions, and Phebe's ingratitude for genuine devotion represent four of the play's limited perspectives on love, the relationship Rosalind builds with Orlando provides a sane alternative. Unfortunately for

Rosalind, however, the precautionary disguise she assumed before entering Arden now prevents Orlando from courting her directly. "Alas the day, what shall I do with my doublet and hose?" she laments (3.2.219). Since, logically, there's no reason for her to conceal her identity any longer, her decision to maintain the role of Ganymede only makes sense as an effort to verify Orlando's love, which so far has only been expressed in the exaggerated rhetoric of courtly love poetry. From Silvius's foolish adoration of Phebe, she understands that is insufficient.

Arden's inhabitants have been amused by the fevered sonnets the love-smitten Orlando has been tacking to every tree. "From the east to western Inde," begins one, "No jewel is like Rosalind" (3.2.88-9). Touchstone, of course, can't resist ridiculing these rhymes by reducing a lover's attraction to its lowest denominator. "If the cat will after kind," he mimics, "So be sure will Rosalind" (3.2.103-4). His reduction of love to the merely physical overlooks love's potential richness that includes sexual desire but also much more as well. To verify that Orlando's love is genuine, therefore, the disguised Rosalind proposes to instruct him on the proper way to woo a girl. Rosalind's catechism demonstrates exactly what the emotional richness of love looks and feels like. For what transpires between these two in Arden is magical, addressing all the emotional shortcomings that plague the civilized world they left behind. Ironically contradicting a situation where a woman is disguised, the catechism is intended to reveal what women are really like.

Because Orlando's sonnets are full of common poetic tropes, Rosalind immediately understands that her lessons need to impart a more realistic view of women and their mercurial emotions. Orlando, however, is incorrigible. He resists any effort to dilute his romanticized vision of love:

    Ros.   But are you so much in love as your rhymes speak?

Orl.	Neither rhyme nor reason can express how much.
Ros.	Love is merely a madness, and I tell you, deserves as well a dark house and a whip as madmen do; and the reason why they are not so punish'd and cur'd is, that the lunacy is so ordinary that the whippers are in love too. Yet I profess curing it by counsel.
Orl.	Did you ever cure any so?
Ros.	Yes, one, and in this manner. He was to imagine me his love, his mistress; and I set him every day to woo me. At which time would I, being but a moonish youth, grieve, be effeminate, changeable, longing and liking, proud, fantastical, apish, shallow, inconstant, full of tears, full of smiles; for every passion, something, and for no passion truly any thing, as boys and women are for the most part cattle of this color; would now like him, now loathe him; then entertain him, then forswear him; now weep for him, then spit at him; that I drave my suitor from his mad humor of love to a living humor of madness, which was, to forswear the full stream of the world, and to live in a nook merely monastic....
Orl.	I would not be cur'd, youth.
Ros.	I would cure you if you would but call me Rosalind. (3.3.396-426)

Humorously acknowledging the volatility of female emotions, Rosalind displays an awareness of the craziness that love inflicts on both women and men, but their exchange contains layers of emotional subtlety. Because he truly enjoys being in love, Orlando resists exchanging his naïve romanticism for Ganymede's exaggerated realism. He refuses to believe that Rosalind could be anything less than perfectly good and consistently loving. He agrees to practice wooing Ganymede-Rosalind, not because he wants to be cured, but because he wants to relive the process of wooing daily. She, on the other hand, pretends to be curing him, not so much to minister to his emotional lunacy but to have a reason to spend precious time with him. Despite the quasi-educational premise for these meetings, the audience is aware that, underneath the dialogue, the flame of love is already roaring-hot, and together they live out some of the very contradictions she mocks. When he is late the next time they meet, for example, she pretends to be cross with him. Later, however, when she learns he's been wounded saving his wicked brother, Oliver, from the jaws of a lion, she faints, all the while trying to explain to her puzzled onlookers why a masculine Ganymede would receive the news as a woman might. The emotional chemistry at work in all this is unmistakable. On stage, it is really quite amusing.

And part of that chemistry is avowedly sexual. In a second session of burlesque wooing, Rosalind mercilessly teases her young charge. When he again pledges unwavering loyalty to his beloved Rosalind, she matter-of-factly suggests that women are just as subject to infidelity as men. And, worse, she warns him, they'll never admit they were wrong:

> Ros. Now tell me how long you would have her after you have possess'd her.
> Orl. Forever and a day.
> Ros. Say "a day" without the "ever." No, no, Orlando, men are April when they woo, December when they wed; maids are May when they are maids, but the sky changes when they are wives. I will be more jealous of thee than a Barbary cock. . ., more clamorous than a parrot against rain. . . . I will weep for nothing, like Diana in the fountain, and I will do that when you are dispos'd to be merry. I will laugh like a hyen, and that when thou art inclin'd to sleep.
> Orl. But will my Rosalind do so?
> Ros. By my life, she will do as I do.
> Orl. O, but she is wise.
> Ros. . . . the wiser, the waywarder. Make the doors upon a woman's wit, and it will out the casement; shut that, and 'twill

		out at the key-hole....
	Orl.	A man that had a wife with such a wit, he might say "Wit, whither wilt?"
	Ros.	Nay, you might keep that check for it, till you met your wife's wit going to your neighbor's bed.
	Orl.	And what wit could wit have to excuse that?
	Ros.	Marry, to say she came to seek you there. You shall never take her without her answer, unless you take her without her tongue. O that woman who cannot make her fault her husband's occasion, let her never nurse her child herself, for she will breed it like a fool! (4.1.143-176)

Much of Rosalind's enduring charm is this witty ability to ridicule the frailties of her sex, which she purposely sets in opposition to Orlando's romantic idealism. If he pledges unchangeable love, she promises maddening contrariness; or a weakness for her neighbor's bed; or the uncanny ability to transform her faults into her husband's. Any woman unable to turn the tables on her hapless husband, she concludes, will raise a fool for her child. But in the process of itemizing feminine weaknesses, she convinces all of us that her self-awareness will make her the exception. Everything about her suggests that knowing where the fault lines are is exactly what will help her avoid them.

    Orlando's unshakeable sincerity together with Rosalind's witty self-awareness creates a picture of two well-adjusted characters who truly enjoy each other's company. Very quickly, the audience sees that they really do belong together. Though she can mock love as thoroughly as Touchstone or Jaques, Rosalind is entirely different from these other two. No sooner has she ridiculed wedded bliss than she makes her confession to Celia after Orlando has left her company. "O coz, coz, coz, my pretty little coz," she begins, "that thou didst know how many fathom deep I am in love! But it cannot be sounded; my affection hath an unknown bottom, like the Bay of Portugal.... I tell thee, Aliena, I cannot be out of the sight of Orlando. I'll go find a shadow, and sigh till he come" (4.1.205-217). Having just delivered a thoroughly anti-romantic catechism to Orlando, Rosalind has established herself as a realistic and therefore reliable observer of human nature, a stature that makes her confession of love all the more believable and genuine. Yet once she's alone, she employs the very same language. These contradictions remain unresolved as they are in life. Every perspective on love is somehow limited, including Rosalind's, but her ability to live with those makes hers the only valid perspective on the topic. So it is entirely fitting that Touchstone comes to meekly accept the value of his wife's simple honesty, that "pearl in a foul oyster." And it is equally fitting that Jaques joins the reformed Duke Frederick who, in the final scenes, retreats to a "life monastic."

Rosalind's balance of realism and genuine emotion qualifies every other partial and incomplete perspective, which lacks her joy, her vitality, her ability to comprehend and accept all of love's crazy contradictions. That is the nature of love: crazy, contradictory, inescapable, necessary, and an essential part of human experience. She sees love wholly and objectively without losing any of the joy that love should bring to life. That is her gift, her magic, and neither Touchstone nor Jaques have the character to duplicate it. That is what differentiates her from the others, and it is what makes her entirely and completely loveable. Because Orlando sees that, accepts it, and loves her for it, he is entirely worthy to be her partner. They belong together because, unlike any of the other characters, they are both fully capable of inspiring each other's love and devotion. This, we come to realize, is romance.

In typical comic fashion, the last scenes of the play bring all the potential couples together: Touchstone accepts his country life with Audrey; Phebe, no longer deceived by Rosalind's disguise, accepts Silvius's love; and, of course, Rosalind and Orlando are finally able to openly pledge their mutual devotion to each other. Frederick, who had set out to arrest and execute his brother, Duke Senior, meets an old religious man who dissuades him from this final wicked enterprise and convinces him to retreat from the world altogether. Civil authority is restored to his deposed brother. Aggression, discord, and selfish desire have all been tamed by love; deception and disguise by plain truth; and wickedness by virtue. Though man will always be vulnerable to the winter winds, both real and metaphorical, life can still be sweet and lovely if simple goodness retains its value. This is, indeed, as it should be and, therefore, as we like it.

As You Like It continues to charm audiences with its captivating heroine, its balanced view of life and love, and its promotion of simple pleasures and basic virtues as antidotes to the corrupting influence of the desire for power, prestige, or pleasure. Mankind is burdened with sufficient freedom to choose what satisfies self-centered desire or what's more in line with what's visibly good in nature, its abundance, its simplicity, its promise of joyful union through love. And with Rosalind, Shakespeare states his argument that some women are able to make the best side of nature visible to others.

Pastoral's dichotomy between urban corruption and rural virtue is a reminder of the potential for innocence that the Biblical story of the Fall documents. That innocence was lost as a result of a desire for something not yet possessed. In the Forest of Arden, nature provides what's needed, its inhabitants rest in that assurance, and the prevailing peace fosters love and its attendant fecundity. Shakespeare doesn't ignore the presence of evil, even here, but he exhibits an awareness not only of a better alternative that can be chosen but of some indwelling force in the world that encourages that choice, that brings seekers to its blessings.

In a compelling little book, Northrop Frye makes the following very astute observation about the difference between Ben Jonson's and Shakespeare's views of nature, particularly the invisible forces capable of disrupting its visible orderliness. In his late masques, Jonson would refer to that force as a form of human magic, a metaphor that Shakespeare uses in a much different way, especially in his later romances, where magic is an acceptable human activity that partakes of something larger and metaphysical.

> This conception of nature as an order threatened, but not essentially disturbed, by witchcraft is in Shakespearean romance too. What Shakespeare has that Jonson neither has nor wants is the sense of nature as comprising not merely an order but a power, at once supernatural and connatural, expressed most eloquently in the dance and controlled either by benevolent human magic or by divine will. ... [T]he myth of nature in Shakespeare [puts the emphasis] not on the visible rational order that obeys, but on the mysterious personal force that commands. (*The Natural Perspective*, 71)

Here, in *As You Like It*, that power, as Frye describes it, may best be described as the force of life. It gives its abundant gifts freely to those, like Rosalind and Orlando, who are intuitively drawn to it. Oliver, Frederick, and Touchstone all want its abundance for themselves and are willing to take by wit or by force what should be freely available from others. Where this life force inhabits a place infused with a generous, selfless, joyful love freely shared, it is opposed by a will to control, to deny, to acquire for the self. This power, therefore, is inherently moral, dividing its goodness from everything evil. As the source of new life, the erotic is connected to this life force, but until it emanates from a generous heart that wants to share its goodness with another, the erotic is easily corrupted by that insatiable desire for self-enhancing pleasure. This selfishness is why Touchstone's attempt to pair with Audry ultimately fails. Rosalind, on the other hand, is aligned with that life force. It is the source of her love and joy. She and Orlando find it in the freedom of Arden, away from the selfishness and greed of a corrupt civilization that foolishly takes for itself what is freely available to all. The only prerequisite for citizenship in Arden is that generous, giving, selfless heart that hungers for love's joy.

As You Like It richly deserves its place in this examination of Shakespeare's artistic development because Rosalind is the first, very clear example of a female character that, by nature and personality, is somehow aligned with this power that Frye identifies in and above nature. Intuitively, she knows its purpose for the world is to be found through her relationship with Orlando, and she takes great joy in cultivating that love, anticipating the blessings that will be bestowed for her faith in its goodness. That supernatural power is visible in nature and, because she so enthusiastically embraces what nature provides her, it is visible in her as well. Rosalind's stature begins in Courtly Love traditions but begins to carry her admirers far beyond those very secular, very worldly implications. While many of Shakespeare's subsequent heroines partake of that same power, the dramatic context in which they function profoundly enriches those implications glimpsed here of nature and mankind's place in it.

While the next play, *Hamlet*, has its roots in the traditions of Senecan revenge tragedy, Shakespeare transforms the inherent melodramatic elements of that subgenre into one of the profound examinations of sin and its personal and social consequences. His awareness of a natural world comprised "not merely [of] an order but [of] a power, at once supernatural and connatural," to adapt Frye's language, made that tragedy possible. In both time and place, Shakespeare argues, evidence of a mysterious benevolence makes itself known. Contrary to the prevalent assumption that Christianity's optimistic belief in redemption obviates the tragic, it is precisely because Shakespeare's work exhibits this awareness of a metaphysical power at work in human affairs that tragedy becomes possible, and it is why his plays possess the kind of intellectual and emotional depth that eludes lesser artists.

In Greek tragedy, the suffering experienced by the protagonists drives them to a recognition of forces largely indifferent to their fates. Suffering in the face of mortality, they question and plead with the gods who never answer. Tragedy reminds us that whatever name a particular culture gives to the force that directs individual destinies and whatever reasons are given for the course of human experience, nothing can adequately explain the essential mystery of either that force or its purposes. It is unknowable and divine and, for all our pretensions to power, we are inherently limited mortals completely inadequate to plumb those mysteries. For Shakespeare, the moral tenets of Christianity, like free will, sin, the possibility of innocence, the necessity of forgiveness, all open a door to the very same questions about human nature, suffering, and death that Greek tragedy explores so effectively. But unlike the inherent pessimism of Greek tragedy, Shakespeare recognizes what Frye terms a mysterious force that commands, and every blessing found in this world somehow seems to align with that presence. Nothing beyond that is knowable.

Hamlet, a play that shows how covetous desire poisons every aspect of life in Denmark, is named for its remarkable and endlessly fascinating central character. Though the ghost of his murdered father commands Hamlet to avenge that death, to call it a tragedy of revenge misrepresents the rich and complex theatrical experience we have been given, for nothing has ever quite matched that play's ability to demonstrate what men of limited insight experience when they are asked to choose between moral absolutes that carry eternal consequences.

Hamlet

In the four centuries since it was written, a convincing interpretation of *Hamlet* has proven notoriously elusive, unsurprising, perhaps, for a play that begins with a question and exudes mystery throughout. In fact, no other work of English literature has generated more commentary than *Hamlet,* usually classified as an example of Elizabethan revenge tragedy, a genre derived from Seneca's Roman dramas. For the critic obliged to reveal the play's significance and cohesion, the problem begins with the absence of any clearly articulated motivation for the delay of Hamlet's promised revenge. Inexplicably, a huge portion of his longest play is a lament for a promise left undone.

Due to its notoriety, the details of *Hamlet's* plot may already be familiar. Hamlet's father, the legitimate king of Denmark, has been secretly poisoned by his brother, Claudius, presumably to marry Hamlet's mother, Gertrude. As the Danes celebrate the marriage offstage, the ghost of Old Hamlet appears and demands that his son, Prince Hamlet, avenge his untimely death. Having just returned from Wittenberg where he studies philosophy with his friend, Horatio, an enraged Hamlet vows to fulfill his father's request. Many problematic circumstances dampen those emotions, however, and his promised revenge is repeatedly delayed. Since the veracity of the ghost is far from certain, Hamlet arranges for a troupe of traveling players to re-enact the murder in front of the royal assembly. Recognizing this as an accusation of his crime, Claudius abruptly interrupts the performance, giving Hamlet the confirmation of guilt he's been seeking. But when the prince happens upon his uncle at his prayers, the ambiguity of what he sees quickly dissipates his renewed determination. Indecision prevails until

Claudius, fully aware now that his nephew is a dangerous threat, sends Hamlet off to England for his prearranged execution. On that trip, however, Providence intervenes to save the prince's life, and he returns to Denmark unharmed. Noticeably changed by his rescue, Hamlet calmly faces his future only to be caught up in another devious royal plot which ends with the deaths of king, queen, and prince. The Norwegian, Fortinbras, who has crisscrossed Denmark at various times during the play, steps in to fill the political void, and order is once again secured.

Based on these details, *Hamlet* is clearly indebted to the revenge genre's conventions, which Elizabethan theatergoers learned from Thomas Kidd's popular *The Spanish Tragedy*. Having already spawned many imitations, Kidd's play had prepared them for a ghost announcing a clandestine murder; a frantic melancholia diverting attention away from the protagonist's strategic maneuvering; the criminal's attempts to evade justice; and a bloody denouement where bodies litter the stage. The assumption *Hamlet* has a place within the revenge genre is therefore entirely reasonable.

But Hamlet's troubling hesitation to avenge his father's murder contradicts this genre's basic premise. Given the way other Elizabethan avengers relentlessly bring events to a final bloody confrontation, Hamlet's reluctance to punish his father's murderer has always been a startling departure from the norm. Until the final moments of the play, Denmark's prince hesitates to punish the perpetrator whose guilt is firmly established by the middle of the third act. Despite many attempts to explain that hesitation, he and his motivations remain enigmas, even to the prince himself who is never able to articulate the cause of this deficiency. Though undoubtedly part of its fascination, the problematic delay suggests Shakespeare's interest in the genre was much different from peers who recognized financial opportunity in its blood-soaked storyline.

A closer examination of *Hamlet* reveals the genre's conventions are an unfortunate distraction from a synergy Shakespeare recognized between Ovid, documentarian of desire's frequently degrading impact on behavior, and Seneca, the Roman author of essays and plays condemning anger and revenge. Both Romans confirm Shakespeare's increasingly evident conviction undisciplined emotions of any kind pose a moral danger with civil implications. First evident in *The Rape of Lucrece,* Tarquin's violation of another man's wife results in his exile and the establishment of the Roman Republic. An inversion of this idea reappears in *Romeo and Juliet* where young love, sparked by erotic desire, leads to a secret marriage that heals Verona's civil discord. In both works, illicit desire, anger, and revenge represent moral and civil hazards.

Interest in Seneca's ideas on revenge motivates a wave of imitators, including Shakespeare who revisits those earlier concerns in *Hamlet* where Claudius's illicit desire for his brother's wife leads to murder, the displacement of the heir apparent's right to the throne, and the prince's desire for revenge. When the dead king's ghost reveals the fratricide instigating all this, Hamlet's initial anger represents the problem the rest of the play must resolve. That resolution determines not only the kind of justice eventually visited upon the guilty but Hamlet's emotional and spiritual welfare as well.

In the play's moral environment, both erotic desire and anger represent dangerous emotions that, left unchecked, initiate violent consequences in the personal as well as the civic environments. The dubious ghost may commit Hamlet to revenge, but as the play's events unfold, Hamlet must abandon the anger motivating vengeance, however understandably felt, because it hinders the empathy that makes extending a deserved mercy possible. Rather than a conventional story of revenge implemented, the process by which Hamlet comes to that realization is the real point of this tragedy. Indicative of the direction the remaining plays on love and desire will take, that moral and spiritual process and its consequences are why this story of revenge needs to be part of a discussion on love.

    The play also makes very clear that Hamlet's moral and spiritual transformation owes much to his awareness of death and judgment. Regardless of what else *Hamlet* may be, it feels very much like a complex meditation on death and its impact on the living. The specter of it hovers over the play like the dark shadow of an avenging angel poised to exact its retribution for mankind's sins. Death and discussions of death are ubiquitous. Obviously, death is a basic premise of a genre where the protagonist is obligated to exact his revenge for a clandestine murder crying out for justice. Nor is the audience ever allowed to forget the murdered victim whose ghost appears at dramatically strategic times. Moreover, Hamlet's black attire is a constant reminder he is mourning the death of a beloved father. His grief is a discomfort to Gertrude and Claudius who, enslaved as both are to the pleasures of this world, remonstrate the prince for his unwillingness to let go. Death, they argue, is common and therefore readily dismissed, which is true enough until it comes for them. And it does, relentlessly, for this royal pair and virtually everyone else. Besides the murdered king, Ophelia, Polonius, Laertes, Rosencrantz and Guildenstern, Gertrude, Fortinbras's nameless soldiers, Claudius, and Hamlet himself are all victims of unexpected but inevitable death. And throughout, the audience hears talk of suicide, how the dust of kings eventually finds its way into the loam stopper of a beer barrel, and, near the end of the story, the unearthed skull of the king's jester becomes one more reminder of the promised end. From first brooding scene to last, death's grim specter never leaves the stage.

    While all these ruminations on life's end provide an appropriately somber atmosphere for tragedy, they also serve the same purpose as Hal's rejection of the playfully unserious

Falstaff and his fascination with worldly pleasures. In the second scene's confrontation between the prince and Denmark's new rulers, the two very different views of grief and death represent two equally disparate approaches to life. Not long after her husband's funeral, which, Hamlet bitterly observes, furnished the meat for her wedding celebration, Gertrude reminds her grieving son that death is common and sorrow should have a reasonable end. Sensing his very visible grief as a silent rebuke of her haste to remarry, she speaks in concert with a new husband so fixated on the world's pleasures he is willing to murder a brother to obtain them. It is entirely consistent that later, as he kneels in penance for his many sins, he is unwilling to forgo what fratricide has purchased, and his crippled prayers are unable to find any avenue to heaven. Like Falstaff, Denmark's rulers hold tightly to things of this world.

Unwilling to forego personal satisfaction, Claudius and Gertrude are so enthralled by the world and the flesh, those shiny baubles of political power, status, wealth, authority, and, implicitly, Ovid's dangerous sexual passion, they have been rendered morally and spiritually unfit. Their similarity to Falstaff, who couldn't resist his own corporeal addictions, should be as obvious as the need to hear Hal's reminder the grave yawns especially wide for those with undisciplined appetites. Inevitable death brings such excesses to an end, the world momentarily rights itself, and something like justice, either here or hereafter, is asserted. Whatever his faults prove to be, Hamlet at least understands worldly pleasures easily distract from significant moral and spiritual truths. While others blithely go about Claudius's business, Hamlet is virtually alone in recognizing something is rotten in Denmark.

In an important foundational essay, Maynard Mack brings attention to the play's ubiquitous questioning which begins with its very first line. Though events will prove the limitations of human perception and logic, Hamlet's philosophical mindset distinguishes him from those whose moral and spiritual laziness explains why the temporary pleasures of the world so easily distract them from death's serious implications. His familiar "To be or not to be" speech reveals a mind contemplating some escape from his troubling obligation, and it sets Hamlet apart from the rest of Denmark, oblivious to the many incongruities that should be obvious. For Hamlet, the unknowable possibilities of the afterlife make the known difficulties of this world bearable. "For in that sleep of death," he begins,

>   What dreams may come,
>   When we have shuffled off this mortal coil,
>   Must give us pause; there's the respect
>   That makes calamity of so long life:
>   For who would bear the whips and scorns of time,
>   Th' oppressor's wrong, the proud man's contumely...
>   When he himself might his quietus make
>   With a bare bodkin; who would fardels bear,
>   To grunt and sweat under a weary life,
>   But that the dread of something after death,
>   ... Puzzles the will,
>   And makes us rather bear those ills we have
>   Than fly to others that we know not of? (3.1.65-81)

The murder of an admired father has circumscribed Hamlet's path to Denmark's crown, but the sense of confinement has other causes as well. Caught between his obligation to revenge and the unknowable, possibly unwelcome judgment that awaits after death, Hamlet feels trapped. "Denmark," he says, "is a prison." Except for the bad dreams that prophesy the inevitability of judgment, he's willing to be "bounded in a nutshell" where he could "count myself a king of infinite space." Since the usurpation has abrogated any expectation of becoming Denmark's ruler, worldly power and prestige are now the least of his concerns. The obligation to revenge exposes Hamlet to far more significant consequences. Confronted by the prospect of eternal judgment, he reluctantly embraces a life of moral obligation. The recalled vision of Hamlet's royal father engaged in trial by combat becomes a fitting icon of this sacrificial life of moral and civic duty. Regardless of the diplomatic competence evident when Claudius defuses the brewing conflict with young Fortinbras at the beginning of the play, the usurper never displays the kind of moral integrity visible in either the old or the young Hamlet.

Resisting the impulse to escape his obligation, Hamlet very rationally makes a decision that encompasses both the physical and the metaphysical realities. His methodical logic represents an alternative to the royal pair's vision of human life driven by the irrational desire for immediate pleasure. A student of philosophy, Hamlet has so far dedicated his life to pursuits of the mind rather than the flesh. His preoccupations have cultivated values and habits very different from those of Gertrude and Claudius. Disciplined activity of the mind, which counterbalances and controls those impulsive emotions, distinguishes man from animals instinctively responding to needs. Reason, he tells Rosencrantz and Guildenstern, not only separates man from beast but makes an exalted, nearly angelic position attainable to the careful and the wise. Those disciplined habits of the mind, he believes, separate man from animal, his life from those of his mother and her new husband.

Because of reason's ability to divide true from false and good from evil, it supports the self-control men like Claudius, who are ruled by their desires, are unable to exercise. The general absence of this, in fact, concerns Hamlet. As he waits for the first view of his father's ghost, he laments the inability of the Danes to moderate their celebratory drinking, the "vicious mole" that undermines their diplomatic stature. Later, in his instructions to the itinerant actors, he reminds them only repetitive practice can eliminate excessive and unnatural emotion from speeches. And he greatly values any evidence of self-control. Isolated as he is within the Danish court, Hamlet acknowledges the "hoops of steel" binding him to Horatio, a man who exhibits the proper balance of reason and emotion. As the conflict with Claudius intensifies, Hamlet is moved by the steady loyalty of his friend who receives such praise with embarrassed silence:

> . . . blest art those
> Whose blood and judgment are so well co-meddled,
> That they are not a pipe for Fortune's finger
> To sound what stop she please. Give me that man
> That is not passion's slave, and I will wear him
> In my heart's core, ay, in my heart of hearts,
> As I do thee. (3.2.68-74)

The contrast between Horatio's valued loyalty and the royal pair's appalling infidelity is one indication Denmark's corruption is related to this lack of self-control. Those who train reason to regulate passions and needs, Hamlet asserts, know how to deal with life's many temptations.

The play, then, very carefully establishes two very different approaches to life and, by implication, to death as well. One, reflecting Ovid's fables of unrestrained desire abusing the vulnerable innocent, is associated with animals, with brutish, undisciplined behavior driven by wants and needs and undeterred by restrictions or any suffering inflicted. Self-involved and selfish, this way of life prefers immediate satisfaction over future consequences here or hereafter, so death and its aftermath are ideas to ignore or avoid. Adherents of this way of life want and take rather than give and share. Vaguely aware of its asocial assumptions, it is compelled to obfuscate its secret shame. It works vigorously to maintain some semblance of the normal, requiring secret stratagems and twisted language to obscure the evil underneath. As Claudius announces his marriage to Gertrude, his speech is rife with contradictions like a "defeated joy" and "mirth in funeral" because the language must account for events that, to the unobservant or unthinking, look normal enough but really aren't.

Hamlet's way of life, on the other hand, is envisioned as rational, self-disciplined, and careful. Striving to operate within commonly accepted norms, Hamlet accepts responsibility and obligations. Because this is a life that values friendships and other relationships, it will be other rather than self-centered. Valuing clarity, it uses language and reason to search out truth rather than hide it. Most importantly, it is willing to sacrifice immediate satisfaction for something worthier in the future, whether here or hereafter. In Hamlet's view, this way of life positions mankind just below the angels. Until the ghost reveals his woeful tale, it is what he admires in Horatio and what he envisions for himself.

But the ghost upends Hamlet's idealistic vision, for the prince's view of human life cannot easily accommodate such disruptive irrational forces as desire and anger. Desire's potential degradation of the human, which Ovid ruefully laments, also finds an interesting parallel in Seneca, the Roman philosopher and dramatist whose plays inspired Kyd's *Spanish Tragedy*, an important predecessor for *Hamlet*. Seneca's essays on anger and revenge, which similarly transforms the civil into the uncivil, were a common topic in Elizabethan moral commentary. As Jonathan Bate observes:

> The Elizabethans were as interested in Seneca the philosopher as they were in Seneca the tragic dramatist. His epistles and his essays, in particular "The Treatise of Anger," which was translated by the dramatist Thomas Lodge, were very widely read and discussed. Crudely speaking, Seneca's ethical writings are about the control of those emotions that in his tragedies explode uncontrollably with catastrophic results. (*How the Classics*, chptr 12)

From both Ovid and Seneca, Shakespeare came to the recognition that any unacknowledged and therefore unregulated need can blind people to the unnecessary cruelty and suffering they inflict. Where desire drives Claudius to murder a brother and steal another man's wife, anger drives Hamlet into equally grievous misjudgments and misdeeds. A father's murder, a mother's betrayal of her marriage vows, the disrupted transfer of political power initiate an anger threatening to overturn the very tenuous emotional balance Hamlet values. A moral hazard no different than the undisciplined compulsion directing Claudius's sexual betrayal, anger blind to a shared humanity easily dehumanizes the noble into a ruthlessness comfortable with cruel murder and revenge. Where the problem is confirmed by Laertes quickly consenting to avenge his father's murder, Hamlet's growing discomfort with a similar obligation reflects an unresolved tension from an idealized self under threat from a required transformation into brutality. As with Laertes, only those moments of heightened emotional extravagance are capable of sustaining his vengeance. Outside of those moments, he vacillates between a lethargic melancholy and a self-flagellating regret for leaving his obligation unfulfilled. Out of this reluctance to act impulsively, however, comes the opportunity for redemption.

  Those moments of angry confrontation easily refute Hamlet's assumption about reason controlling impulsive emotions. Understandably outraged by his father's murder, Hamlet experiences an intense, emotional pressure to implement the promised revenge. After repeated requests not to forget his plight in what sounds like purgatory, the ghost provokes Hamlet's impassioned response:

> Remember thee?
> Ay, thou poor ghost, while memory holds a seat
> In this distracted globe. Remember thee?
> Yea, from the table of my memory
> I'll wipe away all trivial fond records,
> All saws of books, all forms, all pressures past
> That youth and observation copied there,

> And thy commandment all alone shall live
> Within the book and volume of my brain. (1.5.100-108)

His language reflects an unmistakable passion and energy. Grief, the unbridgeable gap between the living and the dead, channels its energy into the anger and the desire for revenge. To fulfill his obligation to a murdered father, Hamlet is prepared to "wipe away" everything he has previously learned. While such consuming anger may be necessary to fulfill his pledge to the woeful ghost, this outrage threatens to reduce a noble and worthy identity into something ugly and brutish. The deliberative personality he admires is under threat.

But some innate caution in Hamlet's nature battles against this initial impetus for vengeance. Sometimes it manifests as habitual questioning while at other times it manifests as self-doubt. Repeatedly, the play documents this internal warfare which is the essence of tragic suffering. Reacting to the player's emotional speech about Hecuba, the wife of a Trojan brutally killed by Pyrrhus in retaliation for the death of Achilles, Hamlet struggles to understand the problematic role emotions should play in his decision to enact his revenge. The actor's tears are seen as a reprimand for his flagging progress toward his goal:

> Is it not monstrous that this player here,
> But in a fiction, in a dream of passion,
> Could force his soul so to his own conceit
> That from her working all the visage waned,
> Tears in his eyes. . . . And all for nothing,
> For Hecuba! . . . Yet I,
> A dull and muddy-mottled rascal, peak
> Like John-a-dreams, unpregnant of my cause,
> And can say nothing. . . Am I a coward? (2.2.551-571)

The actor's tearful response to the verbalized grief of a fictional wife mourning a husband slain by an avenger is certainly an indictment of Gertrude's emotional indifference to her own husband's demise. But the willing avenger, Pyrrhus, also strikes Hamlet as an indictment of whatever remains of his waning anger. That time inevitably diminishes grief does little to assuage the anxiety he feels about fulfilling his obligation. As late as Act V, in conversation with Horatio, he is still bewildered by his inaction.

> Does it not, think thee, stand me now upon—
> He that hath kill'd my king and whor'd my mother,
> Popp'd in between th' election and my hopes,
> Thrown out his angle for my proper life,
> And with such coz'nage—is't not perfect conscience
> To quit him with this arm? (5.1.63-68)

Until the last scenes of the play, his inaction is a source of immense personal dismay that he is unable to resolve on his own. It is only the interrupted trip to England that provides a reason to end this self-flagellation.

Sensitive to the declining intensity of his emotions yet still highly motivated to fulfill his promise to the ghost, Hamlet needs his anger, and every person and incident that bears any taint of royal corruption is an occasion to exercise any remaining outrage, a poison poured most piteously into the innocent ear of his love-interest, Ophelia. Cautioned by both father and brother to "fear" any romantic alliance with a prince on whose "choice depends the safety and health of this whole state," (1.2.16-21) she bears the terrible force of his anger. Their confrontation in the nunnery scene demonstrates the moral danger of unregulated emotions, be they erotic or choleric. Relishing his role as counselor to Claudius, Polonius eagerly accommodates the king's requests for information about Hamlet whose gloomy mood, he assumes, is "the very ecstasy of love" (2.1.99). Placing his daughter where Hamlet will find her, Polonius hides nearby to observe any reaction following his daughter's rejection of the prince's romantic interests. Reading a prayer book, she is the picture of innocence but obediently plays the part of the injured woman. Seeking to return the tokens of affection he once gave her, she falsely accuses him of being unkind. Out of obedience, Ophelia lies, proof that no human virtue is ever pure.

Hamlet's caution is heightened by this strategic lie, and, as it is often staged, he seems to detect Polonius hidden nearby. "Where's thy father?" he abruptly asks, and Ophelia lies a second time, replying, "At home, my lord." This second dishonesty conflates the young girl with the false Gertrude, and all his disgust at feminine weakness—the Biblical Eve's, his mother's, Ophelia's–pours out in a torrent of bitter contempt:

Ham.	Let the doors be shut upon him, that he may play the fool no where but in 's own house. Farewell.
Oph.	O, help him, you sweet heavens!
Ham.	If thou dost marry, I'll give thee this plague for thy dowry: be thou as chaste as ice, as pure as snow, thou shalt not escape calumny. Get thee to a nunn'ry, farewell. Or if thou wilt needs marry, marry a fool, for wise men know well enough what monsters you make of them. To a nunn'ry, go, and quickly too. Farewell.
Oph.	Heavenly powers, restore him!
Ham.	I have heard of your paintings, well enough. God hath given you one face, and you make yourselves another. You jig and amble, and you lisp, you nickname God's creatures and make your wantonness your ignorance. Go to, I'll no more on't, it hath made me mad. I say we will have no moe marriage. Those that are married already, all but one shall live, the rest shall keep as they are. To a nunn'ry, go. (3.1.131-149)

Often considered evidence of Hamlet's misogyny, the point of this misjudgment of Ophelia is more closely related to the play's main concern: how overwrought emotions often serve to degrade the nearly angelic stature he admires. And the consequences of this misjudgment are significant, for an emotionally devastated but largely innocent Ophelia loses both sanity and life. Not just abstractions, those misjudgments and sins have a real cost.

This will not be Hamlet's only mistake, either. This first error of judgment is soon duplicated by his complete misreading of Claudius at his prayers. Unobserved and contemplating the kneeling penitent, who knows he is beyond salvation as long as he is "still possess'd of those effects for which I did the murther: my crown, mine own ambition, and my queen" (3.3.52-55), Hamlet fails to properly decode the moral ambiguities of what he is witnessing. Based on what he thinks he sees, Hamlet once again delays his revenge until there's a moment "that has no relish of salvation in't." Though his words convey a cold and heartless intent, his unwillingness to strike at this opportune moment indicates faulty decisions follow inaccurate perceptions.

Wild emotions will lead him to a third, even more consequential mistake: the murder of Polonius, once again hiding out of sight to overhear what was supposed to be a private conversation between an aggrieved son and his mother. All three misjudgments occur because Hamlet fails to accurately decipher what he sees. Taken together, these misperceptions comprise an extensive examination of the impossibility of seeing accurately and knowing truly. This is so, the play argues, because the eyes are incapable of seeing through the world's opaqueness; because the unprincipled exploit the innocent; because strong emotions subvert judgment; and because a complicated world is made more so when the sinful attempt to hide their misdeeds. Shakespeare's point should be clear: something about mankind's created nature makes his interactions with a complicated world inevitably prone to error, a fact with pertinent implications for revenge. As the *Genesis* story of the Fall asserts, this is existence in a fallen, sinful world, and over and over, reason proves inadequate for dealing with these realities or preventing such mistakes.

In such a morally confusing world, what salvation is conceivable? The answer takes shape in Hamlet's confrontation with Gertrude whose culpability in the murder of her husband is never very clear. The circumstances of this confrontation and those of the earlier nunnery scene are so similar that the two scenes invite comparison. Both involve women who have loved Hamlet; both have a secret observer; both pulsate with emotion; at the center of both, finally, is a passionately angry Hamlet. But one very notable difference is apparent too. Habitually wary of unregulated emotion, Hamlet recognizes the simmering anger provoked by Gertrude's moral culpability requires a degree of self-control that has so far eluded him at crucial moments.

Enraged by Ophelia's perceived duplicity in the nunnery scene, he all but promised to kill the royal couple. This time he prays his actions will prove more benign. "Soft, now to my mother," he begins before continuing:

> O, heart, lose not thy nature! Let not ever
> The soul of Nero enter this firm bosom,
> Let me be cruel, not unnatural;
> I will speak daggers to her but use none. (3.2.393-396)

Referenced twice in this passage, "nature" is a small word Shakespeare uses to capture a plethora of ideas, explored in much greater detail in *King Lear*. One implicates mankind's sinful nature, evident in Denmark's corruption and in Hamlet's own misjudgments. But a second, more positive use of the word identifies a more benevolent nature capable of bonding parents to children, husbands to wives, siblings to each other, friends like Horatio to their intellectual mentors. An essential part of human nature, those bonds are the residue of a prelapsarian condition that, when violated, desecrates the Creator's original intention for His people. Nero, the heartless

Roman emperor who murdered his mother to obtain his position, is the antithesis of a son who, by the nature of those bonds, should love and honor his parent. As the prayer scene proves, Gertrude's ultimate culpability is beyond Hamlet's understanding, so he vows to avoid any violence by controlling his disappointment and anger. Truth will be the weapon employed to encourage repentance in the mother who raised him.

When Polonius, hiding behind the arras, is rashly dispatched, however, intention once again proves insufficient. A mortal error, it sparks another son's vengeance and justifies Hamlet's exile to England where a secret execution has been arranged. Unlike Claudius's failed prayer, however, Hamlet's sensitivity to the nature that binds son to mother is enough to bring Gertrude to something like remorse and reform. The truth about her former husband's murder and her unwillingness to distinguish between the moral worthiness of two very different men begins her transformation.

> Look here upon this picture, and on this,
> The counterfeit presentment of two brothers.
> See what a grace was seated on this brow:
> Hyperion's curls, the front of Jove himself,
> An eye like Mars, to threaten and command. . . .
> This was your husband. Look you now what follows:
> Here is your husband, like a mildewed ear,
> Blasting his wholesome brother. Have you eyes?
> Could you on this fair mountain leave to feed,
> And batten on this moor? Ha, have you eyes?
> You cannot call it love, for at your age
> The heyday in the blood is tame, it's humble,
> And waits upon the judgment, and what judgment
> Would step from this to this? (3.4.54-71)

The passage pivots on Hamlet's comparison of two qualitatively different men. One he likens to Roman gods and a majestic mountain; the other to a corrupted appendage and sheep feeding in lowland pastures. The contrasting images help Gertrude understand her complicity in Denmark's corruption, and she agrees not "to let the bloat king tempt you again to bed" where he might "make you ravel all this matter out, that I essentially am not in madness, but mad in craft." While Gertrude's repentance is one benefit, Hamlet's renewed self-discipline is an avenue to escape the prison of his anger. The ability stems, not from reason alone, but from a rational acknowledgment of the inviolate love between mother and son. Those emotions spark enough compassion to suggest Hamlet can still recover the balance he sees and admires in his friend, Horatio. The bit of mercy extended to a fellow sinner, moreover, shows an appreciation for the mercy a Christian God showers upon an undeserving world. "Treat every man according to his deserts," he had once reminded Polonius, "and who should 'scape whipping?" It is this Hamlet, the one who cares for a sinful mother's remorse and salvation, that Providence deems worthy of protection.

  Nothing comparable occurs in Claudius' heart. Self-involved and unwilling to relinquish queen and crown for his redemption, Claudius never cultivates, and therefore can't demonstrate, any impulse toward a selflessness strong enough to temper his shrewd rationality. He's all about protecting his assets, so his default is strategy and calculation. Lacking sufficient moral authority to openly punish Hamlet, he very deviously sends the prince off to England along with a sealed letter that instructs the recipients to execute Hamlet upon his arrival. Very strategically, Claudius uses Polonius, Ophelia, Rosencrantz and Guildenstern, and finally Laertes to ferret out Hamlet's intentions and to protect what he's unwilling to forfeit in exchange for forgiveness. Always working from a guilt that requires secrecy, his overly complicated strategies are doomed to fail.

  As the play's final moments approach, the dark shadow of death and sacred mystery intensifies until there's an unmistakable sense that larger, metaphysical forces are at work to bring about the required justice. Though a connection between the closet scene and Hamlet's aborted voyage to England is never explicit, it is difficult to avoid the inference promoted by Paul's epistles as well as the Lord's Prayer that mercy extended becomes divine mercy earned, a sentiment voiced more clearly in Portia's speech on mercy to a villain also resolute for retribution. Part way into the voyage, Hamlet discovers the usurper's letter, rewrites it so that his escorts, Rosencrantz and Guildenstern, should be executed in his stead, and then reseals the letter with the royal stamp he fortuitously had with him. Pirates then intercept his ship, and with their help he makes his way back to Denmark.

Enormously significant, these events change Hamlet's demeanor unmistakably. Back in Denmark, he recounts these events to Horatio, who warns Hamlet to be vigilant during the supposedly friendly duel with Laertes. Unaware the duel is meant to remedy what couldn't be accomplished in England, Hamlet exhibits a new sense of peace as he dismisses Horatio's warning:

> Hor: If your mind dislike anything, obey it. I will forestall their repair hither, and say you are not fit.
> Ham: Not a whit, we defy augury. There is special providence in the fall of a sparrow. If it be [now], 'tis not to come; if it be not to come, it will be now; if it be not now, yet it will come—the readiness is all. Since no man, of aught he leaves, knows what is't to leave betimes, let be.
> (5.2.217-24)

Hamlet's response to Horatio's caution is a consequence of how he happened to get back to Denmark. Seen in symbolic terms, the voyage to England is much like any man's life with its predestined, inevitable terminus. That Hamlet's journey was interrupted and aborted doesn't alter the eventual conclusion. Death will come, no matter what fortune or human striving achieves to temporarily avoid the outcome.

Trying to see into the future to punish and kill a murderer is quite pointless since death for him is inevitable, as it is for everyone. This is, therefore, Hamlet's renunciation of the terrible burden of revenge.

But the sparrow reference from Matthew 10:29 is also a recognition that each individual's death has significance for a providential God who cares about his creation. In that Biblical passage, Jesus reassures his disciples that a God who knows and cares about the insignificant death of a sparrow would be with them as they go out into a hostile world to share His good news. "Are not two sparrows sold for a penny?" he asks rhetorically. "Yet not one of them will fall to the ground outside your Father's care." The way a person lives their life matters to a God who will eventually evaluate its worthiness. Echoing Hal's stern warning to the Falstaff expecting his share of royal largesse, Hamlet understands his most pressing obligation is to live life in expectation of that judgment. "The readiness is all."

All the metaphysical anxiety expressed in the famous "To be" speech has finally dissipated. Assured God understands and forgives the many limitations of human nature, assured the revelation of Denmark's hidden truth no longer depends on human effort alone, and assured justice will eventually be served on the guilty, Hamlet is released from the prison of his anxiety, from the necessity of playing multiple uncomfortable roles, and from the administration of a justice that he was, by naturally limited insight and judgment, ill-equipped to enforce. Like that image of Old Hamlet at the beginning of the play, a king who trusted in God's judgment and providential protection as he engaged Denmark's enemies in single combat, Hamlet has reason to trust the good intentions of his loving Father. With spiritual assurance and confidence restored, his transformation is complete. Vengeance is no longer his responsibility. As justice found Rosencrantz and Guildenstern, justice will assuredly find Claudius.

The effects of this emotional liberation are clear. Like the Paul of the Roman epistles, he had always accepted the premise he too lived in sin, "indifferent honest" as he once put it. That makes it easier now to admit to those faults, an acceptance of culpability allowing him to claim, without irony, he did in fact love Ophelia. And he regrets his mockery of Laertes's excessive grief at her grave. "I am very sorry, good Horatio, that to Laertes I forgot myself, for by the image of my cause I see the portraiture of his" (5.2.75-77). As the empathy displayed in Gertrude's closet becomes habitual, Hamlet regains confidence in this identity, and he can now boldly, proclaim "This is I, Hamlet the Dane." Calm, rational, and self-controlled, he no longer fears mistakes, failure, or the judgment that follows death. The contrast with the play's other avenger is instructive. Prepared to cut throats in a church, an outraged Laertes serves as a foil to a prince who found the peace that passes understanding.

To understand the implications of Hamlet's resolution to the problem of revenge, it is useful to compare the final court scene to the one at the beginning of the play where the funeral meats had been repurposed for the wedding of Claudius and Gertrude. That Denmark was a sham, a place where the vicious mole of desire and need undercut the nobility and honor of a king willing to risk his life in personal combat with the nation's enemies. Sin was hidden, guilt was ignored, secret strategies replaced public debate and decision-making, and deception was mistaken for honesty. All these remain operative in the way Claudius manipulates Laertes to participate in the fateful duel with what until the aborted trip to England had been a troublesome and dangerous nephew. That, however, is no longer the Hamlet who accepts the challenge to meet Laertes in what he thinks is a friendly competition with rapier and dagger. The one who walks into a duplicitous king's trap understands Providence alone controls the implementation of a far more perfect justice than he could ever devise.

And so, strangely enough, the match between Laertes and Hamlet does not go as Claudius had planned. The queen drinks from the poisoned chalice before her husband can prevent her, and a wounded Hamlet, realizing his opponent's rapier is tainted, manages to return the favor to Laertes who, dying, confesses the entire devious plot to the assembled court. What was hidden is now known to all. Mortally wounded, poisoned, and facing death because of royal treachery, Hamlet turns on his uncle-father, wounds him with the poisoned rapier, and forces him to drink from the poisoned cup. "Here, thou incestuous, murd'rous, damned Dane, drink off this potion! Is thy union here? Follow my mother!" The poisoned pearl is a fitting end to a royal marriage that had infected the Danish court with its evil disease.

Claudius, the man who used others to covertly implement his evil purposes, has finally been exposed, "hoist by his own petard." Besides the murder of a brother, he is responsible for the deaths of his wife and queen, his nephew-son, indirectly for the deaths of Rosencrantz and Guildenstern, with Polonius's end, as well as his appointed assassin. Claudius's murderous nature has been completely and very publicly exposed, making this very different from private retribution. His obvious guilt makes this much more like state-sanctioned justice. Most importantly, Hamlet enters this final confrontation in complete trust and without a plan for revenge. The deviousness belongs entirely to Claudius. As one final confirmation of God's favor on the prince, Hamlet's earlier desire to catch Claudius at a moment "that has no relish of salvation in't" has been affirmatively answered. Where the wages of sin are death, Hamlet's trust in a caring, protective God's mercy proves to be his salvation, and his friend Horatio quite fittingly proclaims that "flights of angels sing" the prince to his final rest.

Left behind to protect Hamlet's "wounded name," Horatio, the prince's steadfast friend who never had to play a false part, summarizes what led to this carnage: . . .Let me speak to th' yet unknowing world

> How these things came about. So shall you hear
> Of carnal, bloody, and unnatural acts,
> Of accidental judgments, casual slaughters,
> Of deaths put on by cunning and forc'd cause,
> And in this upshot, purposes mistook
> Fall'n on th' inventors' heads. . . . (5.2.379-385)

Treachery was everywhere, Horatio asserts, but Hamlet's relentless questioning, his skepticism, his reluctance to act rashly, his steadfast search for truth, everything, in short, that makes him Hamlet, was anticipated in Providence's divinely ordained resolution.

Providential care extends beyond Hamlet, too. With no one left to restore civil order in Denmark, Fortinbras, a relatively minor character in the play, is named king of Denmark. Like Hamlet, he had lost a father in the single combat with Old Hamlet mentioned in the first act, and his first inclination was to avenge that defeat by raising an army and invading Denmark. Ironically, he is dissuaded from that purpose by Claudius's very able diplomacy. But Fortinbras reappears midway through the play marching through Denmark on his way to some other battle. And he is present, on his way back from that campaign, when the wholesale slaughter of the last act occurs. Therefore, when Fortinbras is named king of Denmark, the very objective of his initial inclination to avenge a father's death has also been achieved without his intervention. As one final symmetry, Providence arranged events to bring about a desired end for the patient, self-controlled Fortinbras, just as it had for Hamlet.

Though *Hamlet* employs the familiar conventions of Elizabethan revenge tragedy, it adapts them in entirely unconventional ways, and in that effort, Shakespeare refashions an old story into a tragedy of the highest order.

Admittedly, the play is not without its problems: at over four hours in its entirety, it's overly long for modern performances; second, dressed in the gaudy clothing of revenge tragedy, it's easy to miss the moral and spiritual transformation of its protagonist; finally, the difference between its ending and the bloody denouements typical of the genre is subtle, especially for secular audiences. All this is exacerbated further by the evaporation of any awareness of Christian metaphysics. But the enduring fascination with this drama over the past four centuries speaks for itself. The classically educated Ben Jonson rightly sees Shakespeare as an equal of those giants of Greek tragedy, Sophocles and Euripides, who wrote very moving tragedies about people caught up unawares in the machinations of fate or the gods. Though they suffer and sometimes perish, an explanation never comes. The mystery of suffering is simply a fact of life. A persistent, stoic endurance is the only possible response.

Shakespeare's view of the tragic is different. Though the Christian promise of salvation supposedly incapacitates the tragic, Shakespeare understood the tragic potential of existence in a fallen world where sin negates that promise and ushers in unjust and unnecessary suffering. He came to believe all sin, be that for another man's wife or for the satisfaction of retribution, stemmed from desire unmitigated by selfless generosity. For him, the tragedy is that none of that is inevitable yet it inevitably happens, a situation that a holy and just God will not tolerate forever. The mysteries of how and why divine intervention occurs in human affairs prompt questions whose answers mankind can only dimly comprehend. In this situation, *Hamlet* argues, moral discipline and trust in God's merciful judgment have to be sufficient.

In the next play examined, The *Merchant of Venice*, Shakespeare elaborates in much greater detail the connection he sees between love and generosity, a conceptualization originating from the moral deficiency observed in Ovid's fables of desire.

The Merchant of Venice

The paradoxical nature of generosity, which is the central concern of *The Merchant of Venice*, made a brief appearance in *Romeo and Juliet* where an emotional Juliet wants to give everything she has and is to Romeo. The pledge expresses a generosity whose benefits, when returned to her greatly multiplied, allow her to give her lover even more. "[T]he more I give to thee," she exclaims, "The more I have, for both are infinite" (2.2.133-135). While this paradox is essential to an understanding of Shakespeare's conception of love, its articulation in this later play with a Jewish villain is hampered by the countervailing expression of numerous antisemitic sentiments. Needless to say, those views are rightly vilified by Karim-Cooper who, to her credit, strives to convey some of the complexity of Shylock's character.

For many, the play's antisemitism clashes with Shakespeare's stellar reputation and cries out, therefore, for some explanation other than ordinary prejudice. Gifted with an ability to dramatize issues and characters from multiple vantages, Shakespeare gives his audience two different but related views of Shylock: in the first unsavory view, he is the unholy Jew, vilified by the Christians of Venice; in the other, he is the angry, vengeful victim of their troubling behavior. The conflicting perspectives, Karim-Cooper suggests, is a deliberate effort to challenge the audience's own assumptions about Jewish culture and religion. "[T]he play is too complex to designate Shakespeare's attitude as either antisemitic or philosemitic," she begins, before continuing. "Shylock is too multifaceted to simply reduce him to an Elizabethan stereotype. Whatever Shakespeare's views, he asks the audience to confront their own attitudes." When viewing character as confirmation of an historical outlook, this position is quite reasonable.

Shylock's presentation, however, also has an instructive theatrical precedent. In 1592, Londoners flocked to see Christopher Marlowe's *The Jew of Malta*, whose evil protagonist was introduced by the hated Italian, Machiavelli, purveyor of conspiracy and poison. The Italian's appearance promised Marlowe's villain would be deliciously familiar. Sure enough, they witnessed Marlowe's Jew manipulate his Christian and Turkish antagonists into various mortal intrigues until he was pushed into a boiling cauldron intended for his last set of victims. Throughout, Barabas's many enemies endure his melodramatic hatred delivered with bombastic oratory. Londoners absolutely loved Marlowe's rhetoric and the dramatic resolution of unadulterated villainy. An immediate success, the play appeared onstage many more times that decade and remained popular for the next fifty years.

The assumption Marlowe's play influenced *The Merchant*'s Jewish antagonist is difficult to avoid. Despite the similarities, including the obsession with money, the insistence on the letter of the law, the charging of interest, the dismay when a beloved daughter elopes with a Christian, and the desire to avenge perceived Christian grievances, the two characters are really quite different. Shakespeare's choices are very deliberate: a less melodramatic and more human villain allows his presentation to gain additional depth from the thematic connections between the play's two parallel plots.

In the main story, the poor but honorable Bassanio has heard of a beautiful, rich heiress in the distant city of Belmont who can only marry when her suitor chooses correctly between three different metal chests, a lottery established by her late father to weed out unworthy suitors. Accepting funds from his friend, Antonio, he sets off to try his luck. Bassanio wins the lady's hand only to learn that his merchant friend back in Venice has defaulted on the loan that financed his successful courtship. Before the lovers have a chance to marry, they return to Venice to assist in Antonio's defense.

Meanwhile, the subplot develops the story of the merchant's contract with the Jewish moneylender, Shylock, who loaned Antonio the funds for Bassanio's courtship. When the merchant cannot repay his debt, Shylock wants to enforce the contract's provision to take a pound of the merchant's flesh. Shylock's insistence on the letter of the law horrifies the Christian community, but the dispute is resolved in a tense courtroom scene, Shylock is humiliated, Antonio is saved, and the play's various couples are finally free to celebrate their nuptials.

To focus narrowly on character or plot or even on the play's antisemitism obscures the thematic implications of the two plots. The attributes of love examined in the main plot, including but not limited to generosity, find their antithesis in the antisemitic tropes that define the contractual dispute with Shylock. That contrast is what Shakespeare cares about, for it allows *The Merchant* to explore the implications of Juliet's paradoxical generosity in greater detail. From that perspective, in fact, Shylock's very legalistic definition of a bond is morally and emotionally insufficient for the marriage bond between the two lovers. From that perspective, *The Merchant* can be seen as Portia's confrontation with and victory over all the potential impediments to a durable relationship with her future husband, Bassanio. Often considered a problem play, this double plotted story with a Jewish villain represents a significant development in Shakespeare's dramatizations of love. Even if difficult to stage today as written, it remains an important milestone in the evolution of Shakespeare's conception of love.

In an interesting analysis of *The Merchant*, John Russel Brown postulates Shakespeare's interest in generosity's paradoxical quality derives from a parable in Matthew 25:14. In that passage, a rich man gives gold to three different servants according to their abilities. The first two put their gold to work and increase what they were given. The third, however, buries his in the ground. After some time, when the master asks each servant the result, the first two are rewarded for their industry while the third is chastised for his fearful caution and cast out of the household.

While no direct influence on the play is offered, the parable makes the point all gifts are to be used to glorify the One who generously provides. Key to understanding the relevance of this to Shakespeare is that the servants are supposed to invest for the master's benefit, not for their own, and to do so with the understanding only he, not they, will decide if a benefit, a punishment, or nothing at all should be conferred. From a Christian perspective, every talent is a blessing, a free gift, intended to benefit others and, through that generous sharing, to make the Creator's lavish goodness increasingly visible. When the investment is made to honor the provider, with no expectation of reward, blessings multiply. The same arithmetic, Shakespeare seems to suggest, applies to love which, when shared, multiplies the benefits of that experience within the relationship. This is the Christian idea Juliet expresses.

But what about that third servant, the one who refuses to invest his gift? Though he doesn't squander his gold, he is severely punished. Shakespeare's sonnets, written early in his career when the theaters were shuttered by the plague, help explain the third servant's relevance to *The Merchant*. The first seventeen so-called procreation sonnets form an extended plea to a young man who, much like the parable's third servant, refuses to invest his obvious virtues in the lives of others, choosing, instead, to be completely indifferent to their attentions. His posture, the narrator fears, may cost a very blessed young man the many benefits of love—things like acceptance, marriage, children, companionship, and emotional security. The narrator clearly values the friendship of this young man who expresses no such need himself, either from the speaker or from the sonnets' nameless dark lady who also vies for the attention of this cold-hearted man.

Maintaining this trifold relationship includes significant emotional risk for the narrator, who can either acknowledge his concern or hide that away, a fearfulness deforming him into the image of both the parable's third servant and the indifferent object of his attention. The emotional distance of this other, nameless man to whom the sonnets are addressed forces the narrator and the dark lady into an uncomfortable and ironic compromise:

> When the sonnets are aware that the friend's faults constitute a threat to the friendship, there is the recurrent accompaniment of ironic self-consciousness, arising, it appears, from a knowledge of the waywardness with which affection, in order to maintain its being in an imperfect world, bestows itself with imperfect cause. It must, at times, debase its currency in order to exist. The alternative to this dilemma is the economy of the closed heart. . . . The closed heart may be poor, but it is at ease. Those men are most content who, though they inspire affection in others, have no need of it themselves. . . . They have the power to hurt, but they are not hurt. Their happiness is their ignorance of their incompleteness. (Hubler 469-470)

Fear of rejection or indifference makes an offer of love a difficult and risky proposition, debasing genuine emotion into something less. The young man's coldness threatens to make the narrator equally cold. The other man's imperviousness to the narrator's admiration, therefore, exacts a cost for both, and the harmful imbalance in emotional vulnerability is what Hubler means by the economy of the closed heart. Since speaking honestly or curbing affection or concern both carry risks, those like the narrator, who are unwilling to compromise their affections, must accept that risking vulnerability may not earn a return. Those unwilling to respond in kind to emotional vulnerability, on the other hand, certainly avoid love's risks but will remain self-contained, self-absorbed, and insulated from its rewards. When the capacity for love is hidden away, like the third servant's treasure, the exponential increase of shared blessings described in Juliet's speech is aborted.

This conception of love as an open-ended investment in others, despite considerable emotional risk, quite naturally lends itself to imagery of money and lending. To explore the complexities of love's paradoxical nature, *The Merchant of Venice* presents two different approaches to investing in the welfare of others. The play's titular character, Antonio, the wealthy Venetian merchant, freely lends money to his friend, Bassanio, who plans to use the proceeds to court the wealthy lady, Portia. The merchant's generosity, however, contrasts with the financial shrewdness of the Jewish moneylender, Shylock, who only lends at interest. With this contrast between usury and generosity *The Merchant* provides a nexus for understanding a complex but important conception of love's risks and love's wealth.

Distasteful as the play's antisemitic tropes are, Shakespeare apparently saw them as an efficient way to clarify a difficult idea. Without the play's financial metaphor to explain the complex associations Shakespeare is making between love and money, the wooing in Belmont seems quite unrelated to the subplot's contractual dispute. But John Russel Brown provides an essential connection with a suggestive insight about the significance of usury:

> It is sometimes argued that Shylock's affairs are so far removed in kind from the affairs of the lovers in Belmont that the play falls into two parts. But in one way the play is very closely knit, for, besides contrasting Shylock with Antonio, the discussion about usury is yet another contrast between [Shylock] and Portia and Bassanio. As we have seen from the sonnets . . ., Shakespeare saw love as a kind of usury, and so in their marriage Bassanio and Portia put Nature's bounty to its proper 'use'. Shylock practices a usury for the sake of gain and is prepared to enforce his rights; the lovers practice their usury without compulsion, for the joy of giving. (64)

As the story's operative metaphor, usury contains a functional ambiguity that allows Shakespeare to draw several insights from the interdependence of money, lending with interest, and affairs of the heart, giving the two plots unexpected cohesion. Shylock's form of usury represents a strategy for avoiding financial risk and increasing material wealth. The lovers, as Brown points out, participate in a different form of usury: they give out their emotional wealth without expectation but receive an abundance of joy in return. Inhabiting a nature constantly at work to counteract dearth, their lack of risk-aversion is rewarded in ways that exceed any conceivable expectation or reservation. Just as the merchant risks his treasure interest-free, the lovers share their gift *gratis*, without interest, and because there's no expectation of return, there's no obligation imposed, no contract.. As metaphor, then, usury suggests love requires a courageous trust in the process of building relationship, a process inherently good precisely because it prospers both without obligation or duty, something that Shylock's insistence on usury denies.

At the beginning, neither lover understands the complexity of this calculus, however. Portia's late father established the casket lottery knowing only a successful suitor could untangle the moral complexities necessary for the proper evaluation of real value or wealth. Bassanio's original motive for traveling to Belmont was to revitalize his "disabled estate" which he had squandered "by . . . showing a more swelling port than [my] faint means would grant continuance" (1.1.123-125). Whether he was overly generous or, like Falstaff, an extravagant, self-indulgent spendthrift isn't clear, but Portia's wealth is what draws him toward Belmont. While his initial motive for the journey is personal reward, only a merchant willing to risk makes the opportunity possible.

Despite his crass, self-interested motives, Bassanio doesn't fearfully hoard or bury Antonio's money but accepts the gift and risks investing what he's been given. And by doing so, Portia's beauty and virtue completely change his initial rationale. Wanting the woman now more than financial gain, he quickly grasps the point of the lottery's relatively straightforward rules. Each prospective husband has one chance to make the right choice among the three chests: one of gold, one of silver, one of lead. Each casket has a cryptic hint suggesting what is hidden inside. For the gold, the hint is "Who chooseth me shall gain what many men desire." For the silver, it is "Who chooseth me shall get as much as he deserves." For the third, lead chest, it reads "Who chooseth me must give and hazard all he hath." Choosing the lead chest would indicate an understanding that giving and risk are operative concepts for a love that endures. After the Prince of Morocco, who selects the gold chest, and the Prince of Aragon, who chooses the silver both fail, we see Bassanio (who is ignorant of the other suitors' choices) select the lead casket and win Portia's love. The first two suitors fail because their choice is based either on what is to be gained from the marriage or what their distinguished stature brings to it. Though some say the ditty Portia sings while Bassanio decides contains a useful rhyme, he succeeds because he alone recognizes the truth embodied in the lead chest: that, to earn love, a person must give and hazard all. Antonio's generosity has prepared Bassanio to risk giving selflessly and unreservedly, the essential quality of a truly loving heart. Because he is comfortable with that, he is the right husband for Portia.

   Portia is similarly transformed by desire. Not a single gallant from the parade of suitors before Bassanio had valued love correctly and thus failed to solve the lottery puzzle. Their failures make her irritable and disconsolate. Not understanding the purpose of her father's lottery, she sees it as an unnecessary hindrance to her right to choose a mate. Before Bassanio, she is "aweary of this great world" because she "may neither choose who [she] would nor refuse who [she] dislike[s]" (1.2.24-25). In conversations with her handmaiden, Nerissa, she mocks her failed suitors, indicating that "there is not one among them" whom she would miss. Unwilling, at first, to trust nature's wisdom about love, she succumbs to bitter resentment of the men who seem to control her fate. Encumbered by her father's gimmick, Portia not only resents her lack of freedom to choose but has come to blame men for their emotional ignorance.

Once desire magically transforms financial ambition into love, Bassanio is able to cure her malaise. Unwilling to wait a moment longer, his passion inflames hers. As he contemplates which casket to choose, Portia reveals her overflowing emotions in an aside that sounds very much like the Juliet who comes to appreciate Romeo's love:

> O love, be moderate, allay thy ecstasy,
> In measure, rain thy joy, scant this excess!
> I feel too much thy blessing; make it less,
> For fear I surfeit. (3.2.111-114)

Instead of scarcity, Portia experiences a blessing in excess of expectation. As her beloved prepares to risk all in the casket lottery, she gives voice to the love she hopes to share. Like a cloud heavy with life-giving moisture, she can barely contain her desire to shower this love upon him. And when he chooses correctly, she promises to pour down abundant love into his life. The language of accounting and finance links this speech to the play's central metaphor.

> You see me, Lord Bassanio, where I stand,
> Such as I am. Though for myself alone
> I would not be ambitious in my wish
> To wish myself much better, yet for you,
> I would be trebled twenty times myself,
> A thousand times more fair, ten thousand times more rich,
> That only to stand high in your account,
> I might in virtues, beauties, livings, friends,
> Exceed account. But the full sum of me . . .
> Is an unlesson'd girl, uschool'd, unpractic'd,

> Happy in this, she is not yet so old
> But she may learn. . . .
> Myself, and what is mine, to you and yours
> Is now converted. (3.2.149-167)

Along with the unmistakable, poignant tenderness here, Portia's use of financial imagery emphasizes the multiplication of tangible and emotional wealth she would gladly deposit into her future husband's account. The speech elucidates the paradoxical usury of true love. Having risked making his choice, Bassanio and Portio both experience how love's abundance enriches both giver and receiver. The one unanswered question now is what will Antonio earn for his generosity?

Once the lottery device settles the proper motivation for love, news of Antonio's predicament reaches Belmont. His ships now lost at sea, he has defaulted on Shylock's loan and the moneylender is demanding his pound of flesh which, quite symbolically, must be taken near his heart. The danger unfolding in Venice now becomes a test of the boundless generosity the lovers have declared in Belmont. How they respond to their benefactor's predicament will prove they mean what they say.

The proof comes quickly. Upon learning the reason for Antonio's contract with the moneylender, Portia vows to pay off the merchant's debt, even if treble the original amount is required to satisfy Shylock's demands. The merchant's generosity that blossomed into love is now being abundantly repaid in kind. Generosity begets generosity. Postponing their wedding night, Portia sends her new husband to save Antonio with the anticipated funds and a betrothal ring he vows never to lose. After Bassanio and his manservant leave, however, Portia and her maidservant Nerissa disguise themselves as young law clerks and set off for Venice to ensure the merchant's safety. Both her money and her time are now invested in the effort to rescue Bassanio's benefactor. The munificence extended to the merchant confirms her appreciation of love's value. While her transformation is complete, its confirmation will become apparent in the courtroom where she will argue the case for mercy, a spiritual form of generosity.

The lavish richness of Portia's joy following Bassanio's lottery success is a form of wealth that has a metaphorical equivalent in the financial well-being of the merchant. The open-ended sincerity of his initial gesture to Bassanio is clear when, after his default, he appears to have lost his legal case to Shylock. Prepared for the death that surely would follow the extraction of that contractual pound of flesh, he refuses to blame his friend for this predicament:

> Bassanio, fare you well,
> Grieve not that I am fall'n to this for you;
> For herein Fortune shows herself more kind
> Than is her custom. It is still her use
> To let the wretched man outlive his wealth,
> To view with hollow eye and wrinkled brow
> An age of poverty; from which ling'ring penance
> Of such misery doth she cut me off. (4.1.265-272)

His refusal to blame Bassanio for his predicament is Antonio's final gesture of generosity. Because he is a "wretched man" who has "outlive[d] his wealth," he laments, death is preferable to years of poverty. Since Antonio never gave with any expectation of reciprocity, he avoids any reference to his friend's theoretical culpability. His gift has been freely given, and the consequences of the decision belong to him alone.

Shylock, however, adheres to an entirely different calculus that has no room for the paradox of generosity, and it dominates everything he does. Never secure or satisfied with what he already has, money is never lent without compounding interest. Contracts minimize risk. Such habitual avarice sets him apart from the rest of Venice. It prevents him from feeding Launcelot, his servant, who complains that he is constantly famished while in Shylock's employ. Shylock, in turn, warns Launcelot, who early in the play is about to change masters and become the servant of the nearly penniless Bassanio, that he will no longer be able to "gormandize, as thou hast done with me." Within the play's elaborate financial metaphor, Shylock's covetousness is a kind of spiritual scarcity that leaves him, in the end, poor, defeated, and alone.

Just as the emotional distance guarding the cold young man of the sonnets should be measured against the narrator's concern, Shylock's greed is meant to be evaluated by the generosity of others nearby. Unfortunately, the anti-Semitic aspects of this contrast tend to obscure a salient point being made about the nature of love. As John Russel Brown notes:

> *The Merchant of Venice* presents in human and dramatic terms Shakespeare's ideal of love's wealth, its abundant and sometimes embarrassing riches; it shows how this wealth is gained and possessed by giving freely and joyfully; it shows also how destructive the opposing possessiveness can become, and how it can cause those who . . . love to [be compelled to] fight . . . for their existence. (74)

The possessiveness of the ungenerous heart is destructive because its sole interest is the enhancement of self without regard for the physical, emotional, and spiritual wealth of the other. It is destructive because, lacking the courage to trust the good intentions of the other, its security is based on legalistic, contractual obligations rather than a union delighting in a fully realized love with abundant riches more than sufficient for both. Love's very survival, in fact, depends upon a disciplined, selfless generosity to ward off the insidious danger of possessiveness. This is to give and hazard all.

Thus, the generosity of Antonio and Portia becomes the standard by which Shylock's acquisitiveness needs to be evaluated. Greed and self-interest spawn his animosity toward the merchant. "I hate him for he is a Christian," Shylock says at one point, "But more, for that in low simplicity He lends out money *gratis*" (1.3.42-44). It is Antonio's generosity, the very generosity that brings Bassanio and Portia to the altar, that offends the moneylender. The hatred and desire for revenge infect his thinking, motivates the contract threatening the merchant's life, and, through the merchant's danger, interrupts the nuptials awaiting the lovers.

The contractual dispute is easily dismissed as entertaining melodrama, but the threat to Antonio's life constitutes a significant test of the lover's commitment to generosity, not just to each other but to their enemies as well, a challenge Jesus posed to his disciples. Shakespeare avoids a melodramatic, cartoonish villain because Shylock's grievances had to have real credence for Portia's defense of mercy to make dramatic sense. Reminding Marlowe's Barabas of the virtues of mercy would be an absurdity. A Shylock sympathetic to his own hurt, however, might realistically be convinced to extend sympathy to others. While Christian opposition to usury, therefore, may be the proximate cause of the Jew's hatred, his antipathy has been further multiplied by the moneylender's mistreatment, which Antonio does not deny. "You call'd me dog for lending with interest," Shylock observes. To which the merchant replies, "I am as like to call thee so again, to spet on thee again, to spurn thee too." Admirable in some respects, the merchant's antisemitism is so repulsive its dramatization has to be intentional.

The sympathy this earns Shylock is enhanced further by his refreshing objectivity. Part of Shylock's charm, if the term properly applies to a villain, is his honest assessment of his Christian neighbors.

> Signior Antonio, many a time and oft
> In the Rialto you have rated me
> About my moneys and my usances.

> Still have I borne it with a patient shrug
> (for suff'rance is the badge of all our tribe).
> You call me misbeliever, cut-throat dog,
> And spat upon my Jewish gabardine,
> And all for use of that which is mine own.... (1.3.106-113)

Nor does he hide the pain their very unchristian behavior has caused. Soon after the contract is signed, his neighbors ask why he should ever want a pound of Antonio's flesh. The moneylender's reply is both ominous and understandable, presaging his arguments later in court:

> I am a Jew. Hath not a Jew eyes? Hath not a Jew hands, organs, dimensions, senses, affections, passions; fed with the same food, hurt with the same weapons, subject to the same diseases, healed by the same means, warmed and cooled by the same winter and summer as a Christian is? If you prick us do we not bleed? If you tickle us do we not laugh? If you poison us do we not die? And if you wrong us shall we not revenge? If we are like you in the rest, we will resemble you in that. If a Jew wrong a Christian, what is his humility? Revenge. If a Christian wrong a Jew, what should his sufferance be by Christian example? Why, revenge. The villainy you teach me I will execute, and it shall go hard but I will better the instruction. (3.1.49–61)

Having endured numerous violations to the humanity shared by both Jew and Christian, Shylock cannot hide the simmering anger, the wounded sense of chronic injustice. For him, the injury of his eye must be redressed by an equivalent injury to the eye of the perpetrator. Though the legalistic logic of equivalency fuels his unhealthy desire for revenge, the causes are completely understandable.

Confident of his rights, he brings his case against Antonio before the Duke of Venice for resolution. Everyone close to the merchant pleads his case, but Shylock remains adamant. What he is owed belongs to him. If the debt cannot be repaid, the law should remedy the loss according to the agreed-upon contract. "What judgment shall I dread, doing no wrong," he begins:

> You have among you many a purchas'd slave,
> Which like your asses, and your dogs and mules,
> You use in abject and in slavish parts,
> Because you bought them. Shall I say to you,
> "Let them be free! Marry them to your heirs!
> Why sweat they under burthens? Let their beds
> Be made as soft as yours, and let their palates
> Be seasoned with such viands"? You will answer,
> "The slaves are ours." So do I answer you:
> The pound of flesh which I demand of him
> Is dearly bought as mine, and I will have it.
> If you deny me, fie upon your law! (4.1.89-101)

The legal bond that makes Christian slaves no more than property, Shylock observes, apply in exactly the same way as the contract he has with Antonio. By Christian example, contractual obligations incur inalienable rights over what is owned, and, because of the default, Shylock now owns that pound of flesh.

Based solely on logic, the law supports Shylock's right to satisfy his grievances in this vengeful way, but the obligations of the heart, the play argues, render the logic of rights insufficient. Wherever there's sin, Christian doctrine insists, forgiveness and mercy become generous gifts that mirror what a gracious forgiving God has provided. Though grievances do humanize *The Merchant*'s villain, the hurt they cause render Portia's subsequent defense of mercy a conclusive test of Shylock's heart, which is in far more danger than Antonio's.

He fails the test because, in contrast to love's irrational paradox, Shylock supports a desire for revenge on the very reasonable assumption laws are enacted to protect contractual obligations. But a strict adherence to law and rights all too easily devolves into a catalog of injustices. A doctrine of generous mercy is the gospel's radical solution to any inflexible adherence to rules. Though the disguised Portia provides him an opportunity to relent, *The Merchant* ultimately refuses to excuse Shylock's unwillingness to soften an obstinate heart. Very cleverly, the courtroom scene serves to knit the two disparate plots together. The defeat of Shylock's adamant refusal to offer mercy for a perceived wrong is not only the defeat of legalism and intractable avarice but the supreme declaration of Portia's fitness for marriage, a sanctuary, supposedly, from self-interest or unbending adherence to rights and rules.

Dejected by Shylock's appeal to the letter of the law, Antonio prepares himself for an agonizing death. But now comes the counter-argument. Disguised as the law clerk, Bellario, Portia reminds the assembled court that the law and justice are not the only considerations here:

> The quality of mercy is not strain'd,
> It droppeth as the gentle rain from heaven
> Upon the place beneath. It is twice blest:
> It blesseth him that gives and him that takes,
> 'Tis mightiest in the mighty, it becomes
> The throned monarch better than his crown.
> His sceptre shows the force of temporal power,
> The attribute to awe and majesty,
> Wherein doth sit the dread and fear of kings;
> But mercy is above the sceptered sway,
> It is enthroned in the heart of kings,
> It is an attribute to God himself;
> And earthly power doth then show likest God's
> When mercy seasons justice. Therefore, Jew,
> Though justice be thy plea, consider this,
> That in the course of justice, none of us
> Should see salvation. We do pray for mercy,
> And that same prayer doth teach us all to render
> The deeds of mercy. (4.1.184-202)

Bellario reminds the assembly that the Judeo-Christian God freely exercises His mercy on behalf of a sinful and undeserving race, that a strict application of His law without mercy would spare no one. Spiritually, everyone is guilty and stands condemned before the law. Mercy is the only way salvation of any kind is possible. If the race created in His image is ever to reflect God's true nature, she argues, human justice must also be seasoned with mercy. She then makes the connection between mercy and generosity: like the rain from heaven, she argues, mercy is a gift that, when given away, blesses both the giver and the receiver. Generosity, mercy and love are all part of the same spirit. Her appeal to divine mercy is both an attempt to persuade Shylock to spare Antonio while also providing an escape from consequences should the moneylender persist in this effort to enforce the contract. But the hurt, the desire for revenge, and the need for satisfaction blind Shylock to this opportunity.

Despite Shylock's probable familiarity with David's *Psalms* which has a lot to say about God's mercy, the moneylender refuses to alter his position, and the disguised Portia now proceeds to apply justice in strict accordance with Shylock's contract. According to Bellario's interpretation, the agreement allows Shylock, fittingly enough, to take his pound of flesh from "nearest the merchant's heart." Encouraged, Shylock praises the wise law clerk, clinging stubbornly to the justice that promises to satisfy his hunger for revenge.

With vengeance tantalizingly close, Shylock refuses even the smallest demonstration of mercy. When the Duke asks Shylock to employ a surgeon to staunch the flow of blood after the grim implementation of his contract, the moneylender objects even to this small gesture of mercy because it is "not in the bond." But it is this insistence on the absolute letter of the law that provides Bellario with the solution to save Antonio's life. After agreeing that Shylock's bond allows him to take a pound of flesh, the law clerk goes on:

> Tarry a little, there is something else.
> This bond doth give thee here no jot of blood;
> The words expressly are "a pound of flesh."
> Take then thy bond, take thou thy pound of flesh,
> But in cutting it, if thou dost shed
> One drop of Christian blood, thy lands and goods
> Are by the law of Venice confiscate
> Unto the state of Venice. (4.1.305-312)

Faced with this insoluble dilemma, Shylock finally relents, but now it is Bellario who insists on the letter of the bond. It is the bond, she insists, or nothing.

When the moneylender is finally ready to capitulate, Bellario levels the next charge: Shylock plotted the death of a Venetian citizen, a crime punishable by forfeiture of his wealth to the victim and the possibility of a death sentence. Though the duke mercifully spares the Jew's life, he rules that Shylock must immediately give away half his wealth to his runaway daughter and her Christian husband. He must also promise to make them his heirs after his death. But the final indignity is that Shylock must convert to the Christian faith. Avariciousness and hatred had sealed Shylock's heart off from any demonstration of love or mercy, and he pays the consequences of those sins. Like the princes who choose the gold and silver caskets, believing they would obtain what they desired or deserved, Shylock walks away empty-handed.

Assuredly, the anti-Semitism in such a thorough humiliation of the Jew is, as Bloom suggests, difficult to ignore (171). To focus only on that historical and cultural problem, however, not only ignores the obvious distaste for revenge in *Titus* and *Romeo and Juliet* but is a distraction from Shylock's larger purpose in this play's design. Much like Falstaff's role within the Henriad, Shylock embodies a specific collection of sins, including self-interest, greediness, a judgmental adherence to rights and rules. All of the play's romantic relationships are under threat from these same sins which can only be averted by the habitual and disciplined application of generous mercy. Love may be a miraculous paradox that doubly blesses a generous heart, but the lead casket and its cryptic message are reminders that its blessings are only available to those willing to embrace its obligations. The defeat of Shylock and everything he represents is a victory for the virtues attendant on love and generosity.

That is not to ignore the wrongs Shylock has suffered from people who now profess a belief in the value of mercy and forgiveness. How the trial unfolds qualifies the supposed virtuousness of the courtroom victors and their application of Christian values. Just as the play's villain rationalizes vengeance by reminding his fellow citizens of their sins and contractual obligations, these believers apply morally sound arguments to save a Christian who owns slaves and despises his Jewish neighbor. No one in this courtroom is above reproach. That these Christians are blind to that fact and to their culpability in his anger and his desire for vengeance is intended to temper any delight their triumph over the ungenerous moneylender might inspire. Generosity's paradox has its obverse in hatred's paradox.

Though the play's villain and the conflict he initiates are resolved by the end of Act 4, rendering the final scenes somewhat anticlimactic, the intrigue played out in Act 5 is an integral extension of what came before. These final events clarify the issue of Portia's ring, given to her husband, Bassanio, who swears never to part with it. Her maid, Nerissa, elicits the same vow from her new husband, Gratiano, to whom she has also given a ring. But after Shylock's trial, the two wives, disguised as law clerks, want the rings as payment for their legal wisdom. Grateful for the law clerks' help, the men can hardly refuse this request, which sets up one final conflict to resolve.

While all this seems anticlimactic, it is not, of course. The request from the disguised women calls for one additional act of generosity, but this time the men's fidelity to the principles of generosity is being ratified rather than Portia's.

As the first four acts show, love's paradoxical logic proves that greed and possessiveness lead to deprivation, whereas a willingness to give generously receives multiplied blessings of love and joy. Given the ethic established by the confrontation with Shylock, the husbands correctly choose to give the rings to the law clerks, despite their vows, from a sense of gratitude and generosity. Since they give them to their disguised wives, only the audience recognizes the false dilemma of the apparently broken vow. As John Russell Brown observes:

> Not recognizing Portia in the young lawyer, Antonio and Bassanio cannot know how deeply he [Bellario, the disguised Portia] is satisfied, how 'dearly' he has given; [the men] do not know that he has acted with love's bounty. Portia chooses to bring this to their knowledge by the trick of asking Bassanio for the ring she gave him at their betrothal. At first he refuses because of his vow, but when he is left alone with Antonio, his love for this friend persuades him to send the ring to the young lawyer. This twist in the plot is resolved in the last act, and still further illustrates the kind of possession which is appropriate for love's wealth. (69)

Love's wealth, of course, accumulates by giving away, by sharing, rather than hoarding out of a fear of losing or not ever having enough. By giving their rings to the law clerks, the men confirm their commitment to generosity and to the flexible application of rules.

The *faux* dilemma is dispelled when the two men return to Belmont where their little treachery is playfully uncovered with much bawdy innuendo from the women, which serves as a subtle promise of marriage's full richness. The final act, therefore, becomes a reminder of the blessing and the obligations that come with the marriage bond. In the end, the difficulties *The Merchant* presents to critic and audience alike can largely be resolved by a careful examination of generosity's paradoxical nature. As John

Russell Brown suggests, ". . . this last act is a fitting sequel to the discord of the trial scene where love and generosity confront hatred and possessiveness; it suggests the way in which love's wealth may be enjoyed continually" (70). Mercy, forgiveness, flexibility, along with good humor, the final act demonstrates, all play a part in the quality of romantic relationships, and in this way it works as a fitting coda to the events that precede this resolution.

The Merchant is a good enough play that it can stand on its own, even without the financial metaphor. Shylock, a sufficiently menacing villain, never topples over into the cartoonish, melodramatic figure that Marlowe's Barabas becomes. Shakespeare takes great pains to give him a recognizable human face. And the love story, with its crucial casket scene, has enough suspense to hold the attention of an audience that doesn't care all that much about thematic cohesion. On stage, the two plots work well on their own. The play is entertaining and delightful. But the money metaphor greatly enriches the play's meaning and provides a thematic consistency that is all too easily overlooked.

Shakespeare seems to have sensed that the dramatic purpose of a metaphor with Biblical roots and an intensely personal significance might be too elaborate and obscure for his audience, for it never reappears again quite so explicitly. But the association of genuine love with generosity persists throughout his subsequent plays. In the context of his entire canon, *The Merchant* is a seminal effort, exhibiting Shakespeare's ability to integrate image or metaphor into drama, pushing it into the realm of literature. As he does here, he continues experimenting with imagery to provide thematic unity without diminishing dramatic intensity.

Because it demonstrates the inherent conflict between the kind of love that risks sacrificing self for another and the insular, selfish nature of sin, *The Merchant* also lays the intellectual and artistic groundwork for his later tragedies. The sonnets initiate this exploration of the open heart's difficulty with those self-possessed individuals who remain content to live with a closed heart. Though it has the structure and feel of the comic, *The Merchant* puts that conflict at the very center of its dramatic soul. Later tragedies, like *Othello, King Lear*, and *Antony and Cleopatra* will explore that conflict between the open and the closed heart further, emphasizing with stunning insight its many paradoxes and ironies.

In the next play, *Twelfth Night*, Shakespeare exhibits a much finer, more subtle comic touch that tones down the villainy and ramps up the zaniness. Nevertheless, it provides a heroine who possesses the same open-hearted desire for genuine, sacrificial love. Her misfortune is to fall in love with a self-absorbed duke, only to become the object of un-looked-for affection herself. In *Twelfth Night*, the absurd randomness of love once again takes center stage, as it did in *As You Like It*, but many of the same themes seen in *Hamlet* and *The Merchant*—appearance and reality, sight and insight, open and closed hearts, and love's wealth—also make their appearance. An example of Shakespearean comedy at its best, *Twelfth Night* is both great drama and great literature.

Twelfth Night

Twelfth Night is an assertion romantic relationships cannot prosper without both honesty and integrity. As always, Shakespeare is developing his ideas about these terms as they apply to the desire for physical and emotional union. Though they have slightly different meanings, the terms are often paired because they work interdependently. An attribute of language, honesty means using words to convey objectively determined truths about inner and outer reality. Since human perception is inherently flawed, honesty is always approximate and never perfect. When speaking about love, however, a desire for union with another only becomes true when the words expressing that desire foster an actual relationship. If the words do not initiate and sustain an actual relationship, the desire expressed is fundamentally dishonest. The speaker's words do not mean what the spoken words normally convey. Integrity, in the context of *Twelfth Night*, is the alignment of objectively and honestly evaluated feelings of desire to actions. What is deeply felt matches what is done. This, the play argues, is as difficult to achieve as honesty and for similar reasons. While love's dilettantes can function with one but will often lack the other, a love capable of enriching is impossible without both. For love to persist, feelings, words, and actions must work in concert. This is the point of *Twelfth Night,* which dramatizes how people dishonest about their feelings and desires can't develop the necessary integrity to form romantic relationships. Unlike *The Merchant*, whose conception of love requires an elaborate financial metaphor, *Twelfth Night* delineates these additional aspects of love by drawing water from the familiar well of Courtly Love. The psychological complexities of desire illuminated here require three rather convoluted but interrelated plots.

The first of these involves a love triangle greatly complicated by disguise, a form of illusion waiting to be comically dispelled. Two twins, Viola and Sebastian, have been shipwrecked and separated near Illyria where Duke Orsino thinks he's in love with Olivia, a rich heiress. As will become clear, her wealth is symbolically important. Since the shipwrecked twins both believe the other has perished, Viola, left to her own devices, decides survival in a strange land requires hiding her gender. Dressing herself as the male page Cesario, she agrees to help Illyria's looney Duke Orsino woo his lady despite having fallen inexplicably in love with him herself. Her attachment is baffling since his absurdly exaggerated desire transforms him into a farcical parody of the gallant but conventionally lovelorn Courtly Lover. Quite sanely, Olivia never takes Orsino's proxy wooing seriously, thereby fulfilling her role as Courtly Love's coldly aloof and stubbornly chaste woman. While Orsino is completely honest about his desire for Olivia, his feelings never go beyond words into action. Trapped in his role as the impassioned, sexually frustrated Courtly Lover, he lacks the integrity to build a viable relationship.

The situation for his love-struck page is equally impossible: though she too is honest about her feelings for her employer, his passion for Olivia and her male disguise make any overt expression of that love impossible. Because circumstances prevent her integrity, Viola assumes the painful role of wooing the woman her beloved desires. Within the first couple of scenes, then, irresistible desire has met immovable obstacles. Given these impediments to romantic success, Viola's disguise is emblematic of the way both she and Orsino present one face to the world while keeping a more authentic one hidden. Lacking the emotional integrity to speak and act honestly on their desire, these lovers know full well what they want but for different reasons are unable to reap desire's full potential.

If the main love story is all about the intractable consequences of pretense, the first of the play's two subplots is a mad, comic celebration of the deflation of dishonest illusion and false posturing. Having recently lost a brother she vows to mourn for the next seven years, the rich heiress Olivia is so indifferent to Orsino's overtures she receives the courier delivering his letters more out of politeness than any detectable interest. Since the spoken vow matches her rejection of Orsino's missives, Olivia has integrity, but the vow allows Olivia to pretend desire has no power over her life. Yet the emotional honesty she sees as Orsino's page woos for her master lights a flame of desire in the wealthy heiress who falls in love with the disguised Viola. Precisely because she's so dishonest about desire herself, it manages to disrupt her plan for seven years of self-imposed chastity. Like Portia, Olivia's wealth is emblematic of the emotional and physical riches she possesses but must learn to share generously before the happiness she deserves can be realized. What is needed for her enlightenment is defined by Sir Toby Belch, her pleasure-loving, acquisitive uncle whose surname suggests the embarrassments that follow gastronomic excess.

Residing with his niece, Sir Toby delights in opportunities to expose Illyria's multiple hypocrisies. His nemesis is Olivia's puritanical steward, Malvolio, a near-homonym of the word "malevolent." Like Orsino, Malvolio secretly longs for the beautiful Olivia, his employer, but his erroneous assumptions about love warp desire into a grotesque parody of what it should be. His ongoing conflict with Toby gradually reveals the reasons for this romantic failure. Permissive and self-indulgent, Sir Toby clashes repeatedly with the judgmental, self-righteousness, and sexually repressed steward who has donned a mantle of authority and moral propriety that chafes Toby's freewheeling personality. When Toby and his companions hatch a plot to convince Malvolio Olivia has responded favorably to his subtle overtures of love, an improbable impossibility, desire's power shreds his self-righteous mantle. Voicing his desire in shockingly selfish and materialistic language, Olivia's steward reveals exactly why he will never deserve the love he wants. But his loss of love's potential wealth is duplicated by Toby's abuse of his niece's generosity and by his deception of Sir Andrew Aguecheek who foolishly pays for advice on winning Olivia's hand. The witty, sophisticated heiress, of course, could have no conceivable interest in a man like Aguecheek, who, as his name suggests, flushes a feverish red at the slightest embarrassment. Both of these plots, therefore, contain male characters whose absurd passions spur their imaginations to pursue women who couldn't possibly return their affections. But Olivia's dishonesty about desire, her willful blindness to love's dominion in her own life, also blinds her to the price poor Aguecheek pays for his desire. Her obliviousness to desire's power allows Toby to enrich himself at the expense of this well-intentioned fool. In the ideal economy of love, which multiplies its riches for giver and receiver alike, her ignorance of desire impoverishes herself and others, a situation repeated in *Othello*. Unwilling to respond honestly to the desire in herself or others, her house could only be ruled by that emotional madman Malvolio, the most emotionally dishonest of them all. His defeat is, in symbolic terms, her liberation into love.

    The final storyline introduces Viola's male twin, Sebastian. Unlike his sister, Sebastian roams the city unencumbered by disguise, helped by his friend Antonio's financial generosity. As in *The Merchant*, when wealth in all its forms is generously shared, unexpected love is facilitated. On one of those excursions, therefore, Sebastian happens to cross paths with Olivia, the object of Orsino's and Sir Andrew's passion. He is astonished but receptive when the rich heiress confuses one twin for the other and boldly confesses her passionate affection. These events begin the process of discovery, and the multiple plots are brought to a comically satisfying resolution, replete with the necessary pairings of appropriate lovers. The authenticity of what Sebastian experiences and expresses, however, not only verifies love's random power but also exposes what denying desire is costing the play's other lovers. Except for the bumbling Sir Andrew, who invests both wealth and dignity in love's cause, every potential lover in *Twelfth Night* chooses safety rather than the risk of sharing a more authentic self, the one replete with all the needs and weaknesses that comprise the reality of human nature. For Shakespeare, only the desire provided by a loving Creator is sufficiently powerful to breach pretense and encourage venturing over the edge into love's deepest joys and commitments. That begins when the desire felt is expressed honestly and offered generously.

The first pretender to appear onstage is Duke Orsino. Endowed with a gift for metaphor, his hyperactive imagination convinces him the verbal expression of desire is the same as real desire. But his frequent proclamations of grand passions never venture beyond moody posturing. For him, desire never goes beyond a display, an act, to impress himself as much as to win the sympathy of others. To relieve the melancholy resulting from frustrated erotic desire, musicians play in the background. "If music be the food of love, play on," he very dramatically declares, "Give me excess of it; that surfeiting, the appetite may sicken, and so die." (1.1.1-3) But, as the rest of the speech indicates, the emotional harmony he pretends to want is not what the duke actually enjoys. What holds his imagination is love's emotional turmoil. Like the vast and tumultuous sea, love, music, and his fevered imagination are all afflicted by storms of heightened excess followed by deflated hope. His imagination seems captivated by desire rising and falling in intensity, which, because it is unrequited, can be enjoyed perpetually as it waxes and wanes. Orsino's pleasure derives, not from a living, breathing woman, but from the metaphors his imagination can spin out of his erotic desire. Since any emotional energy authentic enough to compel a more conventional wooing has been enervated by his self-absorption, his desire has evolved into a love of verbal artifice. For him, love is an excuse for the drama that excites his imagination. **Completely** self-obsessed, he never acknowledges the real Olivia, her needs, or her reasons for rejecting his overtures.

The sad irony of his efforts, despite his familiarity with classical allusions and poetic tropes, is his abject failure to achieve the goal he supposedly wants. The quintessential example of Hubler's closed heart, Orsino is self-obsessed and overly proud. On more than one occasion, he will exalt the strength of his desire for Olivia and lament the cruel impact it inflicts on him. He invokes a highly literary image from Ovid about the hunter, Acteon, who had the misfortune of falling in love with Diana, the goddess of chastity, whom he accidentally observes bathing in a pool. Upset by the intrusion, she transforms him into a stag pursued and brought down by his own hounds. Making the parallel to his own situation, Orsino claims his first encounter with Olivia transformed him into a victim of his own desires:

> O, when mine eyes did see Olivia first. . .
> That instant was I turn'd into a hart,
> And my desires, like fell and cruel hounds,
> E'er since pursue me. (1.1.18-22)

Tellingly, Ovid's tale describes the encounter of a man physically attracted to an unclothed female goddess who has no interest in sexual satisfaction. His allusion is to a story about desire frustrated rather than fulfilled.

Because frustrated desire is the subject that truly interests Orsino, he mistakenly believes his beloved's persistent rejection reflects the superiority of male passion rather than a problem with his reasons for courtship:

> There is no woman's sides
> Can bide the beating of so strong a passion
> As love doth give my heart; no woman's heart
> So big, to hold so much; they lack retention. . . .
> But mine is all as hungry as the sea,
> And can digest as much. Make no compare
> Between that love a woman can bear me
> And that I owe Olivia. (2.4.93-103)

His arrogant conclusion women could never love with the intensity of his passion is disproven when the play's female leads prove far more responsive to desire's irrational demands. Unlike him, they are courageous enough to admit and act upon what they truly feel. Their responsiveness is precisely why they come to understand what love looks, sounds, and feels like. Not so for Orsino. Thwarted by self-absorption and pride, he never musters the emotional or spiritual strength to refocus outward, away from himself and onto another. Doing so would require the kind of spiritual generosity he is never able to exhibit. Instead, an uncontrolled imagination creates this absurd posture of the melancholy lover obsessed with the crazy parabolas of his desire and pain. This imaginative but unrealistic creation of a virtuous emotional self gets savagely mocked in Malvolio's humiliation.

While Orsino's role is to establish an absurd exaggeration of the male Courtly Lover, the next major character to appear onstage is Viola, whose self-imposed male disguise suggests the nature of Orsino's emotional madness: his desire is never more than dramatic proclamation, an act he has no intention of making real. Though she is the first to respond favorably to desire's call, her fear of what she might encounter as a stranger alone in a foreign land causes her to hide her true identity behind a false front. Yet she instinctively knows the dangers of doing so, something she acknowledges when a sea captain provides useful advice after she arrives in Illyria. Grateful for his help, she compliments him:

> There is fair behavior in thee, captain,
> And though that nature with a beauteous wall
> Doth oft close in pollution, yet of thee
> I will believe thou hast a mind that suits
> With this thy fair and outward character. (1.2.47-51)

From the beginning, she admires the integrity of this seafarer whose mind and values are consistent with his outward "beauteous wall." Despite this, she not only falls for a man with virtually no emotional integrity but violates her own better nature by assuming a false identity that prevents her from ever experiencing the love she longs for. The fear that led to an outward disguise begins to multiply her own as well as everyone else's problems. Though she absurdly loves a mad poet who thinks he loves another, a Viola in male disguise is assigned the painful task of wooing an indifferent competitor for Orsino's heart. Though her devotion to her beloved is evident from the selfless diligence with which she carries out this obligation, her disguise violates her admiration for the captain's integrity. Very soon, she will be forced to admit any disguise, including her own, is the handiwork of the devil himself.

    The difference between Viola's and Orsino's response to desire's call is instructive. Though unnatural identities hide more authentic and honest versions of both from the rest of the world, her response to desire is immediate and unqualified, and the validity of her love is evident from her selfless devotion to his needs rather than her own. While Orsino's fascination with his own passion and pain is all-consuming, she cares about his happiness first. Working from a generous and trusting heart, she is willing to risk the relationship she hopes for, fully confident love's good plan will eventually provide their real needs rather than their desires. Where he is self-involved and emotionally selfish, unwilling to invest his passion in an actual relationship, she can sympathize with another's suffering. When her proxy wooing sparks Olivia's desire for a young girl disguised in male doublet and hose, she quickly grasps the predicament her dishonesty has caused the rich heiress:

> Poor lady, she were better love a dream.
> Disguise, I see thou art a wickedness
> Wherein the pregnant enemy does much. . . .
> How will this fadge? My master loves her dearly,
> And I (poor monster) fond as much on him;
> And she (mistaken) seems to dote on me.
> What will become of this? As I am man,
> My state is desperate for my master's love;
> As I am woman (now alas the day!),
> What thriftless sighs shall poor Olivia breathe!
> O time! Thou must untangle this, not I,
> It is too hard a knot for me t' untie. (2.2.26 – 41)

Hiding one's true self is a 'wickedness wherein the pregnant enemy does much,' she comes to understand, because deception leads to cruel and intolerable confusions. The fault, she knows, is hers.

Duplicity, however, is not the only obstacle to love. Olivia has authored her own obstacles, including the idea a brother's death requires seven years of mourning as well as a conviction her beauty will never fade. Both errors reflect a misconception of time, something her wise jester, Feste, argues is a lie. One of his songs, for example, is a somber reminder of time's cruelty and the necessity to respond to love's unexpected intrusions:

> What is love? 'Tis not hereafter;
> Present mirth hath present laughter;
> What's to come is still unsure.
> In delay there lies no plenty,
> Then come kiss me sweet and twenty;
> Youth's a stuff will not endure. (2.3.47-52)

Because joy, beauty, and the desire it inspires never last forever, Feste implores lovers to seize the day and employ these blessings as nature intended. "In delay," Feste reminds us, "there lies no plenty. . . ." Nature's abundant gifts slip away from those who put off love. In another exchange, he challenges her to rethink those seven years of mourning.

> Fe. Good Madonna, give me leave to prove you a fool. . . .
> Oli. Make your proof.
> Fe. I must catechize you for it, Madonna. Good my mouse of virtue, answer me.
> Oli. Well, sir, for want of other idleness, I'll bide your proof.
> Fe. Good Madonna, why mourn'st thou?
> Oli. Good fool, for my brother's death.
> Fe. I think his soul is in hell, Madonna.
> Oli. I know his soul is in heaven, fool.
> Fe. The more fool, Madonna, to mourn for your brother's soul, being in heaven. Take away the fool, gentlemen.
> (1.5.57-71)

Mourning isn't wrong, but a seven-year disengagement from life risks the loss of beauty and love, both of which, the play points out, are fragile and susceptible to passing time. Earthly gifts do not last forever. "Make her laugh at that," Hamlet says as he contemplates Yorick's unearthed skull. Before they disappear, every treasure provided must be invested for the good of the world.

The common Elizabethan refrain of time's passing, the mutability of earthly things, and the urgency of responding to desire's call introduces the complex theme of beauty which, the play argues, is among those precious gifts given to be spent. When Viola-Cesario arrives to deliver Orsino's message, which Olivia virtually ignores, the messenger reminds her that "what is yours to bestow is not yours to reserve," a by-now familiar refrain that withholding nature's gifts from the world is a grievous sin. The most obvious gift, beauty, is subject to the ravages of time, rendering its hold on the male imagination quite tenuous. Though coyly mocking Orsino's conventional praise of her beauty, the heiress agrees to remove the veil she donned to honor her departed brother. Her face fully visible at last, she asks:

> Oli. Is't not well done?
> Vio. Excellently done, if God did all.
> Oli. 'Tis in grain, sir, 'twill endure wind and weather.
> Vio. Tis beauty truly blent, whose red and white
> Nature's own sweet and cunning hand laid on.
> Lady, you are the cruell'st she alive
> If you will lead these graces to the grave,
> And leave the world no copy.
> Oli. O, sir, I will not be so hard-hearted; I will give out Divers schedules of my beauty. It shall be inventoried and every particle and utensil labell'd to my will: as, *item*, two lips, indifferent red; *item*, two grey eyes with lids to them; *item*, one neck, one chin, and so forth. Were you sent hither to praise me?
> Vio. I see what you are, you are too proud. But if you were the devil, you are fair. (1.5.235-251)

Even though Olivia takes obvious pride in what others see in her unveiled face, her catalog of features is a smug dismissal of the conventional praise courtly poets like Orsino pay to feminine appearance. When Viola reminds her listener of beauty's **susceptibility** to corrupting time, she asserts "'[t]will endure wind and weather," a phrase echoed later in the play's mournful final song. Orsino's misguided opinion about the superiority of male desire finds an equivalently misguided conviction in Olivia's ideas about beauty. Beauty's durability, Viola reminds her, is not the only issue for Olivia would be the "cruell'st she alive" if she should take "these graces to the grave, And leave the world no copy." As one of nature's divinely ordained gifts, beauty's purpose in the cosmic dance of desire is to multiply love's wealth.

At the same time, Olivia's nonchalant reaction to Orsino's conventional praise of female beauty suggests a more profound need as well. Like Viola's male doublet and hose, beauty disguises much about what is far more important than pale skin and ruby lips. Behind Olivia's witty mockery of Orsino's obsession with surface appearance is a desire to be known and understood more deeply. She knows what attracts his attention, but she also understands it also distracts from what matters to her. This is the significance of Olivia's wealth, in fact: it represents everything that makes her precious and worthy of male attention. Where Orsino wallows in his self-pity and sexual frustrations, what Olivia possesses is so much more than physical appearance and a capacity to provide sexual satisfaction. As implied by *The Merchan*t's casket lottery, that disparity in evaluations is precisely why Olivia is so indifferent to Orsino and his conventional praise. The very male Courtly Love obsession with female beauty, that wonderful, God-given attribute inspiring male desire, very unfortunately also hinders men from seeing what's more valuable and equally real. His overly narrow conception of love, in fact, compels her to put on a mantle of cold, uncaring aloofness. Olivia quite rightly wants more for both of them. Like gender-hiding clothing, therefore, female beauty ends up disguising a far more authentic and vulnerable self when an ardent suitor's narrow conception of love makes her unwilling to risk courageously engaging with the other.

Despite all these obstacles, romantic love's disruptive force finds a way to overwhelm a reluctant and emotionally cautious Olivia. Instinctively, Viola, the woman hiding herself in male clothing, knows what's needed to solve the problem. Seeing how unwelcome the duke's poetic efforts are, Viola abandons his trite phrases entirely and begins to speak in a far more personal and genuinely emotional language welling up out of her desire for Orsino. As artifice gives way to something more real, those words begin to transform Olivia's heart:

> Vio. If I did love you in my master's flame...
> In your denial I would find no sense,
> I would not understand it.
> Oli. Why, what would you?
> Vio. Make me a willow cabin at your gate,
> And call upon my soul within the house;
> Write loyal cantons of contemned love,
> And sing them loud even in the dead of night . . .
> O, you should not rest
> Between the elements of air and earth
> But you should pity me!
> Oli. You might do much. (1.5.264-276)

But the quality of the emotions expressed ends up subverting the intention to fulfill her commission. Enchanted, finally, by the romance of what sounds very much like genuine longing, Olivia is clearly moved. The honest desire in the words becomes the irresistible food feeding a heart that, until this moment, tried desperately to deny its own hunger. Where the dilettante Orsino plays at love without any direct involvement in an actual courtship, Viola's presence and her words are the thing itself. In this little moment, Viola's hidden, authentic self sneaks out from behind her disguise in language honestly reflecting emotional realities, and the effect, unlike Orsino's conventional tropes and metaphors, is powerful and immediate. Sadly, this is the potential so far unavailable to all the lovers hiding behind their various disguises.

But the multiple ironies in this charming scene also contribute to the play's subtle humor. Obviously very real, Cesario's emotions are triggered by a desire for a person not even in the room, yet the power of that longing moves Olivia to abandon her vow. What she sees and hears is the kind of love she didn't even know she wanted until this moment. It strikes, as Ovid's fables remind, where least expected and in ways that shatter any pretensions of control, a loss with many unintended consequences. Moved by Viola's genuine passion, Olivia muses alone after Orsino's page has left: "How now? Even so quickly may one catch the plague?" Finally acknowledging love's undeniable force, Olivia submits to something greater and more powerful than her own volition. Olivia's attraction to a woman disguised as a man, however, is also a sly and ironic parody of those courtly lovers paying exaggerated tribute to their beloved's outward appearance. Exactly like Orsino, she too is in love with an appearance that belies what remains hidden and thus unknown. Though she scorned Orsino's trivial motives and praise for female beauty, the bewitching appearance of her beloved renders her equally blind to the truer identity underneath. As a consequence of this final, ironic deception, Olivia now tastes the very same bitter medicine she fed Orsino: she has fallen for someone who, it appears, could never requite her affections.

In these events, the play carefully establishes the many ways people inadvertently prevent desire from leading them into romantic relationship. Dishonest about what they want, overly cautious and afraid of the risks of being authentic, they establish various ways to disguise who they are. Such pretensions, however, offer little protection from overpowering desires, sometimes genuinely selfless and good, sometimes selfish and malevolent. Exposing what's foolish about any barrier to desire's potential good is the purpose of the play's two subplots which follow the fate of three very different male lovers: Malvolio, Sir Andrew, and Viola's twin, Sebastian. Like Orsino, Malvolio's desire is deformed by selfish need; Sir Andrew's pursuit of the unattainable makes him vulnerable to the indifferent and the unscrupulous; and Sebastian, willing to accept a benefactor's financial support, is also open to the unexpected gift of love.

In the first of these subplots, Malvolio's humiliation is the result of coveting the benefits more than the obligations of love, what in *The Merchant*'s terms are the gold or silver caskets more than the one made of lead. Underneath Malvolio's mantle of authority and virtue is a desire for wealth, status, and the power to control Toby and his funloving friends. Just as Orsino, Olivia, and Viola hide an authentic self under assumed personas, Malvolio's virtuous posture hides a much different person underneath. Familiar as he is with human sin, Toby senses every lie as a weakness that can be exploited for his amusement. Constantly annoyed by the steward's reprimands, Toby, Sir Andrew, and Maria, Olivia's maid, devise a plot to embarrass him. They compose a letter purportedly from Olivia implying that she has fallen for Malvolio, whose imagination quickly runs wild with the prospect of her love. In a masterfully comic scene, Malvolio finds and reads this letter aloud, unaware that the hidden schemers are listening. With a mad desire for wealth and status firing his imagination, reason and propriety depart, and he fantasizes about what marriage might mean for his position within Olivia's household. Whispering their outrage to each other, the three rogues listen unobserved to the steward's eager ruminations:

Mal.	To be Count Malvolio!
Sir To.	Ah, rogue!
Mal.	There is example for't: the Lady of the Strachy married the yeoman of the wardrobe....
Sir And.	Fie on him, Jezebel!
Mal.	Calling my officers about me, in my branch'd velvet gown; having come from a day-bed, where I have left Olivia sleeping—
Sir To.	Fire and brimstone!
Mal.	And then to have the humor of state; and after a demure travel of regard---telling them I know my place as I would they should do theirs---to ask for my kinsman Toby---
Sir To.	Bolts and shackles!
Mal.	Seven of my people, with an obedient start, make out for him. I frown the while, and perchance wind up my watch, or play with my—some rich jewel. Toby approaches; curtsies there to me---
Sir To.	Shall this fellow live?

Mal.	I extend my hand to him thus, quenching my familiar smile with an austere regard of control---
	. . . .
	Saying, "Cousin Toby, my fortunes, having cast me on your niece, give me this prerogative of speech"—
Sir To.	What, what?
Mal.	"You must amend your drunkenness." (2.5.35-73)

Malvolio's excited emotions obliterate his usual sense of propriety, and, to the hilarious dismay of the hidden plotters, he envisions himself the master of her household, able, finally, to command rather than earn Sir Toby's respect and compliance. Malvolio's imagined scenario reveals his self-absorption, and his desire for power, control, and status. Malvolio loves, not because it requires something from him, but because it provides what he thinks he deserves. His lack of self-knowledge is almost as profound as Orsino's.

Viola-Cesario's dedication to the virtues of service, trust, and patience sets the standard by which Malvolio's selfish desire for wealth, status, and power should be measured. He is nothing like her. His allusion to Olivia lingering on their daybed, exhausted by his sexual prowess, is pure egotism. His insistence on order shows a lack of flexibility and tolerance. Self-righteous and unwilling to forgive Toby, he lacks any capacity for mercy, and without this, joy eludes him, which is why he can never participate in Toby's holiday world. His only consolations, ironically, are the trappings of wealth and status: the titles, the velvet gowns, the "rich jewel," and the wealthy, beautiful, sexually satisfied wife who, he imagines, allows him free reign over their household. Like Orsino's fictional role as courtly lover, Malvolio's vision is a figment of his overheated imagination.

Though he believes he is in love, Malvolio's vision of the future contains no emotional, moral, or spiritual transformation whatsoever. Nothing more than an elaboration of his essential selfishness, the vision demonstrates the

Christian orthodoxy that redemption is impossible without repentance and that repentance is impossible without an admission of guilt, something Malvolio is far too proud to recognize, let alone admit. He is imprisoned within that vision of his own virtue. That every other character except Malvolio is open to change is evidence of what makes them different. Viola discards her disguise. Olivia forsakes her vow. Even Orsino ends his foolish quest to pursue a woman who has no interest in him. By risking honesty and authenticity, by letting go of pretense, they gain the freedom to embrace transformation into romance and love.

Not Malvolio. Instead, the role created by his imagination devolves further into absurd delusion. Lacking any self-awareness, he follows the false advice in the letter and dons a perpetual smile and cross-gartered yellow stocking, both of which are known to irritate Olivia immensely. Because of this apparent madness, Sir Toby and his friends cast Malvolio into a dark cell from which he sends furtive pleas for mercy and release to his intended mistress. As his pitiful pleas are thwarted by the conspirators, the terrifying darkness of his prison mirrors his emotional and spiritual state. Toby, the king of misrule, has subverted the tyranny of Malvolio's imposed order. That defeat ushers in a world revitalized by the holiday joy alluded to in the play's title. To those unfamiliar with Elizabethan holiday traditions, the title references the twelfth and final day of the Christmas season when, to celebrate the newborn baby Jesus, Elizabethans would play-act the gift-giving Magi or local officials only to surreptitiously expose their real, very ordinary identities. This same process of exposing ridiculous disguise is what *Twelfth Night* celebrates.

Sir Andrew's situation explores additional aspects of the delusion irrational desire can cause. The social insecurities implied by Aguecheek's surname combine with Olivia's ignorance of desire's power to create an unbridgeable gap between the suitor and the object of his affection Toby is only too willing to exploit. The money Olivia's uncle extracts from his gull, however, is indicative of what is lost by the unrealistic assumptions about desire and love. The same metaphor will be repeated in *Othello* when the villainous Iago takes Roderigo's money in exchange for advice about seducing the Moor's completely devoted wife. While *Twelfth Night*'s Sir Andrew pursues an unattainable woman, exactly like both Orsino and Malvolio, there is still something a bit admirable within his foolish pursuit. Unlike them, Andrew is willing to invest his wealth, his effort, and his time in the enterprise. His hopes suffer, unfortunately, because he gives his money to the unscrupulous Sir Toby rather than directly to the woman he desires, a misguided trust that mimics Orsino's proxy wooing. And for that misguided trust, he loses his investment, just as Orsino loses his. The penalty for all the pretense is lost time and opportunity. Beauty fades, a potential lover moves on, fate intervenes, loneliness prevails. Like the third servant in the Matthew parable, each of these characters has squandered a precious gift instead of investing it wisely. Each of these characters allows disguise, role-playing, or a lack of self-awareness to impede the fulfillment of that very natural need for love, for honesty, for connection. The poet Orsino, the lunatic Malvolio, and the other unrequited lovers are all victimized by the roles imagination created.

Dispelling illusion is the primary purpose of the third and final plot. The main plot's knotty confusions begin to unravel when **Viola-Cesario's twin brother, Sebastian,** happens to cross paths with Olivia, who mistakes him for his twin, Orsino's disguised page, Cesario, with whom she is in love. Olivia confesses her undying love to the wrong twin, pledges their betrothal which she seals with a pearl ring, and heads off with her entourage to prepare for their wedding. Completely confused but delighted by this overture, Sebastian is enchanted by a city where a rich, beautiful stranger showers her love on him at first sight. He struggles to comprehend this magical turn of events:

> This is the air, that is the glorious sun,
> This pearl that she gave me, I do feel't and see't,
> And though 'tis wonder that enwraps me thus,
> Yet 'tis not madness. . . .
> Yet doth this accident and flood of fortune
> So far exceed all instance, all discourse,
> That I am ready to distrust mine eyes,
> And wrangle with my reason that persuades me
> To any other trust but that I am mad,
> Or else the lady's mad; yet if 'twere so,
> She could not sway her house, command her followers. . . .
> With such smooth, discreet, and stable bearing
> As I perceive she does. (4.3.1-20)

In twenty compact but truly wonderful lines, the play's main ideas about illusion and reality, reason and madness, blindness and insight coalesce. Completely open to love's magic, Sebastian accepts the gift he's been given with wonder and joy. For him, the miracle is real, and Sebastian sounds so genuinely amazed because he understands that where he was lost and shipwrecked is now where he is loved. His language captures everything that is special about love's unexpected intrusion into a life. No artifice or pretense here. Nothing is hidden or disguised. Unashamed desire is answered in kind. There is no calculation, greed, or self-aggrandizement. What is seen and heard in his response is love's truth, and it stands in sharp contrast to everything in the other two plots, and it is this experience that artifice, illusion, and self-deception hinder. Metaphorically, this is what Toby steals from Sir Andrew and what illusion and disguise steal from the other main characters.

Sebastian's experience signals the restoration of a renewed harmony that is a consequence of his free and unfettered openness to love. But in *Twelfth Night* that vision of love's ideal result is not unblemished, for the normal comic ending of happily paired couples and promises of marriage is marred by threats of revenge. The three male lovers, Orsino, Malvolio, and Sebastian stand as a precaution against the dangers of illusion. Confusing one twin with the other in these final scenes, Orsino at first threatens harm to his page, Viola-Cesario, when he witnesses Olivia's love for her brother. Once that confusion dissipates, he somewhat reluctantly accepts the love of the patient and forgiving Viola, whose true identity has finally been revealed. Malvolio threatens revenge, not only because he has been humiliated, but also because Olivia, thinking him mad, never came to his rescue. His illusion of a romantic relationship has created expectations that cannot possibly be fulfilled. The reactions of both men to the vicissitudes of love have been compromised by self-absorption and an unwillingness to let go of illusion.

As the play draws to its conclusion, Viola's patient love for a man only reluctantly willing to separate from his illusions strikes many as an unfortunate and ill-considered sour note. It appears she will pay a price simply because she is not Olivia, the original object of Orsino's affection. But that is an opinion that overlooks the point Shakespeare carefully makes about love's risk. Of all the lovers, Viola is the only one who has voiced an understanding of the wickedness of deceit and the need to put aside all pretense. If Orsino is not yet prepared to let go of the last portions of his illusions, Viola is the only one with the patience and insight to help him through the necessary final steps. And she is willing to take that risk, to extend herself to a seemingly unworthy other, because that's precisely the generous giving of self that love requires. Never showing any surprise at the unexpected intrusion of desire and love, she remains, from first word to last, their patient disciple and ambassador.

Unlike Shakespeare's earlier comedies, the ending of *Twelfth Night* is a mixture of joyful delight and an almost melancholy awareness of the very human difficulty of letting go of illusion and embracing the necessary changes initiated by desire. Given this perspective, it is fitting, that the play ends with a song from the one character whose eyesight has always been clear. Alone on stage at the end of the play, Feste, Olivia's fool, sings this jaunty but melancholy little limerick:

> When that I was and a little tine boy,
> With a hey ho, the wind and the rain,
> A foolish thing was but a toy,
> For the rain it raineth every day.
>
> But when I came to man's estate,
> With a hey ho, the wind and the rain,
> 'Gainst knaves and thieves men shut their gate
> For the rain it raineth every day.
>
> But when I came, alas, to wive,
> With a hey ho, the wind and the rain,
> By swaggering could I never thrive,
> For the rain it raineth every day.

The "swaggering" pride of Orsino and Malvolio leads nowhere and deserves to be mocked. But those elemental forces of "wind and the rain" reprimand Olivia's equally foolish pride in beauty's resilience. Her illusion of control had to dissipate before love was possible. What was real to her then is not what is real in the end. Nature, embodied in the inevitable storms that come with wind and rain, will have its way with false pride and illusion. But time is double-edged: it may steal the bloom off the rose, but it also ushers in another spring. When Olivia and Viola choose to trust time to untie the Gordian knot that hinders them, they have chosen to relinquish any foolish illusions that hide love's truth and the fruitful bounty that it promises.

Whatever joy the play's ending holds, *Twelfth Night* has this unmistakable, somber undertone that signals a shift toward Shakespeare's great tragedies. Love triumphs here, as it should, but the complexity of this play's comic vision also reflects an awareness of evil's persistence in a fallen world. Here, nothing is entirely pure. Even holiday fun is somehow blemished. Malvolio's pride is far more insidious than Olivia's or even Orsino's, but his humiliation and punishment seem unnecessarily cruel too. And though Sir Toby's marriage to Olivia's maid Maria is his reward for exposing Malvolio's hypocrisy, he has benefited at the expense of his friend, Sir Andrew. No part of human existence is free from sin, and in the tragedies the wages of sin are more clearly suffering and death. That awareness of persistent evil brings us to the very doorstep of the tragedies.

Twelfth Night shows its author's deepening insights into the nature and experience of love. That hard-won perspective of essential human qualities under nearly constant threat from contrary behaviors ushers his audience into his mature tragedies, which gaze steadily at this conflict between good and evil. Everything that went into those earlier plays— Ovid, courtly love, his interest in English history, the structural principles of comedy, and, perhaps most importantly, the very Christian awareness of sin and its consequences–have prepared him for this venture into the tragic, which was by no means inevitable. How all these psychological, emotional, intellectual, and moral elements come together in Shakespeare's hands is something of a miracle itself. And contrary to the belief that tragedy and Christianity are incompatible, Christian principles deepen his sensitivity to the ironies and paradoxes of human existence that tragedy asks us to remember, particularly the notion that suffering is sometimes the only way to important insights. Without his understanding of basic Christian principles about the nature of love and sin, his great tragedies would never have happened. Certainly, the very seminal tragedy, *Othello,* the next play examined, is a case in point.

Othello

To suggest its mysterious, irresistible, fascinating dominion within the human imagination, Shakespeare describes the power love and desire exercise on relationships as a form of magic. That association begins with *A Midsummer Night's Dream* where love casts its spell over the poet, the lunatic, and the lover alike with hilarious if ultimately benevolent results. Using that same metaphorical association, *Othello* reverses that relational process toward benevolence to show how desire, perverted by prurient imaginings, can desecrate love into jealousy and brutal murder. Surprising for an author so adept with language, Shakespeare creates a villainous Iago who artfully uses suggestion and insinuation to achieve that odious reversal. As such, *Othello* carries the unmistakable implication that language's capacity for untruth and deception is one tool evil uses to degrade the best within human nature to the unhuman.

Despite the universal susceptibility to language's ability to deceive, many find Shakespeare's story about a Moor married to a white Venetian lady troubling. Though a man of admirable military discipline, Othello is a bewildering and unsympathetic tragic figure who all too easily comes to believe that his new wife has been unfaithful when everyone onstage and in the audience knows the contrary to be true. Based on the circumstantial evidence of a lost handkerchief, his accusation of sexual betrayal appears to be without merit and his revenge, therefore, entirely unreasonable. A few obvious questions could have easily averted this catastrophe. Because his gullibility is beyond puzzling, the usual expectations of a tragedy about heroic nobility undermined by understandable error aren't met, making the play both difficult to watch and difficult to like.

Absent, too, is any evidence of some mysterious, invisible force working to exploit human weakness for unfathomable reasons. Instead, Othello's very human and very nefarious attaché, Iago, has been given that role. He has a place in the story for one dramatic purpose only: to facilitate Othello's change from military leader and husband to deranged murderer. This narrow concentration on psychological transformation creates an impression far more limited and domestic than *Hamlet*'s foreboding atmosphere, where ghosts and musings about death and mortality bring that earlier play much closer to life's unanswerable mysteries. Though the mysterious supernatural may be implicit in the vague and conflicting reasons given for Iago's actions, that hint is largely negated by Shakespeare's very detailed examination of the Moor's transformation. The focus is much more on the human how rather than the metaphysical why.

But the difficulty of appreciating *Othello* increases for enthusiasts of New Historicism's approach to literature: it is, after all, a story about a black African soldier misled by a white subordinate into murdering a woman whose marriage renders her emotionally and culturally defenseless. As such, it raises troubling questions about race, domestic violence, and misogyny. Viewed from this perspective, *Othello* is rich fare for the documentation of racial and gender biases deserving to be exposed, embarrassed, and eliminated.

Except those post-modern concerns do nothing to illuminate what Shakespeare is addressing in his tragedy. What New Historicism misses are the themes *Othello* shares with a play like *Hamlet* which explores the destructive consequences of undisciplined emotions that inflame the imagination and propel the unfortunate into catastrophe. It overlooks ideas shared with *Romeo and Juliet* or *A Midsummer Night's Dream*, which demonstrate the transformative effect of erotic desire; and it misses Desdemona's thematic connection to the loving devotion of Rosalind in *As You Like It* and the patience of *Twelfth Night*'s

Viola. Nor does it clarify Shakespeare's very careful delineation of the complex interplay of language, imagination, and sexual desire in the process of Othello's temptation. Since these are the issues the preceding plays address, it seems obvious Shakespeare would continue to elaborate those concerns here as well.

    Despite its obvious racial and gender components, *Othello* is much more a story about a disciplined military man who, having tasted the pure nectar of desire, finds his fortress reason easily breached by an imagination deliberately inflamed with disturbing images of sexual infidelity. Once reason has been disarmed and overturned, Othello's trust in an innocent wife's marital loyalty is transformed into its opposite. Othello's story exposes in excruciating detail the way the male reduction of love's full complexity into nothing more than sexual desire unleashes a horrifying brutality capable of destroying the innocent and the lovely. Ovid's influence here is unmistakable. Shakespeare's concern is this elaborate process of corrupting a man's rational defenses with language and rhetoric, a sort of evil poetry that knows how to use imagination's limitless powers to envision the entirety of human potential, from the noble to the prurient. Though *Othello* recreates in painful detail the Biblical tragedy of a fall from innocence and faith into sin, the actual fall itself, the murder of Desdemona, is given less emphasis than the process of making such a shocking decision. Both the Bible and Shakespeare return repeatedly to the story of man's fall from grace in all its multitudinous iterations because its causes and processes need to be understood before sin and its consequences have any hope of being avoided.

    Understanding Iago's part in that fall is critical. While his literary pedigree begins with the two-dimensional vice figure of the medieval moralities, the type is modified here so Iago becomes a force credible enough to overcome Othello's resistance. As Bernard Spivack argues in his *Iago: The Allegory of Evil*, Othello's nemesis differs in four specific ways from other Elizabethan vice figures like Marlowe's Barabas or Shakespeare's Richard III:

> [First,] the bravura image of multiple deceit . . . is no longer tandem and episodic, but deftly organized into a single complex intrigue within a comprehensive dramatic plot. [Second,] the amoral humor of the moral personification . . .has become pervasive—a mood and a tone penetrating Iago's role throughout. [Third,] the homiletic dimension of the role. . .is relatively subdued and fragmentary, modified by indirection and mainly limited to sentences and half sentences that twist in and out his more relevant phraseology. [And fourth,] while the stark psychomachia remains. . .it has suffered attrition, and of the original formula only part remains: "I hate the Moor." (Eastman, 352)

Not just a morality play's personification of evil's deceptive nature, Iago's part in what Spivack refers to as this tragedy's psychomachia, its psychological warfare, is integral to its intrigue. His verbal interactions are highly seasoned with sexual innuendo delivered in purposely suggestive sentences, phrases, and questions, all slyly inserted into deceptively normal conversation. The aim is to contaminate Othello's imagination, to fill it with images so perverse that jealousy and rage replace reason and discipline. While this is his mechanism, however, none of this explains why he does what he does. Based on what occurs on stage, the only reasonable explanation for Iago's behavior is that he simply hates Othello. Coleridge's assessment is fundamentally correct: Iago is "motiveless malignity." Since the text makes his methodology of corruption rather than his motives available, the methodology has to be what matters.

Though his motivations are never clear, Iago is able to corrupt Othello's mind because he skillfully intermingles lies with truthful observations, some of which he applies to himself. The strategy works so well because establishing a presumption of honesty enhances the effectiveness of his subsequent deceptions. Early in the play, for example, he describes himself to his supposed friend, Roderigo, who wonders why Iago pretends to serve Othello so diligently when he has already professed his hatred of the Moor. His answer divides those who serve a master into two distinct categories:

> I follow him to serve my turn upon him.
> We cannot all be masters, nor all masters
> Cannot be truly follow'd. You shall mark
> Many a duteous and knee-crooking knave
> That . . . [w]ears out his time. . .
> For nought but provender . . . .
> Whip me such honest knaves. Others there are
> Who, trimm'd in forms and visages of duty,
> Keep yet their hearts attending on themselves,
> And throwing but shows of service on their lords,
> . . . and when they have lin'd their coats
> Do themselves homage. These fellows have some soul,
> And such a one do I profess myself. (1.1.42-55)

What's remarkably ironic about this self-assessment is not only its accuracy but that he's so honest about his motives to a friend from whom he is stealing. Throughout the play, Iago, the master of lies, is paradoxically associated with two attributes: honesty and humorous wit. While the first of these is normally thought to be an ability to align what is said with what is observably true and good, in Iago it is merely an ability to assess the world around him realistically. That objectivity allows him to be keenly observant of himself as well as others and to determine what value that knowledge might have for his purposes. As he plots how to use Cassio to make Othello jealous, for example, he notes that the lieutenant is "a proper man" (1.3.392), which his honorable dealings with Desdemona prove. He also admits that Othello himself is "of a constant, loving, noble nature" (2.1.289), which, despite the play's tragic ending, is true at the beginning of the play. Ironically, Iago's calculated honesty prepares the garden where his *fleur de mal* sink deep roots into fertile soil.

In the play's first scene, Iago practices his dark verbal art for corrupting the imagination of others. Fundamental to this is his awareness of the fear, anxiety, concern, and curiosity others harbor about sexual desire and fulfillment, especially between those separated in racially obvious ways. The very first scene opens with news about Othello's secret marriage to Desdemona. To sow discord in the Moor's new family, Iago and his dupe, Roderigo, rouse Brabantio, Desdemona's father, from his sleep with a profane image of their love.

> Bra. What's the reason for this terrible summons?
> What is the matter there?
> Rod. Signior, is all your family within?
> Iago. Are your doors lock'd?
> Bra.   Why? Wherefore ask you this?
> Iago. Zounds, sir, y' are robbed! For shame, put on your gown;
> Your heart is burst, you have lost half your soul;
> Even now, now, very now, an old black ram
> Is tupping your white ewe. (1.1.82-89)

Rich with imagery intended to provoke, Iago's language insinuates the animalistic nature of sexual passion, the racial differences between husband and wife, and Brabantio's loss of a treasured daughter to a marriage apparently undertaken without his permission. While the news and the manner of its delivery are intentionally disruptive to a father's peace of mind, this vulgar description of the newlyweds' nuptials also reveals a similar contempt for Othello, the "old black ram." The bitter taste from those Ovidian fables of uncontrolled, dangerous bestial passion overwhelming the powerless infuses Iago's language.

Like an insidious poison, this reductive vision of love seeps into the language of Desdemona's father. Later that same night, as he confronts his new son-in-law before the Venetian council, hastily assembled to discuss the threat of a Turkish invasion, the old man resorts to similar racially charged language. Unable to account for his daughter's unexpected alliance with this husband, Brabantio resorts to the only plausible explanation for her puzzling enthrallment:

> If she in chains of magic were not bound,
> Whether a maid so tender, fair, and happy,
> So opposite to marriage that she shunn'd
> The wealthy curled darlings of our nation,
> Would ever have, t' incur a general mock,
> Run from her guardage to the sooty bosom
> Of such a thing as thou—to fear, not to delight! (1.2.65-71)

The introduction of love as a form of magic begins to provide an alternative to Iago's reductive vision of love as well as a thematic explanation for Shakespeare's choice of Othello's race.

Through Ovid, Shakespeare witnessed the irrational nature of love, how the power of sexual desire brings disparate beings inexplicably together, some more or less happily, others not. All the plays already examined indicate desire's ambiguous power constitutes an essential concern of his art. While Othello's blackness does indeed make him different from the other Venetians around him, it functions exactly like the odd features of another alien figure encountered in *A Midsummer Night's Dream*. There, Puck's magic dust causes the fairy queen, Titania, to fall in love with the rustic Bottom, already disfigured with an ass's head. The scene exaggerates what every lover somehow understands: that, regardless of what is visible to everyone else, the lover can only see beauty and virtue in the beloved and is blind to any imperfections. Not necessarily or altogether unfortunate, this blindness to certain obvious realities can be one of love's miracles.

Titania's inability to see Bottom's transformed head is the prototype for Desdemona's blindness to Othello's starkly different appearance. For the uninitiated or unaffected, love is beyond rational and certainly looks a bit like madness or magic, but the emotional dynamic between Othello and Desdemona is identical to the one between the fairy queen and Bottom. Both scenes convey love's miraculous ability to ignore the obvious and to focus on deeper, more important emotional realities. Iago's reductive vulgarity and Brabantio's incredulity are both failures to comprehend this very special, magical quality of love. They are not alone. Though Othello has been lightly touched by this magic, he has not yet been completely transformed by its full power. When circumstances force him to postpone his marriage night, his willingness to give his Venetian responsibilities primacy suggests a man so unfamiliar with the power of erotic desire he might easily be overwhelmed by its affects. In this he is very much like *Twelfth Night*'s Olivia who naively believes her vow to mourn for seven years makes her impervious to desire's unexpected intrusions.

So two very different narratives about love are already underway. The first of these belongs to Iago whose stories incorporate imagery of bestial lust overcoming discretion and decorum. The overwhelming power of the desire his narrative recounts is enough to incite Brabantio's disbelief and anger. At the same time, an alternative narrative about love begins to develop in Othello's stories of dangerous military campaigns in exotic foreign lands, stories that inspire Desdemona's love for the Moor. Rather than the kind of magic in Brabantio's accusation, Othello describes a different kind of magic, verbal in nature, that opened his lady's heart to someone so different from the other very parochial men of Venice.

Her father lov'd me, oft invited me;

> Still question'd me the story of my life
> ...—the battles, sieges, fortunes,
> That I have pass'd.
> ...I spoke of most disastrous chances:
> Of moving accidents by flood and field,
> Of hair-breadth 'scapes i' th' imminent deadly breach,
> Of being taken by the insolent foe
> And sold to slavery, of my redemption thence
> And portance in my travel's history
> .... These things to hear
> Would Desdemona seriously incline
> .... and with a greedy ear
> Devour up my discourse. Which I observing
> ...found good means
> To draw from her a prayer of earnest heart. ...
> My story being done,
> She gave me for my pains a world of sighs....
> And bade me, if I had a friend that lov'd her,
> I should but teach him how to tell my story,
> And that would woo her. (1.3.128-166)

After explaining how his stories affected Desdemona, Othello answers the question about magic:

> She lov'd me for the dangers I had pass'd,
> And I lov'd her that she did pity them.
> This only is the witchcraft I have us'd. (1.3.167-170)

The discussion of magic shows that two different narratives absorbed by two different imaginations with two very different outcomes are at work. Iago tells stories about black rams tupping white ewes to incite discord and hate. Othello's tales about heroic endeavors and terrible sufferings endured captivate a young, impressionable girl who first admires but then loves the storyteller. Differences of race have vanished. Everything that happens in *Othello* demonstrates language's capacity to shape what the imagination envisions and, through that, to determine actions taken. Which of the two narratives enforces its magic on these lovers will determine the play's outcome. It is no exaggeration to claim that *Othello* is very much a demonstration of language's power to shape what the imagination sees.

Later, when Othello is beset by jealousy, the locus of that magic comes to reside in a missing handkerchief that, he thinks, will prove or disprove Desdemona's infidelity. When he tries to explain to her why the lost handkerchief is so important, he too speaks of magic.

>Oth.   Lend me your handkerchief.
>Des.   Here, my lord.
>Oth.   That which I gave you.
>Des.   I have it not about me.
>Oth.   Not?
>Des.   No, in faith, my lord.
>Oth.   That's a fault. That handkerchief
>   Did an Egyptian to my mother give;
>   She was a charmer, and could almost read
>   The thoughts of people. She told her, while she kept it,
>   'Twould make her amiable, and subdue my father
>   Entirely to her love; but if she lost it,
>   Or make a gift of it, my father's eye
>   Should hold her loathed, and his spirits should hunt
>   After new fancies. ... take heed on't,
>   To lose't or give't away were such perdition
>   As nothing else could match.
>Des.   Is't possible?
>Oth.   'Tis true; there's magic in the web of it. (3.4.52-69)

By this time, the magic in his stories, the magic that won Desdemona's heart, the magic that once bound two very different individuals in sacred union, has been reduced to a square of linen. Deeply under the influence of Iago's view of the world, Othello no longer understands the magic that brought two disparate beings into union.

Unlike her husband, Desdemona never shows any desire to withdraw from the spell her husband's magic has cast over her life, refusing to let Othello's original story fade from her imagination. From first to last, her devotion is absolute. When Brabantio asks her to choose between father and husband, her answer, very much like Cordelia's in *Lear*, is clear. She addresses her father:

> To you I am bound for life and education;
> ... both do learn me
> How to respect you; you are the lord of duty;
> I am hitherto your daughter. But here's my husband;
> And so much duty as my mother show'd
> To you, preferring you before her father,
> So much I challenge that I may profess
> Due to the Moor, my lord. (1.3.182-188)

As circumstances grow increasingly dire, that heroic vision of her husband and the commitment it inspires never wanes, even as Iago's provocations make Othello increasingly irritable toward her. After confronting his wife later on about her lost handkerchief, the first token of his affection and evidence, he thinks, of her illicit affair with Cassio, he exits, leaving her bewildered. She refuses to blame him. "Something sure of state," she muses, ". . . hath puddled his clear spirit; and in such cases men's natures wrangle with inferior things though great ones are their object" (3.4.140-145). And when Othello begins talking of revenge for her supposed infidelity, her faithful maid and the wife of Iago, Emelia, tries to console her, saying "I would you had never seen him!" Desdemona gives the only answer her steadfast character would:

> So would not I. My love doth so approve him
> That even his stubbornness, his checks, his frowns. . .
> Have grace and favor in them. (4.3.19-21)

Like Shakespeare's other positive female characters, Desdemona has imbibed deeply of love's magic. As her spirited defense of her innocence later in the play indicates, this is much more than romantic naiveté. It is an integral part of a loving nature that no longer knows another way to see the world or the man with whom she shares it. Her former singular self is gone. She is in wedlock. Though Desdemona's refusal to abandon the spell she's under may look foolishly irrational, her willingness to risk all for her relationship not only proves the strength of the magic she's under but is the contradiction to the narrative of female licentiousness promoted by Iago, who is the essence of disloyalty.

Though responsible for defending the citadel on Cyprus, Othello is unable to protect his commitment to Desdemona from Iago's incursions, for the desire that brought them together also has the power, as Ovid understood, to destroy both reason and self-control. Forced by the Turkish crisis to postpone their nuptials, Othello, his military entourage, along with his wife, arrive in Cyprus to fend off the threat. When that never materializes, Iago seizes the opportunity to undermine the Moor's faith in Desdemona's purity. Thus begins the very detailed illustration of Othello's temptation. Like his mentor, the Father of Lies, Iago's aim is deception and his methodology is sexual innuendo and rhetorical sleight-of-hand. The narrative he constructs is meant to transform Othello's vision of an innocent, faithful Desdemona into its opposite, a cunning, sexually promiscuous lady who has already tired of her black paramour and has chosen a man, Cassio, more to her liking. Because she deceived her father when they married, her truthfulness has already been compromised. Even more crucially, having already felt the flame of sexual passion, Othello's imagination is keenly sensitive to its erotic heat.

Ironically, the Othello who won Desdemona with stories of an arduous, military life abroad is undone by Iago's false narrative of an affair that never happened. Both men are poets, weaving fantastical images with airy words that have the power to transform people's thinking and behavior. While storytelling, like love, is a form of magic Shakespeare himself employed for the stage, he seems increasingly aware of the moral ambiguities inherent in both language and desire. The two are inextricably intertwined: desire is an expression of need that often benefits from language, just as language is enhanced by emotion. Both entail risk because both have the power to enrich and build up or to debase and destroy. Which of these will prevail depends upon the state of the heart, whether it is closed and self-protective or open, other-directed and willing to risk everything as it clings tightly to the conviction that love is steadfast in its capacity to forgive real and sometimes perceived wrongs. This is what Desdemona has, what Othello lacks, and what he comes to understand only too late.

  The amoral substructure of Iago's villainy is suggested by what seems like an insignificant and strangely unrelated thread of the unfolding story. Roderigo, described in the *dramatis persona* as "a gulled gentleman," pays Iago to help win Desdemona's love, an arrangement reminiscent of the one between Toby and Sir Andrew in *Twelfth Night*. And like Falstaff's gluttony or Shylock's usury, Iago's villainy is actually a form of self-interested greed, a desire to obtain more of what is believed to satisfy. Such self-interest is often very proficient at identifying opportunities for satisfaction. Objective and very self-aware, Iago understands that any desire for what isn't already possessed represents a susceptibility to manipulation. By marrying his calculating objectivity to an imagination actively searching for advantage, he quickly identifies where desire opens opportunity for profit. As Iago empties the gulled gentleman's purse, Roderigo's need for satisfaction becomes the type for Othello's. Both, consequently, are easy targets for manipulation.

  And Iago is masterful at finding vulnerabilities to exploit. Disgraced by a drunken incident that offends the

Moor, Cassio accepts Iago's offer to help reclaim Othello's favor with the assistance of his wife. Just as Iago uses Roderigo's desire for the unattainable Desdemona to enrich himself, Cassio's need to ingratiate himself provides half the opportunity Iago has been waiting for. The other half presents itself when Othello's love and physical desire for Desdemona is on clear display. Hypersensitive to such nuances of human need, Iago could hardly turn away. After a short conversation between husband and wife, Othello, who has already been infected by the villain's insinuations, watches Desdemona leave and muses absentmindedly as Iago listens:

> Excellent wretch! Perdition catch my soul
> But I do love thee! and when I love thee not,
> Chao is come again. (3.3.90-92)

A troubled Othello senses he is on the cusp of a decision, and this is an insight Iago immediately seizes upon to further his stated goal. He follows Othello's statement with a question meant to agitate.

> Did Michael Cassio, when [you] woo'd my lady,
> Know of your love? (3.3.94-95)

The question, of course, insinuates some unrecognized historical rivalry for Desdemona's hand, a suggestion intended to point the Moor toward that path to perdition. Through similar questions and phrases and half-sentences, Iago multiplies Othello's emotional insecurity. And by encouraging Cassio to approach Desdemona for help overcoming her husband's displeasure, he is able to intensify that insecurity further still. The more her good nature tries to assist, the easier that assistance can be mistaken for infidelity.

The deception reaches a shocking nadir during the crucial middle scene of the play. Very subtly, Iago discredits Cassio to Othello while simultaneously encouraging him to seek Desdemona's help to regain the Moor's favor, all the while feeding Othello's intensifying suspicions with vivid images of their illicit lovemaking. The same imagination that had once secured his wife's heart now inflames his jealousy, that "green-ey'd monster" (3.3.166), until the Moor is hungry for revenge.

> Oth. Like to the Pontic Sea,
> Whose icy current and compulsive course
> Nev'r feels retiring ebb, but keeps due on
> To the Propontic and the Hellespont,
> Even so my bloody thoughts, with violent pace
> Shall nev'r look back, nev'r ebb to humble love
> Till that a capable and wide revenge
> Swallow them up. [He kneels.] Now by yond marble heaven,
> In the due reverence of a sacred vow
> There engage my words.
> Iago.   Do not rise up yet. [Iago kneels.]
> Witness, you ever-burning lights above...
> Witness that here Iago doth give up
> The execution of his wit, hands, heart,
> To wrong'd Othello's service! Let him command,
> And to obey shall be in me remorse,
> What bloody business ever. [They rise.]
> Oth.   I greet thy love,
> Not with vain thanks, but with acceptance bounteous....
> Within these three days let me hear thee say
> That Cassio's not alive.
> Iago. My friend is dead; 'tis done at your request.
> But let her live.
> Oth. Damn her, lewd minx! O, damn her, damn her!
> Come, go with me apart, I will withdraw
> To furnish me with some swift means of death
> For the fair devil. Now art thou my lieutenant.
> Iago. I am yours forever. (3.3.453-480)

The image of the surging sea on its "compulsive course" captures the intensity of Othello's resolve. Desdemona's fate is now clearly sealed.

But a closer examination of this scene deepens the shock, for the audience bears witness to a grim mockery of a wedding, replete with vows, commitments, and promises of love. Following their pledge of fealty, the two men are hooped together in their desire to assuage a perceived wrong. There is no love for wife, no commitment to marriage, no mercy for her kind, faithful, tender and forgiving heart. If anyone in the play betrays his marital fidelity, it is Othello, not Desdemona. Though she has done nothing to deserve the ambiguous title of "fair devil," a deceived Othello exchanges a loving marriage for a union with the demonic Iago, who knows quite well the way to perdition and chaos.

As Othello prepares for what is now an inevitability, Desdemona's physical presence in their marriage bed very nearly dissuades him from killing her. After kissing her as she sleeps, he confesses that her "balmy breath . . . doth almost persuade Justice to break her sword" (5.1.16). He has been wronged, he believes, so revenge has become the justice that will end the agony of his jealous heart. Convinced by Iago's narrative rather than Desdemona's, he has forgotten, or never fully grasped, his wife's essential value.

It is all too easy to view Desdemona as romantically naïve, inattentive to the danger her husband's growing jealousy represents. But once she understands that danger, she is absolutely clear about her innocence.

> Oth. Think on thy sins.
> Des. They are the loves I bear to you.
> Oth. Aye, and for that thou di'st.
> Des. That love's unnatural that kills for loving. . . .
> Oth. Peace, and be still.
> Des. I will so. What's the matter?
> Oth. That handkerchief which I so lov'd, and gave thee, Thou gav'st to Cassio.

> Des. No, by my life and soul!
> Send for the man and ask him. (5.1.39-49)

Unfortunately, Othello believes that Iago has already murdered Cassio. Her alibi gone, Othello smothers her only to have her return briefly after Emilia, hearing the commotion, returns to their bedchamber.

> Des. O, falsely, falsely murder'd!
> Emil. O Lord, what cry is that?
> Oth. That? What?
> Emil. Out, and alas, that was my lady's voice.
> Help, help, ho, help! O sweet mistress, speak!
> Des. A guiltless death I die.
> Emil. O, who hath done this deed?
> Des. Nobody; I myself. Farewell!
> Commend me to my kind lord. O, farewell! [dies]
> (5.1.117-125)

The return from beyond the grave happens too often in Shakespeare's tragedies to be mere coincidence. Juliet is the first instance, but it occurs here and in *King Lear*, with allusions to similar associations of love and death in *Hamlet* and *Antony and Cleopatra*. Here, it reinforces the idea that love's mysterious magic is powerful enough to transcend even death. Her words from beyond the grave contrast with Iago's self-imposed silence as he's hauled off to prison and torture.

Though Othello laments his mistake and takes his own life as punishment for his failure, that suicide seems insufficient proof that he has fully grasped what he has lost. His focus remains, not on his innocent wife, but on his legacy.

> Speak of me as I am, nothing extenuate,
> Nor set down aught in malice. Then must you speak
> Of one that lov'd not wisely but too well;
> Of one not easily jealous, but being wrought,
> Perplexed in the extreme; of one whose hand
> (like the base Indian) threw a pearl away

> Richer than all his tribe.... (5.2.342-348)

Beyond the acknowledgment that he has thrown away a pearl of great value, the speech seems strangely devoid of self-awareness so late in the play. Loved too well? Not easily jealous? This is one more reason Othello is so difficult to like as a tragic protagonist. By way of contrast, Desdemona's momentary resurrection includes the wondrous absolution of Othello, despite his obvious shortcomings. It is the essence of her love, this generous forgiveness, this ever-fixed constancy, and it is precisely why she can return from a place where her magic derives its power and meaning.

Othello fails Desdemona because he mistakenly sees magic in an unworthy object—the handkerchief—while failing to believe in the far more valuable magic his wife embodies. For a short while, he experiences love's magic only to permit a cunning and calculating rhetoric to debase that into something shameful, a reductive vision of love where the old black ram is tupping the white ewe. It is a vision that leaves no room for Desdemona's magic. In his very fine analysis of the play, *Magic in the Web*, Robert Heilman addresses the use of that metaphor in the play:

> Wit and witchcraft: in this antithesis is the symbolic structure of *Othello*. By witchcraft, of course, Iago means conjuring and spells to compel desired actions and states of being. But as a whole the play dramatically develops another meaning of witchcraft which forces itself upon us: witchcraft as a metaphor for love. The magic in the web of [Desdemona's] handkerchief... extends into the fiber of the drama. Love is a magic bringer of harmony and may be the magic transformer of personality; its ultimate power is fittingly marked by a miraculous voice from beyond life. Such events lie outside the realm of "wit"—of the reason, cunning.... Wit must always strive to conquer witchcraft.... Whatever disasters it causes, wit fails in the end: it cuts itself off in a demonic silence before death, while witchcraft—love—speaks after death. (225)

Because Othello allows Iago to sow doubt on the fertile soil of his imagination, he fails the test every lover eventually faces in some form: is this love real? The question is a test of faith, commitment, and sometimes forgiveness, and only those who respond to a magic that makes no rational sense are able to eliminate those fears and doubts that lead to failure. Two types of magic: one, worked by Desdemona, is marked by constancy, trust, and generous forgiveness, and it promises infinite blessings; the other, worked by Iago, is marked by deceit, self-interest and gain, violence, and destruction. The first of these is a miracle. The second is a sin that can only end in death. Othello's tragedy is that he chooses the second when he so easily could have enjoyed the first. With the serpent whispering in his ear, he is Adam standing before the tree in the garden, unable to hold on to innocence.

Unfortunately, Othello's blackness in a tragedy from a white seventeenth-century European has become a formidable critical challenge. As morally repugnant as real racism is, however, that is not what *Othello* represents. To read *Othello* as one early example of a European racial bias that needs to be identified and shamed is an error of two sorts: first, it makes the treatment of Othello's blackness onstage a significant but correctable sin when the sin the play actually cares about is so deeply embedded in human nature, in the way mankind has been created, that it deserves to be labeled "original." The label is accurate precisely because it defies human correction and can only be acknowledged and lamented Second, it ignores Shakespeare's lifelong interest in love's magical ability to bridge differences, heal division, and bring joy, which is clearly evident in a text so very aware of both false and true magic.

Make no mistake, this is not simply a benign difference of critical methodology. The danger of these errors to an appreciation of Shakespeare's achievements is very real, as the former director of education for London's Globe Theater, Farah Karim-Cooper, observes:

> . . . students at Yale University petitioned to "decolonize" the literary canon demanding that pre-1800/1900 courses encompass a study of "literatures relating to gender, race, sexuality, ableism, and ethnicity." Around the same time, students at the University of Pennsylvania removed a portrait of Shakespeare replacing it with a printed photo of Audre Lorde the Black feminist poet and novelist in order to protest the overemphasis in English degrees on white male authors. What these protests reveal is that the elite exceptionalism that has been built, with Shakespeare as its talisman, can feel oppressive.

The saddest of ironies is that these earnest demonstrations for racial equality and justice, gender fairness, and anticolonialism reveal no awareness of Shakespeare's appreciation for feminine strength, his promotion of mercy and forgiveness, his deep understanding of the intricate mechanisms of evil, his admiration for generosity of the heart, for selfless service to others in need, the ubiquity of human pain and suffering, the growth that only comes by way of tribulation, and the joys of every aspect of love, including the sexual. In many discussions today, all that seems to matter is the presence of a black African in a play written by a white European. It can only be regarded as a profound pedagogical failure that, in the zeal and earnestness of youth, values delineated so clearly in play after play remain invisible.

  The intricacies of temptation and sin, which are the driving forces in *Othello,* provide the subject matter for all the great plays that follow. While the Moor's susceptibility to Iago's wicked manipulations may undercut his stature, his story dramatizes the complex process, mechanisms, and consequences of evil, which very adroitly exploits the limitations of language to disguise its intentions. In the two following plays, *King Lear* and *Macbeth*, neither male protagonist is capable of accurately decoding the verbal expressions of the women who claim to love them. In both cases, desire for something they don't already have infects their imaginations so they hear what they want to hear. Opposed against this dynamic is the mysterious, magical power of love, offered as the only available remedy for the plagues unleashed by the wicked. The following two tragedies will stage this opposition with far greater assurance, but those plays would have been quite different without *Othello*'s examination of language's limitations.

King Lear

●●●●●●●●●●

  As in other Elizabethan moral histories including *The Mirror for Magistrates* and his own *1Henry4*, *King Lear* argues personal vices have public consequences. In this, perhaps his most wrenching tragedy's two parallel stories, an elderly king's rejection of his favorite daughter over a linguistic misunderstanding is mirrored by a duke who commits an almost identical misjudgment. In a fallen world, sin afflicts everyone equally. While the consequences of Gloucester's error are largely personal, Lear's rejection of his good daughter, Cordelia, and the trust he mistakenly confers on those wicked daughters Goneril and Regan unleashes their indifference and cruelty upon everyone subject to their rule, including the now powerless Lear. Though both plots involve fathers and their children, such cautionary stories were meant to remind civil authority the welfare of ordinary citizens is determined by the quality of a ruler's character.

  What differentiates *King Lear* from moral history, however, is its conviction the experience of both good and evil reflects an unseen warfare between much larger, unseen forces. Both Greek and Shakespearean tragedy recognize suffering is somehow deeply rooted in the inadequacies of human perception, largely unaware of this spiritual warfare and where allegiance belongs. This unfortunate intersection of an opaque metaphysical struggle with men of limited reason and insight is reflected in two rhetorical devices common to tragedy. Irony, a device where words convey unintended meanings, reflects the complexity of perceived reality, as does paradox, a device where two contradictory meanings may both seem equally true. Any adequate discussion of *Lear* must take note of its heavy load of both irony and paradox, which intentionally point to unanswerable mysteries of human existence. According to Normand Berlin's *The Secret Cause,* these mysteries are the subtext of tragic art.

> Einstein, the clearest of thinkers, believed that "the most beautiful experience we can have is the mysterious. It is the fundamental emotion which stands at the cradle of true art and science." A serious examination of the tragic tradition confirms the validity of this view. It is the fundamental emotion and contains the very seed of tragedy and religion and science. However, whereas religion offers answers to the mystery, whereas science strives to comprehend answers to mystery, tragedy enhances the mystery by dramatizing portions of the mystery. (2)

Whatever else may be said about tragedy as a genre, its purpose is not to provide answers to life's mysteries but to remind us that those unanswerable mysteries exist. *Lear* brings us face to face with an evil that is demonstrably pervasive and therefore inescapable. While its causes can be anatomized, doing so utterly fails to explain why men continue to pursue its false promises or why a loving deity assumed to be involved in human affairs would tolerate its existence. Suffering, given symbolic confirmation in the play's relentless storm, imposes a kind of disproportionate supernatural correction for the folly of pride and impatience that, because the suffering inflicted defies rational explanation, feels grossly unfair.

Directly confronting the many paradoxes of suffering and death, tragedy poses questions about life under such preordained conditions. As Berlin implies, a Christian tradition that promises salvation might easily have eliminated the possibility of tragedy altogether. But Shakespeare's awareness of contrary impulses toward either sin or redemptive love, both battling for man's soul, is precisely what ushers in the tragic. That these possibilities co-exist in the particular, that the resulting suffering is not just a spiritual abstraction but is felt in bone and marrow, opens rather than closes the window to a tragic vision that counterbalances his equally firm grasp of the comic.

Rather than unrelieved pessimism, Shakespeare's tragedies reflect a conviction those good but imperfect human qualities opposed to evil and suffering are evidence of divinity's tender regard for the world, a belief differentiating him from Greek tragedians offering only stoic endurance. This is so because his plays originate from a culture convinced the world had a moral design that preferred what's good but provided the opportunity to choose otherwise. While worldly justice is limited by human failings, nature's design abhors every vestige of evil and works to restore a more equitable order from the subsequent chaos. Within that terrible metaphysical dynamic between good and evil, love's opposition to cruelty in this world dimly reflects those mysterious powers engaged in an endless battle for dominance. Because neither choice is immune to suffering, the choice is actually between temporary satisfactions or a joy that endures.

To convey the significance of Lear's experience, Shakespeare's examination of the love between father and daughters uses five themes, each associated with a set of related images: imagery of sight and blindness identify why perceiving what's truly important is so difficult; imagery of clothing and nakedness draws distinctions between outer and inner and exposes the costs of an honest emotional and moral vulnerability; differentiating the human from the bestial suggests familiar ideas about the danger of undisciplined desire; the morality of justice is examined in three interrelated courtroom scenes; and, finally, references to reason and madness indicate evil only temporarily triumphs because it is ignorant of powerful, more durable forces found in the heart, beyond the reach of logic and language. While this belief in the innate value of human emotion contradicts Ovid's emphasis on their dangers, it gives the opening and final scenes of *Lear* their extraordinary symmetry.

While this intense examination of love continues to explore familiar ideas about generosity, risk, and desire, *Lear*'s opening scene repeats *Othello*'s detailed examination of language's capacity to deceive and degrade. Afflicting both sides of linguistic transactions, the danger is manifested in the deceitful ways language can be employed as well as the way expectations affect what is heard. As the play begins, Lear has gathered court and family to announce his retirement from royal duties and the division of his kingdom between his three daughters. Before receiving their parcels, each child must provide him a public declaration of love. The assumptions behind this odd request are erroneous in multiple ways: first, Lear assumes spoken words will truly reflect intentions; second, he assumes he will recognize the truth when it is spoken; and third, he assumes his reaction to the truth will be dispassionate and fair. Since none of these prove true, the tragic consequences are all but inevitable.

Those errors are compounded further by two others. Having relinquished any power to enforce his expressed needs, Lear's belief respect and care will continue in his dotage depends entirely on accurate knowledge of his daughters. At the same time, however, a father's apparent generosity is flawed by qualifications reflecting a deeply felt insecurity about being vulnerable without authority. Marred by this smidgen of self-interest, his request each child should take turns entertaining him and his hundred knights tarnishes whatever generosity inspired the division of his kingdom. Compared to the complete selflessness of Cordelia's eventual return, the intentions behind this gift have been compromised by Lear's small but detectable grain of self-regard. That tiny grain, what Hamlet calls "a vicious mole of nature," contributes to the ruin visited upon the garden.

Out of these spiritual deficiencies comes the rejection of Cordelia, the favored daughter. "Tell me, my daughters," he begins, ". . . which of you shall we say doth love us most, that we our largest bounty may extend where nature doth with merit challenge?" His eldest daughters, Goneril and Regan, happily oblige him with the frothy rhetoric typical of manipulative excess. "Sir, I love you more than words can wield the matter," begins Goneril, though she continues despite this professed inadequacy of words. "Dearer than eyesight, space, and matter, Beyond what can be valued. . . ." Following this performance, Regan can only mimic her sister's words. "I am made of that self metal as my sister, and prize me at her worth. . . Only she comes too short." Unfortunately, Lear believes the words but is blind to the defective nature of the speaker.

Lear's expectations are highest when it is his favorite daughter's turn. Her suitors, the Duke of Burgundy and the King of France, are present to witness what follows. "Now our joy," he says, "what can you say to draw a third more opulent than your sisters'?" Looking for opulence, her unadorned answer proves devastating:

> Cord. Nothing, my lord. . . .
> Lear. Nothing will come of nothing, speak again.
> Cord. Unhappy that I am, I cannot heave
> My heart into my mouth. I love your Majesty
> According to my bond, no more nor less.
> Lear. How, how, Cordelia? Mend your speech a little,
> Lest you may mar your fortunes.
> Cord.   Good my lord,
> You have begot me, bred me, lov'd me; I
> Return those duties back as are right fit,
> Obey you, love you, and most honor you.
> Why have my sisters husbands, if they say
> They love you all? (1.1.87-100)

If Cordelia's words were not an echo of Desdemona's to her disappointed father, assigning Lear's youngest daughter some portion of blame for subsequent events, as some critics do, might make sense. But exaggerated claims of love for a father would be disastrous in front of suitors bringing offers of marriage, so Cordelia simply refers to the Biblical commonplace in Matthew 19:5 that a child taking a spouse must leave parents behind, as her married sisters have already done. In accordance with the fifth commandment, love for a parent doesn't cease but to truly become one flesh, the priority must rightfully shift from parent to spouse. This is an essential part of the transition from daughter to wife Cordelia not only understands better than Lear but is brave enough to state honestly, in contrast to the hypocrisy of her sisters.

A display of charity deeply marred by invalid assumptions and self-regard suggests why Lear lacks the emotional and spiritual resources to rise above those disappointed expectations. Grievously hurt and unable to find the mercy that "becomes the throned monarch better than his crown," Lear's lack of emotional and spiritual discipline is exposed before the assembled court. Embarrassed by Cordelia's inability to "heave [her] heart into [her] mouth," his response is swift, decisive, and angry:

> . . . thy truth then be thy dow'r!
> For by the sacred radiance of the sun. . . .
> Here I disclaim all my paternal care,
> Propinquity and property of blood,
> And as a stranger to my heart and me
> Hold thee from this forever. (1.1.108-116)

With these fateful words, Lear severs ties with his favorite and offers her penniless to whoever will take her. Withholding Cordelia's portion of the kingdom as well as her wedding dowry, Lear not only punishes Cordelia twice over but proves the proceedings were a thinly veiled *quid pro quo*. This ceremony really had very little to do with unqualified generosity. Expectations in ruins, he has now placed himself entirely at the mercy of his remaining daughters. Whether vibrant or moribund, the private virtues of kings will eventually ripple out into public consequences.

From a different vantage, Lear's error results from an improper evaluation of his daughter, a bit like choosing the wrong casket in *The Merchant*'s lottery. Though once his favorite, Cordelia gives her father the lead chest when he was looking for the gold one, and, disappointed and angry, he misconstrues her actual value. The association of the plain-spoken Cordelia with an empty dowery is certainly no accident. Although Burgundy, like Lear, doesn't see her real worth, the king of France does. Of the two suitors present, he alone recognizes her relationship priorities are in the right order. And like *The Merchant*'s Bassanio, he risks choosing the lead casket, the one others reject because, despite appearances, France correctly assesses the worth of what Lear has just thrown away.

In language reflecting the paradox of love's valuations, he comforts her:

> Fairest Cordelia, that art most rich being poor,
> Most choice forsaken, and most lov'd despis'd,
> Thee and thy virtues here I seize upon. . . .
> Not all the dukes of wat'rish Burgundy
> Can buy this unpriz'd precious maid of me. (1.1.249-259)

Two men have made two very different assessments of the same woman. One, the father who should have loved her unconditionally, proves to be emotionally and spiritually impoverished and, as a result, is unable to evaluate her words correctly or forgive this perceived refusal to flatter. Devoid of any sincere generosity, his love is conditional. The gift only comes with interest. The other, the French suitor, evaluates her worth correctly and leaves for home enriched by a loving wife who only looks poor. The evaluations differ because what each man values determines what he is capable of seeing. Though Lear briefly remains in the ascendancy, which of the two made the right choice becomes painfully obvious soon enough.

The imagery of sight becomes one vehicle for speaking about Lear's deficiency. Because the anger from unmet expectations blinds Lear to his daughter's true worth, the play immediately identifies the old king's misjudgment as a failure of insight. Appalled by Cordelia's sudden fall from favor, Kent, Lear's faithful advisor, is the first to point to this fault. "Be Kent unmannerly," he begins, "when Lear is mad," a foreshadowing of Lear's coming ordeal on the heath. He continues the confrontation with brutally frank language:

> What wouldest thou do, old man?
> Think'st thou that duty shall have dread to speak
> When power to flattery bows? To plainness honor's bound
> When majesty falls to folly....
> Thy youngest daughter does not love thee least....
>
> Lear. Kent, on thy life, no more.
> Kent. My life I never held but as a pawn
> To wage against thine enemies....
> Lear.   Out of my sight!
> Kent. See better, Lear.... (1.1.145-159)

The sight imagery is not limited only to Lear's misapprehension of Cordelia's value, either, but carries over into his inability to distinguish between truth and lie. As the previous chapter indicates, the verbal dynamics between Othello and Iago reveal a growing distrust of language's inherent inaccuracy, which too often provides unfair advantage to the unscrupulous. Like Cordelia's, Kent's truth tastes like plain fare compared to the sweet froth Lear prefers from his eldest daughters. While truth is most effective precisely because it usually lacks the "opulence" Lear expected from Cordelia, his preference for the ornamental rather than the emotional and verbal authenticity of honest language is another symptom of a deficient understanding of value.

Human perceptions of reality, therefore, are crippled in multiple ways. Evident as both symbol and plot device, *Lear*'s use of eyes and sight and blindness continues to be part of a nuanced commentary on the problems of human perception. As Robert Heilman writes in his excellent study of *King Lear*:

> In fact, the whole content of the sight pattern is resolved into the Sophoclean paradox that the blind may see better than the proudly keen-eyed. But the play also attacks the problem of seeing and understanding from another direction: it presents elaborately the obstacles which interpose between human sight and its objects. We are made fully aware that man faces obdurate materials, efforts to deceive, and his own tendency to reconstruct the objective world according to his own preconceptions. (67)

Heilman notes three ways the truth about existence is difficult to see: first, the complexity of the world obscures meaning and value; second, people find ingenuous ways to deceive; third, people prefer their own preconceptions about the world to its sometimes harsh realities. Like Othello, Lear's discernment of internal as well as external truth is severely limited by all the factors Heilman identifies, perhaps especially by a fragile hope all his daughters love him equally. But that construct is imaginary because it is based on what he wants to see rather than what is.

The play's subplot is a proposition these problems are universal and not particular to Lear. As the play opens, the Duke of Gloucester and Kent are involved in a conversation about Lear's proposed division of the kingdom. The topic soon switches to Edmund, the duke's illegitimate son, who is riding silently with them.

> Glou. ... Do you smell a fault?
> Kent. I cannot wish the fault undone, the issue of it
>   Being so proper.
> Glou. But I have a son, sir, by order of law, some

> year elder that this, who yet is no dearer in my account. Though this knave came something saucily to the world before he was sent for, yet was his mother fair, there was good sport at his making, and the whoreson must be acknowledg'd. (1.1.16-24)

While it may be tempting to applaud Gloucester's even-handed affection for his two sons, he fails to grasp that, because there was "good sport at [Edmund's] making," the young man's position outside the "order of law" poses a danger to his family. Like Lear, Gloucester opens himself to disappointment because he sees only what he expects to see: his love for Edmund will be returned in kind. Unaware of Edmund's secret intention to trick him into disinheriting Edgar, the duke's lawful son, neither traveler can penetrate the dark heart of the villain riding beside them as they speak. Illegitimate and effectively disinherited, Edmund will soon falsely implicate Edgar as the mastermind of a plan to murder Gloucester and split the estate between them. Though the accusation is false, the enraged duke issues an arrest warrant for Edgar, who has since fled into the night. Like events in Lear's court, Gloucester's inability to distinguish true from false will lead to a misjudgment with consequences almost as dire as those awaiting the king. Both men think they know and understand what's in front of them, but both are gravely misled by that obdurate world, by deceit, and by hopeful expectations that prove unrealistic.

Initially, *Lear* posits two possible explanations for these failures of insight. The first of these proves grossly insufficient. Arriving onstage after Cordelia's rejection, Gloucester glibly attributes the discord he has witnessed to "these late eclipses of the sun and moon." From this view, men may be flawed, but since their essential goodness is only warped by forces outside their control, they bear little responsibility for evil or suffering. This very Greek explanation, however, is clearly inadequate since Lear's irrational rejection of Cordelia results from a recognizable spiritual deficiency. Edmund's explanation is the alternative.

> This is the excellent foppery of the world, that when we are sick in fortune— often the surfeits of our own behavior— we make guilty of our disasters the Sun, the moon, and stars, as if we were villains on necessity, fools by heavenly compulsion, knaves, thieves, and treachers by spherical predominance; drunkards, liars, and adulterers by an enforc'd obedience of planetary influence, and all that we are evil in by a divine thrusting on. An admirable evasion of whoremaster man, to lay his goatish disposition on the charge of a star! . . . I should have been that I am, had the maidenl'est star in the firmament twinkled on my bastardizing. (1.2.118-133)

More introspective, rational, and self-aware than either king or duke, Edmund dismisses such evasions of moral responsibility with a delightful realism. But while this objectivity and moral honesty have a certain charming appeal, the villains of this story are eventually undone by a similar naivete regarding the forces, natural and supernatural, directing a person's fate. As clear-sighted as he is, his deep need for legitimacy is an irrational hunger that not only motivates slandering a brother and misleading a father but drives him into simultaneous and therefore dangerous, illegitimate relationships with both Goneril and Regan. While ambition and cunning momentarily gain the advantage, rational objectivity alone, it turns out, cannot deter those unrecognized desires of the heart from leading the unwary down the unanticipated path.

    As part of the sight theme, Gloucester's journey towards moral clarity provides useful perspective for Lear's more tragic sojourn through the dark night of the soul. Initially a man overly deferential to those in power, Gloucester's behavior exhibits the evasion of moral responsibility mocked by Edmund. A peacemaker who dislikes confrontation, Gloucester is eventually forced to recognize just how abhorrent the behavior of Lear's eldest daughters has become. The recognition does not come easily. When Regan's husband, the Duke of Cornwall, offends Lear by placing the king's messenger in the stocks, Gloucester wants to pacify a justifiably outraged Lear by saying," You know the fiery quality of the duke." Aware of who really exercises power after Lear's abdication, Gloucester tries to soothe his former king while maintaining some influence with the daughters and their husbands. He will soon learn that he cannot serve two masters. A world marred by unchecked selfishness requires making a judgment, taking a stand. Sympathetic toward an old king exiled to stormy heath, he chooses to assist Lear "bearing a torch," a light in a dark world. As a bearer of light, of a certain kind of truth about kindness and personal authenticity, Gloucester dispels a darkness that is both real and symbolic.

Gloucester's kindness to Lear offers no protection from evil, and Cornwall will put out Gloucester's eyes. The eighteenth-century critic, Dr. Johnson, found this violence grotesque and morally offensive, but Shakespeare is thinking thematically rather than realistically here. Paradoxically, the loss of Gloucester's physical sight, as Heilman noted earlier, marks the beginning of his insight. He calls out for Edmund to avenge his suffering only to learn from Regan," …thou call'st on him that hates thee. It was he that made the overture of thy treason to us. . . ." Gloucester's reply to this revelation begins his transformation. Relinquishing any impulse toward self-pity as well as a short-lived request for vengeance, his first thought is of the harm he caused his good son: "O my follies! Then Edgar was abus'd. Kind gods, forgive me that, and prosper him!" Having doubted the legitimate bond uniting him to the child of his flesh, Gloucester's insight necessarily begins with conviction of sin and the necessity of repentance. Paradoxically, having lost his eyes, Gloucester sees Edgar more clearly, which becomes his road to salvation. Lear will need to follow a similar path.

This paradoxical sight imagery highlights the limitations of physical vision and the moral significance of insight, that crucial ability to distinguish between good and evil, between what's true and what isn't. Such insight, however, is all too easily corrupted by superstitious belief or rationalization. Instead of unreliable input from eyes and ears, those basic, pre-verbal impulses driving individuals toward connection are better at preventing unfortunate, sometimes disastrous misreading of words or events. References to smell, taste, and touch carefully move the audience in that direction. After Gloucester's blinding, Regan taunts him by suggesting he can now "smell his way to Dover." Common throughout the play, such phrases suggest those basic feelings ingrained deeply in human nature and felt before they are understood sometimes deserve primacy over those other unreliable perceptual senses. Symbolically, eyes are more closely tied to a complex and misleading world. Smell, Regan inadvertently suggests, is the more reliable guide. Ironically, the play's resolution confirms her observation, meant to be sarcastic but truer than she knows.

Gloucester's experience illustrates the blind do see better than those with eyes, who remain enthralled by the world's illusions. In the absence of sight, more basic faculties begin to predominate. After his cruel blinding, for example, Gloucester is led away by a nameless old man. Fearing his alleged treason might endanger his guide, Gloucester tries to send him away. "Good friend, be gone," he says:

        Thy comforts can do me no good at all;
        Thee they may hurt.
Old man.   You cannot see your way.
Glou.   I have no way, and therefore want no eyes.
        I stumbled when I saw. . . .O dear son Edgar,
        The food of thy abused father's wrath!
        Might I but live to see thee in my touch,

> I'ld say I had eyes again. (4.1.14-24)

The comfort Gloucester receives from his guide's attention awakens an appreciation for the selflessness of such men. It inspires an instinctive concern for others, including an innocent son. Thus, sight imagery is linked to basic feelings like touch and taste. This synesthesia, a rhetorical device intermixing senses, suggests deeply held feelings, active but beyond words, can make fallible sight more reliable.

Although Ovid's stories are all about passion's dangerous side, Shakespeare understood desire for what's good enables the blessings of marriage, children, and profound contentment. The blessings aren't available without the possible risk of dangerous emotions. The contrast between what's recognizably human and dangerous brutality is an argument that a fully engaged life requires both the rational and the irrational components of our created nature, regardless of the significant moral, emotional, and spiritual risks. While self-serving impulses hungry for satisfaction require discipline, an empathy for shared experience and emotions must enlighten whatever rational process exerts control. The necessary balance differentiating moral human and amoral animal nature becomes one of the central motifs of the play's conception.

Lear's ordeal raises important questions about human nature, especially those troublesome needs that shape identity, purpose, and decisions. Among the play's many ironies, those rational, calculating daughters so impervious to compassion and sympathy are eventually undone by the moral complexities of passions they neither understand nor have the discipline to control. Lear's frequent use of animal and sexual imagery reveals a struggle to understand how desire undisciplined by compassion exchanges humanity's best nature for its opposite. After Goneril attempts to reduce the number of Lear's attendants, he curses this "detested kite" with a frightful prayer:

> Hear, nature, hear, dear goddess, hear!
> Suspend thy purpose, if thou didst intend
> To make this creature fruitful.
> Into her womb convey sterility...
> And from her derogate body never spring
> A babe to her! If she must teem,
> Create her child of spleen, that it may live
> And be a thwart disnatur'd torment to her. (1.4.275-283)

No longer blind to his eldest daughter's indifference to any need but her own, Lear's un-human language describes what he now sees. And when Regan follows her sister's lead, he points to his heart and claims she too "hath tied Sharp-toothed unkindness, like a vulture, here." Unable to comprehend such cruelty, Lear can only curse their self-centered unkindness with references to the unhindered sexual impulses of animals, red in tooth and claw. Later, that connection re-emerges in his mad discussion with the blind Gloucester who, remember, begot Edmund between unlawful sheets:

> When I do stare, see how the subject quakes.
> I pardon that man's life. What was thy cause? Adultery?
> Thou shalt not die. Die for adultery? No,
> The wren goes to't, and the small gilded fly
> Does lecher in my sight.
> Let copulation thrive, for Gloucester's bastard son
> Was kinder to his father than my daughters
> Got 'tween the lawful sheets.
> To't, luxury, pell-mell, for I lack soldiers. (4.6.108-117)

Though Gloucester's blindness disproves the ironic assertion of Edmund's alleged kindness, a mad king urges wanton copulation to generate soldiers who will punish his daughters' wicked cruelty. Cruelty begets anger, which begets thoughts of revenge and the eventual chaos of conflicting needs.

The amoral assertion of need exposes the vulnerability of the powerless, which is explored through the juxtaposition of clothing with nakedness. In the play's intricate thematic conception, clothing carries multiple implications. At times, it defines a role with its attendant responsibilities. The fool, for example, schools Lear on the folly of taking off his crown and giving it to his daughters:

> Fool. Nuncle, give me an egg, and I'll give thee two crowns.
> Lear. What two crowns shall they be?
> Fool. Why, after I have cut the egg I' th' middle and eat up the meat, the two crowns of the egg. When thou clovest thy crown i' th' middle and gav'st away both parts, thou bor'st thine ass on thy back o'er the dirt. Thou hadst little wit in thy bald crown when thou gav'st thy golden one away.
> (1.4.155-163)

Symbolizing authority and power, the crown had at one time sheltered Lear from filial malice. Though his divestiture is already in the unchangeable past, the fool reminds Lear the act defies reason and logic. Hope made a fool of him. He may struggle with the reality of that, but none of that changes the fact he will never have the power and authority to protect himself again.

As a form of protection, clothing also functions much like those humble shelters Lear discovers after being expelled out into the wild storm on the heath. A bit of humble material or a modest lean-to is enough to provide a bit of comfort, some safety, or shelter from the world's many afflictions. "Our basest beggars," Lear reminds Goneril who is about to eliminate his entire entourage of knights

> Are in the poorest thing superfluous.
> Allow not nature more than nature needs,
> Man's life is cheap as beast's. Thou art a lady;
> If only to go warm were gorgeous,
> Why, nature needs not what thou gorgeous wear'st,
> Which scarcely keeps thee warm.... (2.4.264-270)

Having been a king, Lear must first lose everything before he comprehends what should be valued. Clothing's symbolic significance, therefore, amplifies what its loss will mean. In their imminent nakedness, both Edgar and Lear experience the kind of defenselessness that will teach them who they must become. Stripped to the minimal, both Tom O'Bedlam and Lear become visual evidence of the price the defenseless pay for their misfortune. The humiliation is a necessary part of the reformation.

Threatened with arrest after losing his father's trust, Edgar disguises himself as the mad beggar, Tom of Bedlam. After discarding everything except a loincloth, knotting his hair, and besmirching himself with filth, Edgar transforms himself into elemental man:

> Whilst I may scape
> I will preserve myself, and am bethought
> To take the basest and most poorest shape
> That ever penury, in contempt of man,
> Brought near to beast. . . . Poor Turlygood! Poor Tom!
> That's something yet: Edgar I nothing am. (2.3.5-21)

Echoing Cordelia's "nothing" to her father's request for opulent flattery, Edgar is similarly reduced to "the basest and poorest shape." With flesh exposed to the elements, Edgar becomes "unaccommodated man," and heads out into the stormy heath where Lear is now wandering with his fool and the loyal Kent, disguised as the servant, Caius. Leaving an established identity behind and escaping into a wilderness where animals fight for subsistence, Edgar begins to exercise those virtues defining authentic authority. By choosing selfless service to a suffering father, Edgar is fashioning an identity fit for public service. Cultivating private virtue is the prerequisite for public authority.

While the trajectory of Lear's transformation is different, he too must relinquish everything standing between him and his salvation. Both stories confirm the very Christian paradox a man must first lose his life to find the one he's been promised. The undressing begins in that first court scene where Lear announces to the assembled court he will "now. . . .divest us both of rule, interest of territory, cares of state." Though his hundred knights are symbolic of a fond hope he might still retain a semblance of authority and respect, his divestiture of things royal initiates his journey toward a vulnerability that concludes with his disrobement on the heath.

Imitating Tom O 'Bedlam, Lear casts off his garments to give his vulnerability dramatic reality. During this first confrontation with Edgar, paradoxically disguised by his nakedness, Lear's imagination begins to focus on Mad Tom's lack of clothing:

> Thou wert better in a grave than to answer with thy uncover'd body this extremity of the skies. Is man no more than this? Consider him well. Thou ow'st the worm no silk, the beast no hide, the sheep no wool, the cat no perfume. Ha? Here's three on's [pointing to the fool, Kent, and himself] are sophisticated. Thou art the thing itself: unaccommodated man is no more but such a poor, bare, fork'd animal as thou art. Off, off you lendings! Come, unbutton here. [Tearing off his clothes.]
> Fool. Prithee, nuncle, be contented, 'tis a naughty night to swim.
>   in (3.2.101-110)

As Lear strips down to essential man, symbol, event, and language merge into a tightly integrated, artistic whole. Clothing makes man too "sophisticated." Underneath are those essential human attributes he once failed to comprehend but that matter intensely now. Desperately hungry for answers, Lear's focus begins to change from the obvious outer, the opulent, to the inner. Both symbol and fact, clothing is becoming superfluous.

Lear's defenselessness is fodder for the king's jester who has accompanied his master into the night. Wittily tutoring the old king with jests and puns, the fool will frequently use clothing imagery to remind Lear of his folly. "When thou gavs't them the rod and put'st down thine own breeches," he quips, "Then they for sudden joy did weep." His clothing reference implicates the fateful role reversal initiated by Lear's decision to divest himself of authority and power, transforming ambitious daughters into parents eager to use the rod. The unnatural reversal of roles contributes to his newfound sympathy for the powerless.

In this sense, a nearly naked Edgar is the lesson that Lear, the student, contemplates:

> Poor naked wretches, wheresoe'er you are,
> That bide the pelting of this pitiless storm,
> How shall your houseless heads and unfed sides,
> Your loop'd and window'd raggedness, defend you
> From seasons such as these? O, I have ta'en
> Too little care of this! Take physic, pomp,
> Expose thyself to feel what wretches feel,
> That thou may'st shake the superflux to them,
> And show the heavens more just. (3.4.28-36)

As he contemplates his past misjudgments as king, Lear's nakedness leads to a very personal, keenly felt awareness of a shared vulnerability, a sympathy entirely lacking when Cordelia was dismissed for her honesty.

None of this, however, can assuage the sense of outrage. "I am more sinned against than sinning," Lear laments. If vulnerability inspires empathy, being wronged unfairly quite naturally leads to questions of justice. Inside the hovel with Kent, the fool, and the naked Tom O 'Bedlam, Lear's mad imagination assigns each of his companions a role in a mock trial of his thankless daughters. The ironies are profound:

Lear.	I will arraign them straight.

        [To Edgar] Come sit thou here, most learned justice;
           [To the Fool] Thou, sapient sir, sit here. Now you she-foxes—

Kent. . . . How do you sir? Stand you not so amaz'd. Will you lie down and rest upon the cushions?
Lear. I'll see their trial first, bring in their evidence.
    [To Edgar] Thou robed man of justice, take thy place,
    [To the fool] And thou, his yoke-fellow of equity, Bench by his side. [To Kent] You are o' th' commission, sit you too.
Edgar. Let us deal justly . . . . Purr, the cat is grey.
Lear. Arraign her first, 'tis Goneril. I here take my oath before this honorable Assembly, she kick'd the poor king her father.
Fool. Come hither, mistress. Is your name Goneril?
Lear. She cannot deny it.
Fool. Cry you mercy, I took you for a joint stool.
Lear. And here's another, whose warp'd looks proclaim What store her heart is made an. (3.6.19-54)

In his madness, Lear isn't working with hard evidence of crime. His concern is not legal but moral. For him, his daughters' crime is cruelty: they "kick'd the poor king her father." He is focused on whatever makes his daughters' hearts impervious to those natural feelings of sympathy and love. "Let them anatomize Regan," he concludes, "See what breeds about her heart." What is the nature of the evil that cries out for punishment? Yet while this mock trial raises profound questions about evil and justice, the proceedings in a hovel on a stormy heath are the occupation of a madman, a beggar, and a joint stool. They can only lead to nothing, that same word again. In its odd mixture of penetrating questions and gross absurdity, the scene parodies all the inadequacies of earthly justice.

Following Lear's mock trial, Gloucester's blinding confirms the problems of human justice. Conducted by Regan and her husband, Cornwall, this second trial confuses justice with the exercise of raw power in the service of rationalized need rather than public good. Afraid that a mad and naked Lear might awaken public sympathy, the ones now in power impose their brand of justice to protect their interests. In this second court, logic is a tool to justify punishing Gloucester for his kindness to Lear:

> Though well we may not pass upon his life
> Without the form of justice, yet our power
> Shall do a court'sy to our wrath, which men
> May blame but not control. (3.7.24-27)

Like the proceedings in the hovel, this trial is a mockery of any reasonable standard of justice. Since Gloucester cannot be executed without a public trial, an angry Cornwall can only secretly torture the old duke. But a glimpse of a far more equitable justice comes when a servant outraged by the cruelty mortally wounds Regan's husband.

The wrong endured by Cordelia suggests why that same injustice now inflicts its sorrows throughout Lear's former kingdom. Devoid of power and authority, a mad king dressed in weeds and wildflowers meets the blind Gloucester, an encounter imbued with a sad nostalgia. Recognizing Lear's voice, the old duke asks," Is't not the King?" To which Lear replies with exquisite irony, "Ay, every inch a king." Though naked vulnerability has brought insight, power and pomp are gone forever. All that is available to him now is the spiritual and emotional transformation Cordelia will soon bring with her from France.

Evil's eventual failure is explored in the contrast between reason and madness. Admittedly, madness on stage is difficult for modern audiences to accept unreservedly, but the play carefully prepares us for this eventuality. Unable to fathom the cruel disregard of his eldest daughters, Lear struggles to maintain his grip on reality. He repeatedly warns those attending him that his distress will make him mad. When the nearly naked Tom O 'Bedlam emerges from the hovel, Lear finally slips into the madness he feared. But this is madness with a purpose, for it seems to free Lear's imagination from the restrictive logic of false quantification that once ruled his decisions. He begins to freely associate bits of perceived reality with thoughts from his internal turmoil. "Didst thou give all to thy daughters?" he asks mad Tom, as if the cause of his particular mental chaos is the only explanation for all human misery. Throughout his ordeal, the essential question has been," Is there any cause in nature that makes these hard hearts?" Little wonder then, that when Lear is encouraged to enter the hovel, he points to mad Tom and responds," First, let me talk to this philosopher." Though the irony is profound, it is there, somewhere beyond the rational, that man is able to come to a valid understanding of the love and generosity capable of redeeming madness.

Since it was Lear's imagination and heart that were deficient, the transformation occurs outside the rational and in a very fluid realm where ideas and images collide, setting off fiery sparks of anger, bitter regret, even calls for revenge upon those "thankless daughters." But the anguish takes Lear beyond Gloucester's despair. Overhearing Lear's ramblings, Edgar says," O, matter and impertinency mix'd. Reason in madness!" As Heilman notes:

> The madness pattern. . .is concerned with the ways in which men interpret phenomena, the meanings which they find in experience, the general truths which they consciously formulate. . . . Its materials are men's philosophic attitudes,. . . their grasp, more specifically, of the problem of evil. Lear's madness is, in one respect, a result of his inability to bring an obdurate universe under intellectual control. . . (180)

The storm that Lear endures out on the heath, of course, reflects this mental turmoil, but having slipped out of his old habits of thinking, his imagination is free to recast his understanding of such problems in new ways. That he doesn't flinch from the investigation of such questions nor from any of the possible answers differentiates him from Gloucester, who eventually attempts to escape his despair through suicide. For Lear, the pain of his daughters' cruelty drives him toward a wide range of moral and emotional truths, no matter the cost.

In a world ruled by Goneril and Regan, a world where personal vendetta is disguised as justice, the defenseless cannot avoid suffering. When the play's two victims, the mad Lear and the blind Gloucester, finally meet on the heath, cruelty's desecration of justice and human relationships is at the forefront of Lear's mind. Though the sight theme figures prominently, what's striking is how the passage blends several of the most basic human senses:

> Glou. O, let me kiss that hand!
> Lear. Let me wipe it first, it smells of mortality.
> Glou. O, ruined piece of nature! . . . . Dost thou know me?
> Lear. I remember thine eyes well enough. Dost thou squinny at me?
> No, do thy worst, blind Cupid, I'll not love. Read thou this challenge, mark but the penning of it.
> Glou. Were all thy letters suns, I could not see. . . .
> Lear. . . . No eyes in your head, nor no money in your purse? Your eyes are in a heavy case, your purse in a light, yet you see how this world goes.
> Glou. I see it feelingly.
> Lear. What, art mad? A man may see how this world goes with no eyes. Look with thine ears; see how yond justice rails upon yond simple thief. Hark in thine ear: change places, and handy-dandy, which is the justice, which is the thief? (4.6.132-154)

The difficulty of seeing and understanding whatever lies beneath the impenetrable surface of an obdurate world is the fixed and unchangeable condition of fallen man. In such a state, Gloucester is right: the blind man must see the world feelingly, with his heart open and vulnerable to pity, for all are sinners and all require mercy. Lear's reply, heavy with irony, acknowledges the price people who make themselves vulnerable will pay when the strong prey upon the weak: "What, art mad?" As Cordelia's fate will show, undressing into vulnerability is indeed a kind of madness. Lear is surely a "ruined piece of nature," no longer capable of much more than sharing those insights with the blind. But that does not make those insights any less valid, especially in a world so tolerant of sin.

The paradox of the madness theme is that what looks like madness actually leads a man like Lear to undeniable truths while what looks pragmatic and reasonable contains an element of madness. Lear's troubles began when he attempted to evaluate and measure what, ultimately, could not be measured. "Tell me how much you love me," he had insisted. Reneging on their pledge to let Lear keep his hundred knights, his eldest daughters use this same flawed calculus to control their suddenly powerless father. "What need you five and twenty? ten? or five?" asks Goneril, to which Regan adds "What need one?" Having consolidated all power from their father, they now blame him for permitting "these not-to-be-endur'd riots" of his knights and his "all-licens'd Fool." They rationalize what they want to do.

And for these sisters, rationalizing what pleases them is habitual. After Lear leaves his daughters to face the pitiless storm, those who now wield the power explain their decision to Gloucester, who is very uneasy with these events:

> Corn. Whither is he going?
> Glou. . . . I know not whither.
> Corn. 'Tis best to give him way, he leads himself.

>   Gon. My lord, entreat him by no means stay.
>   Glou. Alack, the night comes on, and the bleak winds
>   Do sorely ruffle; for many miles about
>   There's scarcely a bush.
>   Reg.   O sir, to willful men,
>   The injuries that they themselves procure
>   Must be their schoolmasters. Shut up your doors.
>   He is attended with a desperate train,
>   And what they may incense him to, being apt
>   To have his ear abus'd, wisdom bids fear.
>   Corn. ... tis a wild night, my Regan counsels well.
>   (3.1.296-309)

Reasonable arguments are served up as excuses for bad behavior. Where bonds of filial love and gratitude are absent, the rationalization of self-interest replaces the minimal duty and respect owed to aged fathers.

Because Edmund's view of the world is likewise based on self-interest, his allegiance to these sisters is not surprising. In an early aside, Edmund describes how he deceived both father and brother:

> A credulous father and a brother noble,
> Whose nature is so far from doing harm
> That he suspects none; on whose foolish honesty
> My practices ride easy. I see the business.
> Let me, if not by birth, have lands by wit. ...
> (1.2.179-183)

To those who calculate for their own benefit, innocent credulity and a noble nature look like "foolish honesty." Virtues make Gloucester and Edgar vulnerable to deception and manipulation and therefore such credulousness, to follow Edmund's logic, ought to be shunned. Every decision, every encounter is weighed according to the possible advantages to be gained. For those, like Edmund, who use their wits to improve their fortunes, the principles Edgar follows are worse than useless. They impede advancement. It is perfectly rational, therefore, Edmund should eventually betray his father to gain favor with Regan and Cornwall.

But this self-conscious calculation for personal gain carries the seeds of its own annihilation. Though the selfishness of ambition and greed may temporarily gain control of circumstances, self-regard remains unaware of the basic emotions, the bonds, that unify families and communities. It is immune to the enlightenment suffering and vulnerability bring to the play's two old men. Again, quoting Heilman regarding the Goneril-Regan-Edmund trio:

> . . .to Lear's reason-in-madness there is opposed their tainted reason, a self-confident, unshackled sharpness of mind, shrewd and penetrating as far as it goes, but incapable, ultimately, of detecting its own frailty and limitations, of formulating a workable pattern of existence, and of bringing to them the saving insights of men of imagination. (284)

The evil at work in *Lear* is, ultimately, based on a kind of madness in reason. It cannot build anything of lasting value because the nature of evil lacks the comprehensive and inclusive quality of the good, that willingness to acknowledge and respond to the value of others. Ungenerous, its only concern is self-regard.

As the play's events unfold, each of the rationalizing characters succumbs to passions they fail to anticipate because they neglected to cultivate any understanding of them by experiencing them. Blind with fury because of Gloucester's perceived treason, Regan's husband enacts a cruelty so offensive a servant is moved to kill the perpetrator. That Cornwall's cruelty ends because of a servant's genuine sympathy is a warning lost on Goneril, Regan, and Edmund. Their self-centered rationalizations have no insight into the irrational forces beyond their control. They mistake anger for justice and lust, in the case of Goneril and Regan, for love. Goneril falls for the charismatic Edmund and forsakes her husband, the Duke of Albany, who has gradually come to the realization his wife is "not worth the dust that the rude wind blows" in her face. Since Regan, whose husband succumbed to the wounds suffered during Gloucester's blinding, has also fallen in love with Edmund, the wicked sisters poison each other in an escalating war of jealousy.

If these events expose the madness of rationalized self-interest, Lear's rescue from madness is proof that the irrationality of virtue is ultimately the more logical choice. As Cordelia prepares to return from France to relieve her father's suffering, Lear cannot resolve the conflict between his need for compassion and his lingering desire for revenge. On the heath, Lear comes to understand a justice almost inevitably tainted by self-interest is never perfect and therefore requires the exercise of mercy. Schooled in the errant ways of justice he can now say, "none does offend, none, I say, none." Endurance is the only help for the defenseless:

> If thou wilt weep my fortunes, take my eyes.
> I know thee well enough, thy name is Gloucester.
> Thou must be patient; we came crying hither.
> Thou know'st, the first time that we smell the air
> We wawl and cry. I will preach to thee. Mark. . . .
> When we are born, we cry that we are come
> To this great stage of fools. (4.6.176-183)

Because no one can avoid the consequences of their sinful nature, tears are inevitable from the moment of birth.

Although he promotes patience to Gloucester, a man recently contemplating suicide, Lear's sanguine mood does not hold for long. Only a few lines later, Lear returns to his desire for revenge. "When I have stol'n upon these sons-in-law, Then kill, kill, kill, kill, kill, kill!" The hurt, the anger, the helpless frustration persist. By this time, Lear has learned much about suffering, pity, justice, the limitations of sight, and responsibility, but expiation eludes him until he is finally reunited with Cordelia, his joy.

Balancing one of the cruelest scenes in literature, Gloucester's blinding, is one of the most tender, Cordelia's rescue of her tormented father. The first demonstrates how self-interest degrades mankind's ideal nature into the subhuman, driven by need and red in tooth and claw. The second demonstrates the healing balm of human kindness and love. Very efficiently, the play draws a clear distinction between the natures and the consequences of good and evil. Motivated by self-gratification, the wicked end in violence, division, and death, evident in the mortal jealousy of the evil sisters. Cordelia's sacrificial love, on the other hand, risks all, unselfishly, to comfort an abused father. The purity of her motives measures the compromised generosity Lear exhibits when he sought to divide his kingdom among his three daughters. Cordelia risks all, gains nothing for herself, by returning to rescue her father. The return is illogical because it is completely selfless and loving.

Remarkable for its love and compassion, their reconciliation is a moving tribute to the decency of which man at his best is capable. With his ordeal on the heath finally behind him, Lear has been sleeping. As he awakens, he recognizes Cordelia, who asks," How does my royal lord?" to which he replies," You do me wrong to take me out o 'th' grave." When she asks for his blessing, he tries to kneel at her feet. His heartfelt words reflect a hard-won humility:

> I am a very foolish fond old man,
> Fourscore and upward. . .
> And to deal plainly,
> I fear I am not in my perfect mind.
> Methinks I should know you. . .
> Yet I am doubtful: for I am mainly ignorant
> What place this is. . . .
> Do not laugh at me,
> For as I am a man I think this lady
> To be my child Cordelia.
>
> Cor.   And so I am, I am.

> Lear. Be your tears wet? Yes, faith. I pray weep not.
> If you have poison for me, I will drink it,
> I know you do not love me, for your sisters
> Have (as I remember) done me wrong;
> You have some cause, they have not.
> Cor. No cause, no cause. (4.7.59-73)

In remarkable symmetry with the play's opening self-deposition scene, Cordelia's unadorned reply of "no cause" cancels the misguided equivalency where kingdoms are the reward for rhetorical opulence. An argument for love as more verb than noun, the emotional and spiritual richness of this moment renders language unnecessary. Recalling the paradoxical implications of the financial metaphor in *The Merchant*, where giving away enhances wealth, Cordelia's freely given absolution includes no additional interest. This unsullied forgiveness is the moment of Lear's expiation. Re-enacting the Christian miracle of salvation, she accomplishes what he could never achieve on his own. The Biblical connection is not at all far-fetched. The association to the sacrificial servant of the gospels is clear when Cordelia, having just arrived in England to save Lear, remarks," O dear father, It is thy business that I go about," echoing a twelve-year-old Jesus explaining why he left his parents to teach in the temple. The allusion is particularly apt because, from a Christian perspective, that was the historical moment God's redemptive grace began to illuminate a dark and spiritually ignorant world. Shakespeare clearly wants to suggest that, for Lear, Cordelia's return is equal parts salvation, expiation, and the comforting light that will finally dispel the darkness of the world's evil.

This moment of forgiveness is also when Lear lets go of every lingering vestige of his royal identity. From this moment on, nothing else matters except this bond with the daughter he once angrily dismissed with the phrase "nothing will come of nothing." Her full worth now obvious, she has become his whole world. When her French army is defeated and they are taken off to prison, Cordelia calmly asks, "Shall we not see these daughters and these sisters?" But Lear has no interest in them any longer. "No, no, no, no!" he replies:

> Come, let's away to prison:
> We two alone will sing like birds i' th' cage;
> When thou dost ask me blessing, I'll kneel down
> And ask of thee forgiveness. So we'll live,
> And pray, and sing, and tell old tales, and laugh . . . .
> And take upon 's the mystery of things
> As if we were God's spies. . . . (5.3.8-16)

Reliving over and over again that moment when his one good daughter forgave him is where Lear finds meaning and joy. Why some hearts are so hard and others are tender enough to forgive must surely be part of "the mystery of things" known only to God. In the end, such things are beyond human comprehension. Sin, evil, kindness, and forgiveness—these can be identified and classified and appreciated for their consequences, but why they are part of the human experience, ultimately, cannot be understood. In his despair, Gloucester had once said, "As flies to wanton boys are we to th 'gods, they kill us for their sport." Inexplicably, though, Edgar's kindness finds a way to mitigate that despair. Nor can the indifferent supernatural realm contemplated in Gloucester's speech explain a Cordelia. In her defiant, unwavering love, she is the precious mystery that is just as much a part of nature as evil. In its vulnerability, virtue has no power to eliminate the world's evil. Its small victories of the heart are merely a brilliantly shining alternative bravely offered.

But despite the good evident in Cordelia's return, she and Lear seem to share the same fate meted out on the cunning for the cruelty inflicted on the credulous and the noble. Many people find it difficult to comprehend why, despite her integrity and virtue, death comes for her just as it does for the evil characters. In deference to judgments like Dr. Johnson's,

Nahum Tate remedied this problem by saving Cordelia and marrying her to Edgar. Shakespeare's tragic resolution, however, is far richer in its complex implications than such an easy and obvious resolution. He understood this is a fallen world where forgiveness and love afford no protection from the scourge of death, an inescapable, universal consequence once sin sullied the world. After Edgar, disguised this time in armor, defeats his illegitimate brother in a trial by combat, Edmund renounces his sins but not before he has set in motion the imprisoned Cordelia's murder. His confession comes too late to save her, and Lear enters carrying the lifeless body of his favorite child in his arms. From the very deepest grief, far beneath the calculus of reason, Lear mimics the sound of an animal in wounded agony:

> Howl, howl, howl! O, you are men of stones!
> Had I your tongues and eyes, I'ld use them so
> That heaven's vault should crack. She's gone forever!
> I know when one is dead, and when one lives.
> She's dead as earth. Lend me a looking glass,
> If that her breath will mist or stain the stone,
> Why then she lives. . . . .
> This feather stirs, she lives! If it be so,
> It is a chance which does redeem all sorrows
> That ever I have felt. (5.3.258-268)

Where Ovid laments desire's power to transform gods into animals, Shakespeare inverts Ovid's sentiment to indicate the inexplicable sorrow of love lost. Lear's unhuman noises reflect a grief arising so deep within those prerational feelings of love that it cannot be rendered into human language. He looks frantically for signs of life, but the feather is not stirring.

What comes next, however, gives voice to a profound ambiguity:

> And my poor fool is hanged! No, no, no life!
> Why should a dog, a horse, a rat have life,
> And thou no breath at all? Thou'lt come no more.

> Never, never, never, never, never.
> Pray you, undo this button. . . .
> Do you see this? Look on her! Look her lips.
> Look there, look there! [Lear dies] (5.3.306-312)

Like his mistaken conviction his eldest daughters loved him, what he sees on her lips may very well be an illusion of desperate hope. Ironically, his inarticulateness mirrors exactly what Cordelia faced in that first scene, but now it is Lear who finds it impossible to adequately express feelings, to heave his heart into his mouth. Evidence of life is everywhere except where he needs it most, and the finality of her passing is more than he can bear. The final truth is harsh. Yes, suffering may bring insight. Forgiveness may produce momentary joy. Yet neither can preserve the very precious opportunity man has been given because life is fragile. Everything beneath the heavens, both good and bad, is subject to the grave, but this is precisely why the hard work of defining meaning and value accurately is vitally important: those matter to the ones we profess to love.

And yet, what is to be made of his illusion that her lips are whispering one final thought to him? It is no coincidence that every Shakespearean tragedy contains a similar final scene where love and death merge. An apparently dead Juliet inspires Romeo to follow her beyond the grave. The concept is there in the pun on "union" Hamlet makes to point out Claudius's poisoned pearl that inadvertently kills his beloved wife. Convinced of Desdemona's infidelity, a jealous Othello strangles his innocent wife, who returns from death to defend her honesty. When the Macbeths resort to murder, the pattern of a love victorious over death is reversed. And Antony's death inspires the mercurial Queen of Egypt to commit fully to the man she loved. In each instance, love seems to function as an invisible connection that transcends the worst death can do. Death may be the "bourne from which no man returns," as Hamlet says, despite the ghost's multiple appearances, but

Shakespeare's tragic denouements suggest love gives meaning to the passage from life into whatever lies beyond. Perhaps love cannot preserve life, but somehow it endures and inspires and guides, even from beyond the grave. Despite suffering and evil, this is cause for great joy, for it provides a reason to choose what's right and good. For Christians like Shakespeare, it also explains why a good and loving creator provided this wonderful yet terrible gift of desire.

To some who consider tragedy the pessimistic and comedy the optimistic genre, this reading of *Lear*'s ending may seem too spiritually hopeful. On this, Heilman again has the final word:

> Pessimism does not consist in seeing evil injure good; it is instead the inability to see good; or it is to conclude only that evil is mistaken for good; or to discover total depravity, but no grace. To find the play painful or shocking is to be unable to grasp quality as quality, and to substitute success for quality; it is to think in terms of the naïve expectation that longevity, as well as invulnerability to mortal ills, is the reward of virtue. This is the error of Lear at the beginning of the play— the introduction of irrelevant quantitative standards. Quantity of life or quantity of immunity to suffering has, alas, no relationship to moral integrity. . . . To assume or to seek such relationship is to substitute reward for merit, accident for substance; it is to move from tragedy to melodrama. (290)

Where melodrama offers simple moral distinctions and simplistic resolutions, tragedy looks at human existence in all its complex but richly suggestive paradoxes and never blinks, regardless of the painful truths that emerge. But it sees more than suffering, too. In the end, tragedy is the more hopeful genre because, like *King Lear*, it recognizes grace when it sees it, even amid wickedness, and insists on its relevance to human life. Though magic is never referenced explicitly in this play as it is in several others, Shakespeare clearly shows in this immensely moving examination of human nature that any proper evaluation of it must account for the magic of Cordelia's love.

Macbeth

◆•◆•◆•◆•◆•◆•

In Portia's remarkable speech on mercy, she makes a rather startling observation about the gift of mercy which, she says, "blesseth him that gives and him that takes." In previous chapters, love succeeds when the hearts of women share generously from their material, emotional, physical, and spiritual wealth. But the relationship also succeeds because worthy men are grateful for what they receive. Those that gratefully "take," like *The Merchant*'s Bassanio and *Twelfth Night*'s Sebastian, both surprised by the unexpected gift of love, are also blessed. The Macbeths fail in their tragic quest to become Scotland's rulers because Lady Macbeth deems the generosity Duncan shows her husband to be inadequate. Harmony is the product of two equally important virtues: generosity and gratitude. Based on the false promises of the witches, Lady Macbeth tries to harness her warrior husband's innate brutality to take what she thinks they deserve.

The shortest and bloodiest of Shakespeare's tragedies, *Macbeth* follows the tradition of Elizabethan moral history popularized by *The Mirror for Magistrates*, stories recounting the many ways flawed character brings ruin upon princes. The similarities are undeniable: the fall of the play's Scottish warrior briefly focuses on the psychological process of temptation but spends considerable time on the social, psychological, and spiritual consequences of choosing evil rather than good. With efficient precision, it demonstrates how temptation originates from a desire given shape and form by the imagination, how those mental visions intrude into the mind where they subvert reason and judgment, eventually negating the better inclinations of human nature. Yet Macbeth's story also includes a wife who at the most obvious level is a type for the Eve who misleads Adam. She is, however, much more than mere symbol. Comparisons of Lady Macbeth with selfless women like Cordelia who love in divinely inspired ways introduces interesting and far richer reasons to appreciate her purpose in the play's moral architecture. Lady Macbeth, in fact, is a reminder of the intricate ways evil works to corrupt a love originally intended for good, making the story of the Macbeths the obverse of what happens in *Romeo and Juliet* or *Antony and Cleopatra*.

While both *Othello* and *Macbeth* demonstrate the detailed process of temptation, the Moor's downfall is the result of one very devious human antagonist with malignant motives. Limited to human interactions only, the tragedy has a peculiarly domestic spirit. Though another domestic pair are at the center of *Macbeth,* the presence of larger supernatural forces opposed in a war for human souls gives this play a much different feel. Macduff's revenge certainly seems like divine retribution, but as the embodiment of ever-vigilant evil powers, the three witches recognize Lady Macbeth's dissatisfaction as an opportunity to encourage a disavowal of her uniquely feminine virtues, turning marital love into a weapon to cow her hesitant spouse into unnatural submission.

Unlike the protagonists of familiar Greek tragedies, Macbeth is no innocent victim ensnared by unresolvable moral conundrums. He knowingly and repeatedly makes self-serving, evil rather than morally good choices. Nor is he blind to the possible consequences of his decisions. He covets a position that doesn't belong to him, and he acts on that desire, hoping more than believing that bold action will bring success, that the expected earthly consequences can be avoided, that the pleasure of earthly success will help him endure whatever punishment might come after death. Within the Christian context of Shakespeare's culture, Macbeth is the unrepentant sinner who suffers the inevitable consequences of a heart indifferent to everything good and holy. Endowed with free will, his moral culpability is absolutely clear. Despite the seductive ambiguities of the witches' prophecies, he could have made a different decision. He doesn't, in large part, because his wife's desire for what they don't yet have corrupts who she should be within their marriage.

His companion, Banquo, who also receives his own ambiguous prophecy, proves the point, for he does not make the same choice as Macbeth. Nevertheless, despite the clear moral responsibility of both husband and wife, it remains impossible not to sense the presence of an ongoing spiritual war between good and evil for Macbeth's soul. Near the end of the play as he approaches the witches one final time to discover his fate in the coming battle against his amassing enemies, the hags wind up their charms in preparation for his visit:

> Great business must be wrought ere noon:
> Upon the corner of the moon
> There hangs a vap'rous drop profound,
> I'll catch it ere it come to ground;
> And that, distill'd by magic sleights,
> Shall raise such artificial sprites
> As by the strength of their illusion
> Shall draw him on to his confusion,
> He shall spurn fate, scorn death, and bear
> His hopes 'bove wisdom, grace, and fear;
> And you all know, security
> Is mortals' chiefest enemy. (3.5.22-33)

Macbeth is being seduced by a heady concoction of his own desire for the crown, equivocal promises from the witches, and morally specious reasoning as he debates the way forward. But the witches invoke powers beyond his control to create the necessary confusion preventing reason and conscience from leading him to the right choice. The relationship between the witches and Macbeth becomes a symbiosis of respective weaknesses. Aligned with the demonic, they have no power to force his decisions. All they can do is exploit any unfulfilled desires or hopes he happens to harbor. Normally a virtue, the desire to maintain the good opinion of his beloved spouse becomes a most unlikely weakness those powers are able to exploit.

Unencumbered by any subplots, *Macbeth*'s story is uniquely straightforward. As the play begins, Duncan, the victorious Scottish king, is surveying a battlefield gradually going quiet. His royal forces have prevailed. Macbeth, Scotland's bravest warrior, has fought valiantly to protect his nation from rebellion and invasion. Generous and grateful, Duncan rewards Macbeth with the title of the defeated rebel leader, an event that three witches had already shared with the valiant warrior. Though Macbeth is all but convinced the weird sisters can accurately foresee the future, their message is also troubling: while they suggest Macbeth would eventually become king, they also claim no child of his would ever succeed him. Instead, his friend, Banquo, would father a long line of Scottish kings that, according to legend, included King James himself. Despite this puzzling ambiguity, ambition now flames hot in his own and his wife's imaginations. Since his determination wavers as the crucial moment approaches, Lady Macbeth challenges him to murder Duncan, which he does. Afraid for their own lives, Duncan's sons flee and are therefore blamed for their father's death. Consequently, Macbeth is crowned and begins to settle into his new role. But troubled by predictions of an uncertain future, Macbeth's relentless anxiety disrupts the façade of calm normalcy he tries but fails to maintain. Despite his wife's plea to hide his restless imaginings, their lives drift apart. Resolving to murder anyone who might jeopardize his future, Macbeth initiates a series of bloody actions that cost him peace of mind, sleep, his marriage, friends, political stability, and eventually his life. Unlike his wife, his behavior is not the result of guilt. Like an animal obsessed with survival, he no longer has sufficient emotional energy to stay connected to his wife. As her marriage disintegrates, Lady

Macbeth descends into madness, quickly followed by death which comes shortly before the avenging Scottish nobles defeat and kill her husband. Duncan's son assumes the throne and peace returns to Scotland.

One implication of the tragedy is clear enough: time brings Macbeth's bloody reign to an end, replacing it with stability and peace. First performed for King James, who not only dabbled in occult mythology but personally witnessed the Gunpowder Conspiracy trials, Shakespeare's play was confirmation God often uses good men like Banquo and MacDuff to root out evil and restore a nation's harmony, a view of history that is Biblical as well as comforting. Judging from *1 Henry 4*, Shakespeare saw time as the divine workshop where society is continually redeemed from the effects of human frailty and sin. As the play's events unfold, the children who haunt Macbeth's imagination convey this notion of evil's inevitable defeat, coming in a future beyond his control. While the world's punishment may be inevitable, avoiding the worst spiritual consequences requires only confession and repentance.

But the Thane of Glamis's choices put him beyond redemption. In *Macbeth*, time is redemptive only to men of good character. Because he has deliberately and repeatedly forsaken his best nature, Macbeth's experience of time is entirely different from those who have rescued Scotland. As the avenging army advances toward the castle where he is trapped, he hears the last shriek of his dying wife, consumed by grief and despair. Preparing to engage his enemies, Macbeth reacts to the event with the nihilism of a man who has lost everything, including his soul:

> Sey. The Queen, my lord, is dead.
> Macb. She should have died hereafter;
> There would have been a time for such a word.
> To-morrow, and to-morrow, and to-morrow,
> Creeps in this petty pace from day to day,
> To the last syllable of recorded time;

> And all our yesterdays have lighted fools
> The way to dusty death. Out, out, brief candle!
> Life's but a walking shadow, a poor player,
> That struts and frets his hour upon the stage,
> And then is heard no more. It is a tale
> Told by an idiot, full of sound and fury,
> Signifying nothing. (5.5.16-28)

The lines capture the emotional and spiritual desolation of a man whose life is now devoid of any significance. Ambition led to murder which led to additional bloodshed, isolation, despair, and death. With Macbeth's future now obliterated, this particular life has been bled dry of both purpose and meaning. Except for his wife, no one else in the play expresses such deep despair. But the despair is not universal. Since those who have suffered under his rule are fighting to restore honor and respect to their community, their efforts are blessed with significant meaning. Macbeth's enemies know what their purpose is. Murdering Duncan, though, removes everything of value from the lives of both husband and wife. They have lost respect, trust, friends, community, peace, sleep, and the companionship and love of a devoted spouse.

His life was not always so bleak. As the play opens, a sergeant provides an account of his ferocious confrontation with the leader of the Scottish rebels trying to overthrow good king Duncan:

> . . . brave Macbeth. . .
> Disdaining Fortune, with his brandish'd steel
> (Like Valor's minion) carv'd out his passage
> Till he fac'd the slave;
> Which nev'r shook hands, nor bade farewell to him,
> Till he unseam'd him from the nave to th' chops,
> And fix'd his head upon our battlements. (1.2.16-23)

Impressed by Macbeth's valiant efforts, Duncan decides to reward his captain with the defeated rebel leader's title, Thane of Cawdor. But the play's first description of Macbeth is itself ambiguous. On one hand, Macbeth bravely supports a noble king who is associated with generosity, abundance, and grace. But the image is also of a bloody man who "meant to bathe in reeking wounds," a foreshadowing of his coming reign of terror. Which of these is the real Macbeth? "There's no art," Duncan observes, "to find the mind's construction in the face." Capable of either good or evil, the true character of any man is hidden within, opaque to human vision, until action reveals the character within. For better or for worse, one Thane of Cawdor rebels and another takes his place. The first is defeated, confesses in "deep repentance," and bravely accepts his punishment. "Nothing in life," says Duncan's son Malcolm, "became him like the leaving it." As the death of the first Thane of Cawdor shows, the fate of those who rebel against legitimate authority is certain. It is a lesson that the second Thane of Cawdor should not ignore but does.

The difference between the valued warrior at the beginning of the play and the dry husk of a man at the end is evidence of Macbeth's decline. A life full of promise has been replaced by deep spiritual desolation. Like all men, Macbeth had been endowed with a variety of gifts, including his skills in blood and death which, quite remarkably, nature can use for good. A generous king willingly repays him for employing all these to preserve Scotland's order. Where Duncan's benevolence had once showered rewards upon a brave and valiant man willing to risk his life in service to his king and nation, the man at the end is encircled by the consequences of his bloody reign. Even the last vestiges of freedom have disappeared. "They have tied me to a stake," he laments. "I cannot fly but bear-like I must fight the course." The how and why of that change is the real substance of *Macbeth*. Like the lost paradise of *Genesis*, *Macbeth* recreates the oldest story of all: the fall from grace into the horrid consequences of sin.

That degeneration begins with the three witches, equivocating agents of darkness, who provide Macbeth with a blurred glimpse into the future. Their message is misleading because it is also partially true. But desire, in the form of ambition for the crown, prompts him to hear what's true and ignore the danger even he suspects. Fresh from his victorious battle against rebel forces, he encounters the three witches on the heath. The first greets him with his present title, but the remaining two greet him with titles that have yet to be bestowed:

> 1W. All hail, Macbeth, hail to thee, Thane of Glamis!
> 2W. All hail, Macbeth, hail to thee, Thane of Cawdor!
> 3W. All hail, Macbeth, that shalt be king hereafter!
> (1.3.49-52)

At this juncture, Macbeth has no insight into how this will come about. Since no mortal can see into the future, the encounter is fraught with the kind of dangerous moral ambiguity that promotes confusion, a state where "fair is foul, and foul is fair." And the sowing of confusion is exactly what the incantations of these witches anticipate. Within the uncertainty they create, the moral compass loses direction, and desire's imagined visions of royal power all too easily lead Macbeth down into the darkness of sin and damnation. Because equivocation fosters the moral confusion that renders the wrong choice more attractive than experience proves it to be, it is all too easy for desire to participate in the corruption of Macbeth's soul.

But man has also been endowed with a conscience to counter the dangers inherent in free will. At first, that conscience actively resists the idea of Duncan's murder, so the temptation, which occupies the play's first two acts, occurs in stages. When Duncan rewards Macbeth with the defeated rebel's title, Thane of Cawdor, the witches' ability to predict the future seems confirmed. But both Macbeth and his companion, Banquo, recognize the moral dangers in the witches' prognostications. Turning to Macbeth, Banquo warns that these predictions "Might yet enkindle you unto the crown," which is followed by the admonition, ". . . oftentimes, to win us to our harm, the instruments of darkness tell us truths." In a private moment a few lines later, Macbeth wrestles with exactly that problem:

> This supernatural soliciting
> Cannot be ill; cannot be good. If ill,
> Why hath it given me earnest of success,
> Commencing in a truth? I am Thane of Cawdor.
> If good, why do I yield to that suggestion
> Whose horrid image doth unfix my hair,
> And make my seated heart knock at my ribs,
> Against the use of nature? (1.3.130-137)

The battlefield image of Macbeth from the play's first scene describes a man who knew that rebellion was evil and must be repelled. But the witches have already planted a seed in Macbeth's imagination, and it will take root as the same ugly weed of desire for illegitimate power that motivated the first Thane of Cawdor. As we see in Macbeth, that process begins when moral certainty is replaced by moral indecision, a condition already evident in Macbeth's assessment that the prophecy "cannot be ill; cannot be good." Craving some resolution, his imagination creates a "horrid image" of a murder "against the use of nature," a phrase suggesting nature's design included a standard of right behavior. Recoiling from the thought of what he might do, Macbeth's conscience is still delicate enough to resist such an unnatural act.

Shakespeare's very Biblical model of a nature imbued with understandable principles of the good helps to define the Macbeths' depravity. Offsetting their unnatural cruelty is a nature of harmony and fecundity that the Macbeths violate in word and deed. As Duncan and his entourage approach Macbeth's castle, he comments that the fortress, nestled in the bucolic Scottish countryside, "hath a pleasant seat, the air nimbly and sweetly recommends itself/Unto our gentle senses." To which Banquo remarks:

> This guest of summer,
> The temple-haunting martlet, does approve,
> By his lov'd mansionry, that the heaven's breath
> Smells wooingly here; no jutty, frieze,
> Buttress, nor coign of vantage, but this bird
> Hath made his pendant bed and procreant cradle.
> Where they most breed and haunt, I have observ'd
> The air is delicate. (1.6.3-10)

The author of *Genesis* understood that the bleakness of sin's many consequences would stand out more sharply against the perfections of Eden. Superficially, the nature that both men observe restores nerves chafed raw by the stress of recent battle. But this seemingly superfluous exchange points to the other, more spiritual battle that is ongoing. Paradoxically, the very castle where death awaits also provides safe haven for the birds that make their nests among the battlements. The vision is emblematic of the essential moral quandary life outside the original garden presents. What the two men observe is a nature struggling to assert its abundant fertility against the encroachments of chaos and blood, the opposition between good and evil. In opposition to death, new life emerges from the beds and "procreant cradle[s]," where the martlets can "breed and haunt." It is a scene that embodies the tension between life's abundant goodness and death's various negations of life. The struggle between these forces is cyclical, and just as Macbeth repeats the mistake of the previous Thane of Cawdor, the battle between life-enhancing forces and death is the perpetual struggle of human experience.

This dichotomy is enhanced further by Duncan's affiliation with the forces of life. After hearing of Macbeth's battlefield valor, Duncan greets his champion with language that is rich with agricultural images of husbandry and new growth:

> Welcome hither!
> I have begun to plant thee, and will labor
> To make thee full of growing. (1.4.28-30)

Far from passive, a good king works to cultivate the prosperity of others. Rich with the promise of future abundance for all that serve him well, Duncan's generosity aligns him with the natural fecundity observed outside Macbeth's castle. Both the title and Duncan's liberality are the fruit of the king's "labor," for each is meant to enrich the other. As seen in many previous plays, giving selflessly and generously multiplies love's wealth, so when both king and citizens put all God-given gifts to use, both giver and receiver are enhanced. As an extension of nature's bounty, Duncan's royal generosity reflects the will of a Creator who designed nature to overwhelm the agents of death with new life and abundance. Consequently, when Macbeth decides to murder Duncan, he alienates himself from this nature and all its promised wealth.

Though at first the witches' message intrigues him, Macbeth knows full well the moral decision he faces. In a remarkably complex soliloquy, he contemplates which path to follow. A rich amalgam of the rational and the imaginative, the argument attempts to evaluate worldly and supernatural consequences of such a heinous act before reaching its apocalyptic conclusion. As servants are preparing a table for Macbeth's royal guest, he examines one possible consequence of murder: the possibility of escaping detection altogether:

> If it were done, when 'tis done, then 'twere well
> It were done quickly. If th' assassination
> Could trammel up the consequence, and catch
> With his surcease, success; that but this blow
> Might be the be-all and the end-all---here,
> But here, upon this bank and [schoal] of time,

>We'ld jump the life to come. (1.7.1-7)

If all the consequences of murder could be gathered up and managed successfully in this world, then Macbeth would be willing to risk whatever consequences might follow in the afterlife. Ironically, these first lines contain an echo of John 13:27 where, at the Last Supper, Jesus speaks to Judas and tells him," What you are about to do, do quickly." The Biblical allusion, which subtly equates Macbeth to Judas, provides immediate moral orientation since, as it was for Jesus, this too will be Duncan's last supper. But Macbeth continues:

> But in these cases,
> We still have judgment here, that we but teach
> Bloody instructions, which, being taught, return
> To plague the inventor. This even-handed justice
> Commends th' ingredience of our poison'd chalice
> To our own lips. (1.7.7-11)

As Bolingbroke learned when he overthrew Richard II, deposing a rightful king taught others how to assert their rights in exactly the same way. Rebellion begets more rebellion. So even if supernatural consequences could be avoided, judgment in this world cannot be escaped. Since punishment is unavoidable, therefore, the passage transitions to the social preclusions against murder:

> He's here in double trust:
> First, as I am his kinsman and his subject,
> Strong both against the deed; then, as his host,
> Who should against his murtherer shut the door,
> Not bear the knife myself. (1.7.11-15)

Besides the recurring cycle of violence that regicide would incite, Macbeth knows that Duncan's murder would also violate social and cultural norms. His conscience is certainly troubled by these significant cultural arguments against murder. What follows, however, acknowledges the moral and spiritual dimensions of such a "horrid deed."

> Besides, this Duncan
> Hath borne his faculties so meek, hath been
> So clear in his great office, that his virtues
> Will plead like angels, trumpet-tongued, against
> The deep damnation of his taking-off;
> And pity, like a naked new-born babe,
> Striding the blast, or heaven's cherubin, hors'd
> Upon the sightless couriers of the air,
> Shall blow the horrid deed in every eye,
> That tears shall drown the wind. (1.7.15-24)

This powerful and frightening vision should give anyone pause. With its apocalyptic imagery, the concluding lines of Macbeth's soliloquy complete the transition to the spiritual consequences of the contemplated murder. Evil cannot be hidden. It will be proclaimed and punishment will inevitably be meted out. When good is measured against evil, Duncan's virtues will speak with trumpet tongues, and either pity or heaven's cherubim will stride through the coming storm of tears, announcing Macbeth's sin for all to hear. The deed will be exposed and judged, either by his kinsman or by avenging supernatural powers. Dissuaded from his contemplated purpose, his conclusion follows:

> I have no spur
> To prick the sides of my intent, but only
> Vaulting ambition, which o'erleaps itself
> And falls on th' other--- . (1.7.25-28)

Since ambition rather than any recognizably just cause is his only motive, the plan to murder Duncan will inevitably fail. At this point, Macbeth is fully cognizant of the consequences following Duncan's murder. Every aspect of human nature, including its social, moral, and spiritual norms, argues against it, and he resolves not to commit such a heinous act. Though the play's opening scene describes the warrior Macbeth, who "unseam'd" Scotland's enemies "from the nave to th' chops," he shows himself equally capable of reasoned moral contemplation. Which of those two male natures eventually predominates, one violent and bloody, the other rational and moral, is largely determined by the woman who professes to love him.

Following Macbeth's very rational rejection of a contemplated sin, Lady Macbeth deliberately decides she must wear the identity of her warrior husband who, she believes, "wouldst not play false, yet wouldst wrongly win." To eliminate such ambivalence, she's willing to eschew her own identity to look more like the bloody battlefield warrior described as the play opens. That process begins when, reading her husband's letter about the witches' prophecy and the king's imminent arrival, she offers a chilling, demonic prayer to the agents of darkness:

> The raven himself is hoarse
> That croaks the fatal entrance of Duncan
> Under my battlements. Come, you spirits
> That tend on mortal thoughts, unsex me here,
> And fill me from the crown to the toe topful
> Of direst cruelty! Make thick my blood,
> Stop up th' access and passage to remorse,
> That no compunctious visitings of nature
> Shake my fell purpose. . . . Come to my woman's breasts,
> And take my milk for gall, you murth'ring ministers,
> Wherever . . . you wait on nature's mischief! (1.5.38 – 50)

As the first crucial step toward murder, Lady Macbeth asks for fierce cruelty to replace those gentle, nurturing inclinations nature assigns to women fearing compassion might dissuade her from the bloody deed required to win the crown.

Steeled for the inevitable confrontation with her husband, Lady Macbeth quickly projects this assumed identity when he informs her he can't and won't murder Duncan.

Challenging the valor and manhood of the one who just saved Scotland from traitorous rebels, her response is swift and aggressive:

> Lady M. Was the hope drunk
>   Wherein you dress'd yourself? Hath it slept since?
>   .... From this time
>   Such I account thy love. Art thou afeared
>   To be the same in thine own act and valor
>   As thou art in desire? ....
> Macb. Prithee peace!
>   I dare do all that may become a man;
>   Who dares [do] more is none.
> Lady M. What beast was't then
>   That made you break this enterprise to me?
>   When you durst do it, then you were a man.
>   (1.7. 35-49)

This domestic confrontation begins an extended examination of what it means to be a man. Where a courageous, battle-tested Macbeth has already demonstrated the moral efficacy of reason, his wife works to provoke a defensive, emotional reaction. To win her husband's compliance, she challenges him to act upon "desire" rather than conscience. She then goes on to assail any lingering reluctance by challenging his devotion to her. Asserting he has already proven he will "do all that may become a man," she calls him a "beast" for disappointing her. Inverting both Ovid and doctrinaire Christianity, she suggests a husband who frustrates a wife's expectations by letting conscience discipline desire forsakes the loving man he pretends to be and becomes the unthinking, uncaring brute.

In the topsy-turvy world where "fair is foul, and foul is fair," where kindness and morality are weaknesses and cruelty is manly and good, Lady Macbeth convinces her husband by denying her own feminine nature and dressing herself as the bloody warrior. But this inversion of natural gender associations descends even further into the demonic when she envisions evil spirits sucking gall rather than nourishing milk from her "woman's breasts." Along with the theme of manliness, this allusion initiates a second elaborate web of associations, this time to young, vulnerable babies that serve to define the cruelty of the Macbeths. To confirm his resolve, she transforms a particularly maternal moment into an image of ghastly brutality:

> I have given suck, and know
> How tender 'tis to love the babe that milks me;
> I would, while it was smiling in my face,
> Have pluck'd my nipple from his boneless gums
> And dash'd the brains out, had I so sworn as you
> Have done to this. (1.7.54-59)

Remarkable for its poetic and prophetic efficiency, Lady Macbeth's imaginary babe brutalized to prove her masculine *bona fides* anticipates the murder of Macduff's children as well as the apocalyptic infant announcing her husband's horrid deed throughout the world, for those murders inspire a father's revenge, bringing Macbeth's bloody reign to an end. Equally remarkable, this unnatural reversal of gender roles where the woman sheds her normal compassions and assumes her husband's warrior-like indifference to suffering and death is indicative of the moral inversions governing these life-altering decisions. The influence of Ovid, who shared this same dismay for indifferent cruelty, lingers here, even in this late tragedy.

But the moral truths Shakespeare detected in the architecture of a loving God's creation are not so easily dismissed. While her husband is murdering Duncan, Lady Macbeth nervously admits that "had [Duncan] not resembled my father as he slept, I had done't." Though she is ultimately unable to sustain this pretense of unfeminine cruelty, her dreadful image is still enough to shock her emotionally vulnerable husband into compliance. "Bring forth men-children only," he concludes, "for thy undaunted mettle should compose nothing but males." Since he too now equates such heartless cruelty to manliness, it is clear that a morally confused Macbeth has succumbed to her arguments. Her temptation complete, she very diligently lays out the details of their plot.

  Where the early *Romeo and Juliet* is a somber celebration of love's ability to transform people and society, *Macbeth* inverts that proposition into a warning that love corrupted has the power to deform not only husband and wife but the society they temporarily rule. Engaged in a collaborative selfishness to take Scotland's crown, the Macbeths pervert love into something entirely alien. It isn't exactly the opposite of love, which would be hate, an emotion neither Macbeth expresses. As the emotional center of the conspiracy, what Lady Macbeth espouses actually has many of the characteristics of love but might more properly be termed anti-love. Like Juliet and Portia, she wishes herself more than what she is in the expectation they both will be enriched. She is loyal, transparent in her ambition, generous about giving all of herself to her husband, aware of his gifts. What this marriage of true minds could have been, though, is destroyed because Lady Macbeth's specious reasoning can't disguise this fact: each wants for themselves something they shouldn't have. And in a weirdly inverted way, this anti-love, similar to genuine love, imparts its anti-blessings on both. Instead of union, they reap separation; instead of joy, they reap despair and madness; instead of respect and admiration, they reap anger and hatred; instead of communion, they reap alienation and isolation; and instead of abundant life, they reap death.

  Just as his wife cannot escape her own nature, Macbeth's response to murder similarly confirms the innate moral structure of the world, for his conscience continues to activate a deep sense of guilt. When he returns from Duncan's room where he has murdered the king, he is fixated on the blood he has spilled. Looking at his hand in horror, he asks, "Will all great Neptune's ocean wash this blood clean from my hands?" The answer he provides suggests the enormity of his guilt: "No; this my hand will rather the multitudinous seas incarnadine." Blood, life-giving and precious, has now dyed the entire world with the unnatural color of sin. Because guilt this enormous is impossible to hide, Lady Macbeth's attempts to assuage it are pitifully inadequate. "Consider it not so deeply," she implores, but the words betray her inability to face the horror of what they've done, for thinking deeply on it can only aggravate that relentlessly nagging conscience.

Because she was so focused on obtaining the crown that she failed to appreciate her husband's deeply moral nature, she never anticipates the depth of his guilt and can do very little after the murder to mitigate it. She tries to manage those feelings by focusing very narrowly on the incriminating details of the murder scene, but, in the end, the cruelty she reawakened in her husband begins to separate them. While her guilt overwhelms and drives her toward madness, the very battle-hardened, masculine bravery she had taunted now battles against conscience and the consequences that had once argued against the murder. Unlike Lady Macbeth, courage and cruelty were always a part of his nature, so warrior-like, he now dares "fate into the list" so it can "champion me to the 'utterance." Though they are now on two separate but equally destructive spiritual paths, the first fruit of evil, division, is already at work.

By murdering Duncan, the Macbeths placed their interests before the common good. That selfishness is the essence of their sin, and that all-consuming self-interest will come to dominate their thoughts, their actions, their lives, even their sleep until there is no more room for anything of real and lasting value. Unwittingly, Lady Macbeth has unleashed the brutal animal that once fought for a good and gracious king but now fights for their survival, and this battle gradually empties Macbeth's heart of any human kindness until no feelings are left, even for his once beloved wife. Their complete isolation from each other is the personal consequence of sin. Their isolation from the community becomes the social and political consequence. Whether they yet realize it, the Macbeths have passed through the very gates of Hell, which the irritable porter humorously acknowledges the morning after the murder as he answers the persistent knocking of Duncan's entourage:

> Here's a knocking indeed! If a man were porter of Hell Gate, he should have old turning the key. (Knock.) Knock, knock, knock! Who's there, i' th' name of Belzebub? . . . . But this place is too cold for hell. I'll devil-porter no further. I had thought to have let in some of all professions that go the primrose way to th' everlasting bonfire. . . . (2.3.1-20)

There is no turning back anymore. The king has been murdered. Life can never be poured back into what's dead and gone. The Macbeths have stepped onto the primrose path to hell. Confession and repentance are the only options to return to nature's good graces now, but time, as subsequent events will show, is no longer on their side.

For the Macbeths, repentance never happens. As the necessary precursor to murder, the repudiation of human nature's moral and nurturing qualities becomes increasingly difficult to reverse. The first sin makes successive ones easier until they become habitual. The answer to Lady Macbeth's demonic prayer came instantaneously, but the remainder of the play traces this hollowing out of everything that was once good in her husband. Fittingly, that process involves his war against children, who embody the future he can still only dimly perceive. Previously, Lady Macbeth had used the imagery of vulnerable babes to define the depraved cruelty required for murder. Now children, who threaten to avenge the wrongs they've suffered, become the cause of his relentless anxiety and restless sleep.

Because the king's sons, Malcolm and Donalbain, feared for their own lives and fled, they are blamed for their father's murder, but they eventually become instrumental in Macbeth's defeat. But the play's other children are also instrumental in time's redeeming retribution. Because they remained in Scotland, Banquo and his son, Fleance, are of more immediate concern. Since the witches prophesied that Banquo's descendants, not Macbeth's, would comprise a long line of Scottish kings, Macbeth decides that they too must be eliminated. Though the thugs he hired succeed in killing Banquo, Fleance escapes, an outcome that intensifies Macbeth's concern about the future. "The worm that's fled," he observes, "hath nature that in time will venom breed, no teeth for th 'present" (3.4.29-30). Though harmless for the moment, young Fleance represents the vengeance that the future will eventually bring to Macbeth's doorstep, and that vengeance is personified in the child who escaped.

Besides Macbeth's obsessive anxiety about the future, the consequences of sin are manifested in other ways as well. One of those is the disruption of sleep which is nature's way of healing mind and body from life's ordinary cares. When Macbeth emerges from the chamber where he murdered Duncan, he admits hearing a voice cry "Sleep no more! Macbeth does murther sleep. . . ." From that point on, neither he nor Lady Macbeth enjoys the kind of sleep "that knits up the ravell'd sleave of care." Her last appearance, in fact, has her sleepwalking through the castle trying to wash away the "damn'd spot" from her hands. Though she had once counseled her husband that "a little water [will clear] us of this deed," guilt will not allow either of them to forget the blood that has permanently stained their hands. With guilt large enough to dye the green sea red, such deeply troubled minds can never enjoy the necessary balm that sleep normally provides.

Deception and secrecy are other consequences of their sin. Having tried mightily to hide their guilt and shame, their effort to project a façade of normalcy causes a familiar divergence between surface appearances and a hidden truth. It begins when Lady Macbeth advises her husband to "look like the innocent flower, But be the serpent under it." Later, when he explains why the attendants in the king's chamber were also killed, a suspicious and wary Malcolm remarks to his brother, Donalbain, "to show an unfelt sorrow is an office which the false man does easy." Again, as his waiting guests are seated for the dinner where Banquo's ghost appears, Lady Macbeth tries to ease her husband's troubled soul, imploring him to "sleek o'er [your] rugged looks, Be bright and jovial. . . ." Throughout *Macbeth*, starting with the equivocal statements from the witches, a misleading innocence cloaks the evil underneath. But nature's inherently moral design will not allow sin to remain hidden for long.

As in *Hamlet*, the ghost of a murdered father is the first indication a secret, abhorrent sin will be exposed. When Banquo's ghost disrupts the assembled nobles at Macbeth's dinner, it is clear that something in nature detests Scotland's unnatural violence and wants these terrible secrets to be revealed and addressed so the wounds can be healed. The morning after Duncan's murder, in fact, the Scottish nobles arriving to escort the king to his next destination report events that imply nature's revulsion:

> The night has been unruly. Where we lay, our chimneys were blown down, and (as they say) lamentings heard i' the' air; strange screams of death, and prophesying, with accents terrible, of dire combustion and confus'd events new hatch'd to th' woeful time. The obscure bird clamor'd the livelong night. Some say, the earth was feverous, and did shake. (2.2.54-661)

Unnatural love initiates a murder disrupting nature's normal order, and that disruption cannot be allowed to persist. Divinely designed for order, peace, and abundance, nature waits to be healed by the truth implied by Banquo's ghost.

When Macbeth's confused and frightened guests leave his banquet prematurely, therefore, a false display of camaraderie and social bonding is revealed as a lie. Murder has and will continue to undermine community until the murderers are brought to justice. The appearance of Banquo's ghost is the eruption of Macbeth's bloody sin into the light of day, an event that will trigger Scotland's deliverance from the shackles of tyranny. Despite every effort the Macbeths make to hide their sin and bend fate to their liking, the truth eventually emerges like the naked, newborn babe blowing the horrid deed into every eye. Though evil currently rules the land, the young eventually bring future justice into the present.

Undaunted, Macbeth continues to struggle against the inevitable. The vision of Banquo's ghost prompts him to once again seek out the weird sisters for another glimpse into a future that he desperately wants to control. Once again, though, he is allowed to see only partial truths. The witches provide three more veiled prophecies. He is told to "beware Macduff." He is told that "no man of woman born shall harm" him. And he is told that he can never be defeated until "Great Birnam Wood to high Dunsinane hill shall come against him." As the witches indicated early in the play, their method is to provide their victim with a false sense of security, the purpose for which these latest prognostications are designed. To enhance that false promise of security, the obvious solution to the first warning is another murder, this time of Macduff. And because the remaining two prophesies seem impossible, his future safety and security seem within his grasp. Like the other prophecies, though, these prove to be equivocal as well. Desperate for the security his sin has precluded, Macbeth now hears what he wants to believe. Reckless hope blinds him to the realities that have begun to envelop him.

The first of these prophecies sets Macbeth's resolve to murder not only Macduff but his entire family. Macduff, however, has left for England to encourage Duncan's sons to raise an army that would free Scotland from bloody oppression. Unfortunately, this leaves his wife and children unprotected. When news of their murders reaches Macduff, his emotional response initiates an exchange with Duncan's son Malcolm that describes manhood much differently than Lady Macbeth's earlier perverted definition:

> Mal.   Be comforted,
>   Let's make us med'cines of our great revenge
>   To cure this deadly grief.
> Macd. He has no children. All my pretty ones?
>   Did you say all? O hell-kite! All?
>   What, all my pretty chickens, and their dam,
>   At one fell swoop?
> Mal.   Dispute it like a man.
> Macd.   I shall do so;
>   But I must also feel it as a man:
>   I cannot but remember such things were,
>   That were most precious to me. Did heaven look
>   on,
>   And would not take their part? Sinful Macduff,
>   They were all strook for thee! Naught that I am,
>   Not for their own demerits, but for mine.
>   (4.3.213-226)

Here, the loss of a wife and her precious children is cause for deeply felt grief and remorse because he wasn't there to protect them. Where Lady Macbeth had once prayed to "stop up th 'access and passage to remorse," Macduff suffers the loss of his family with genuine and heartfelt grief. An expression of sorrow does not make him less of a man. Moreover, his sense of moral responsibility for their safety enhances rather than detracts from his understanding of what it means to be a man, a father, a husband. Manhood does not prohibit emotions like grief or tears for the loss of loved ones. It is an indication, in fact, of a deeply felt human connection to family.

         Lady Macbeth's demonic prayer to dash the brains of her nursing child contrasts the vulnerable helplessness of babes with the unnatural cruelty she aspires to. But the murder of Macduff's little boy, who bravely defies his assassins, establishes once again that children will embody future vengeance. Banquo's son Fleance, supposedly the ancestor of King James, begins that theme. But Macduff's nameless son becomes the play's most vivid example. In his illuminating essay "The Naked Babe and the Cloak of Manliness," Cleanth Brooks writes:

> The logic of Macbeth's distraught mind . . . forces him to make war on children, a war which in itself reflects his desperation and is a confession of weakness. Macbeth's ruffians, for example, break into Macduff's castle and kill his wife and children. . . . But the pathos is not adventitious; the scene ties into the inner symbolism of the play. For the child, in his helplessness, defies the murderers. Its defiance testifies to the force which threatens Macbeth and which Macbeth cannot destroy. (400)

Macbeth's expectation that a babe would somehow blow the horrid deed in every eye is fulfilled by the death of Macduff's child. Time, anthropomorphized in Banquo's Fleance and Macduff's defiant little boy, will indeed redeem the Scottish nation. As Brooks suggests, the play's defiant juveniles constitute a corporate force that, despite their temporary helplessness, becomes the power that the perverse masculinity of Macbeth cannot possibly defeat.

Moreover, the genuine grief and anger of a father for the loss of a child, the very feelings Lady Macbeth sought to expunge, are essential parts of that universal force. As Malcolm implores his distraught countryman, "Be this the whetstone of your sword, let grief convert to anger, blunt not the heart, enrage it." And as the witches foresaw, Macduff, who comes to avenge his murdered child, will confront Macbeth in his final battle. The truth hidden in the witches' prognostication, the truth that the bloody tyrant could not comprehend, was that a cesarean procedure had ripped

Macduff "untimely" from his mother's womb. Since he is the man never born of woman, a man now full of righteous anger for his brave little boy's death, Macduff enacts justice upon a once brave and noble man whose crimes have left him isolated and completely dispirited.

This gradual devaluation of Macbeth's original stature is amplified further by images of a man who is too small for the robes in which he has been dressed, a child, ironically, wearing adult clothes. The first use of the image suggests a status that doesn't belong to him. "Why do you dress me in borrowed robes?" he asks Duncan's messengers who greet him as Thane of Cawdor, a title the witches had predicted would be his. Later, that image is enhanced as Macbeth's enemies discuss the impending confrontation with Scotland's bloody tyrant:

> Now does he feel
> His secret murthers sticking on his hands;
> Now minutely revolts upbraid his faith-breach;
> Those he commands move only in command,
> Nothing in love. Now does he feel his title
> Hang loose about him, like a giant's robe
> Upon a dwarfish thief. (5.2.17-22)

As king, Macbeth has broken all faith with his people. Despite his effort to wash away the blood, the incarnadine stains, "sticking on his hands," persist for all to see. As a result, he can no longer inspire love from those he commands, and the oversized cloak of royalty loosely covers "a dwarfish thief." This image of an overly large, ill-fitting garment on a child-like figure transforms the once manly warrior of the play's first scene into an absurd thief of royal authority. By deliberately choosing to devalue his ordained nature, this once noble person is reduced to a farcical version of the original. The true manliness of Macduff is meant to be measured against this ridiculous, dwarfish figure.

Even at this late date, however, repentance is still possible. Just as the thief crucified next to Jesus was forgiven at the moment of death, Macbeth's predecessor, the first Thane of Cawdor, regained some of his lost honor by repenting before his execution. But Macbeth's sins are so grievous they circumscribe his options and he believes he has little choice but to soldier grimly on. As the armies of his numerous enemies gather nearby, a desperate Macbeth senses defeat but cannot see any direction that could provide an escape from a life that has become devoid of meaning:

> For mine own good,
> All causes shall give way. I am in blood
> Stepp'd in so far that, should I wade no more,
> Returning were as tedious as go o'er. (3.5.134-137)

There is emotional exhaustion in that word "tedious," for having released this river of blood, he is unable to decide whether continuing to spill more is better than repenting and paying the consequences of his terrible misdeeds. The moral confusion initiated by witches still affects his thinking. Macbeth has reached this moment of weary nihilism because he yielded to equivocation, ambition, specious moral logic, and the repetitive murders that dulled his conscience so that even the horrid scream of his dying wife fails to affect his hardened heart. As he prepares for his final battle, he understands exactly what has been lost:

>   This push
> Will cheer me ever, or [disseat] me now.
> I have liv'd long enough: my way of life
> Is fall'n into the sear, the yellow leaf,
> And that which should accompany old age,
> As honor, love, obedience, troops of friends,
> I must not look to have; but in their stead,
> Curses, not loud, but deep, mouth-honor, breath,
> Which the poor heart would fain deny, and dare not.
>   (5.2.20-28)

Until now, Macbeth's cruelty had cowed every heart into sullen compliance, but resentment and dissension multiplied all around him. Community was destroyed. When the Macbeths chose to murder Duncan, they forfeited the blessings that come with righteous living, with living according to nature's design. There are consequences for sin, as Macbeth knew from the beginning, but he allowed the witches' half-truths and his wife's spurious moral logic to subvert his reason and overpower his conscience.

Entering with the tyrant's head, the victorious Macduff announces that, finally, "the time is free." Duncan's son Malcolm, now hailed as Scotland's king, thanks his loyal followers with language that promises a return to the benevolent nature of his murdered father:

> We shall not spend a large expense of time
> Before we reckon with your several loves,
> And make us even with you. . . .What's more to do,
> Which would be planted newly with the time,
> As calling home our exil'd friends abroad. . .
> This and what needful else
> That calls upon us, by the grace of Grace,
> We will perform in measure, time, and place. (5.9.27-39)

Free of Macbeth's bloody reign, Scotland can once again experience the blessings they had enjoyed from the good and generous Duncan. Under Malcolm's rule, loyalty and bravery will be repaid with royal largesse, exiled friends will be brought back home, and everything necessary will be "planted newly with the time. . . by the grace of Grace." Grace, God's restorative instrument, has redeemed both time and the Scottish nation.

Ironically, given the thematic, emotional, and spiritual prominence Shakespeare gives to many of his women characters, the evil side of the spiritual war waged against Macbeth is implemented largely through the weird sisters and his wife. Both exert the type of magic that deceives, coerces, and eventually damns a promising man's soul. Without much evidence of the countervailing magic of love, it is difficult to escape the sense of unrelieved doom in *Macbeth*. Having devoted two major plays to the process of temptation, Shakespeare turns his attention once more to a story about the dual morality of erotic desire, its ability to reduce and deform the sexual down to the elemental, which exists alongside its ability to inspire and transform. The next play, the tragedy of *Antony and Cleopatra,* reasserts Shakespeare's conviction about the nature of love and the role women play in teaching men its value. Though it is set in the pagan world of ancient Rome and Egypt, with no reference to Biblical verses or to God at all, the light of the divine still shines brightly through the play's magnificent female protagonist, Cleopatra. Rather than a denial of God's presence in the world, it's as if Shakespeare wanted to be very clear that, even if everything else in the world shows no evidence of the New Testament's loving Creator, that presence is always visible through the woman who gives herself wholeheartedly and generously to the man she loves. If God's presence can't be seen anywhere else, Shakespeare seems to be saying, it is visible there.

Antony and Cleopatra

Although the title suggests that *Antony and Cleopatra* has two main characters, the play is really about the effect the famed Egyptian queen has upon Antony, the Roman general who gave a pivotal speech in the earlier *Julius Caesar*. In a striking departure from the preceding tragedies with their male protagonists, Cleopatra emerges as the main character in this later play. In some respects, *Antony and Cleopatra* is closer to *Romeo and Juliet*, the only other Shakespearean tragedy named after two lovers, than it is to *Hamlet*, *Othello*, *Macbeth*, or *Lear*. Both are about couples who believe they're in love; both make distinctions between reductive and richer views of love; both end with deaths that are as much celebratory as somber.

But this play also has important differences from the exuberant, joyful love of Romeo and Juliet, so aptly captured in the courtly love poetry of the sonneteers. In that youthful tragedy, love is largely foiled by misfortune. An ongoing feud and a delayed letter outlining the plan to reunite Juliet with her husband are circumstances beyond the lovers' control. Except for those unfortunate events, love might very well have triumphed. But *Antony and Cleopatra* replaces that first, exciting blush of teenage romance with a sober awareness of the difficulties resulting from human fallibility that love must struggle to overcome. Compared to Romeo, Antony is hardly as clear-sighted about his feelings for Cleopatra, whose mercurial temperament mystifies him for most of the play. Moreover, misfortune has minimal impact on these middle-aged lovers who become ensnared in the political intrigues of men vying for power and control. The expansive scope of their language reflects a view of the world and their place in it that is based on an experience of authority. These are people who command the known world. They are rarely if ever victimized by fate or chance in any ordinary sense of that word. When Cleopatra asks the honest Enobarbus who was responsible for the disastrous naval retreat that begins Antony's decline, his answer is clear: "Antony only, that would make his will lord of his reason" (3.13.4-5).

Most probably written around 1606, a year or so after *Lear*, *Antony and Cleopatra* reflects Shakespeare's interest in Roman history, most of which he learned through Sir Thomas North's translation of Plutarch's *Lives*. Experimenting with transitions of unusually short scenes, which follow in quick succession to convey the chaos of battle, Shakespeare condenses ten years of political maneuvering into a rapid flow of events. No subplot impedes the play's relentless forward progress. Even the main plot is relatively simple. Antony dallies with Cleopatra in Egypt until his Roman wife, Fulvia, forms an alliance with Antony's brother to foment rebellion in Syria. Though the rebellion is quickly put down, Caesar assumes Antony had some part in the turmoil, and he is forced to return to Rome to explain his lack of attention to family and empire. To patch up their differences, Antony agrees to marry Caesar's sister, Octavia, even though he already longs to return to his Egyptian lover. Though Caesar explicitly warns Antony not to, he goes back to Alexandria, which gives Caesar an excuse to consolidate power by eliminating all his rivals. When the Roman army enters Egypt, Antony manages to lose two crucial naval battles by following Cleopatra's retreating forces. As Caesar's troops approach, Antony hears a false rumor that Cleopatra is dead and attempts to commit suicide. Mortally wounded and near death, he learns that Cleopatra is still alive and implores his attachés to bring him to her. Hiding high up in her pyramid, she pulls him up and tries to comfort him before he dies. Though Caesar promises to respect Cleopatra's wish to remain in Egypt after her lover's death, she correctly anticipates his plan to humiliate her by parading her through the streets of Rome. Partly to avoid this shame but mostly to fulfill her dream of becoming Antony's wife, she joins him in death by committing suicide. While Shakespeare's retelling of the story incorporates many of North's details, his version not only avoids North's moral condemnation of the Egyptian queen but transforms her death into a celebration of her steadfast love for Antony.

As *Macbeth* indicates, Shakespeare could make very clear distinctions between right and wrong behaviors, showing that tragic consequences usually follow when will or desire subverts judgment and conscience. Consequently, it may seem quite reasonable to assume, as Enobarbus does, that the sins of these two aging lovers make them responsible for the dire consequences that engulf them. In a very good essay on *Macbeth*, Dolores Cunningham concludes her analysis by applying *Macbeth*'s straightforward moral perspective to *Antony and Cleopatra:*

> Unless one accepts the distorted modern view of the play as a sermon on the glories of a noble love transcending everything in this world and the next, one sees that Antony and Cleopatra are presented as being so accustomed to the worship of sensual love as an absolute that they would rather lose everything than change their ways. The tragic outcome of *Antony and Cleopatra* is as firmly shaped as that of Macbeth by the failure to alter misguided affections and destructive choices. Both plays end in tragedy because the heroes and heroine give their hearts completely to those things (worldly glory, worldly love) which, however attractive, are defined in the plays as unworthy of such ultimate allegiance.... (79-80)

The judgment being applied here certainly sounds morally rigorous, but it isn't Shakespeare's. Projecting the lessons of *Macbeth* onto a very different play distorts the theatrical experience derived from the contrast between Rome's pragmatic emotional coldness and Egyptian warmth. Oblivious to the details and themes of earlier plays as recounted in previous chapters, such negative evaluations of the lovers never make clear why the Roman world is a better choice. Nor do they account for why this play devotes its final act to the Egyptian queen. Instead, it seems far more appropriate to point out a crucial similarity to this play's older sibling, *Romeo and Juliet,* which also distinguished streets marred by violence and juvenile bawdiness and a lyrical garden where reverence and love could bloom. In the end, there is remarkable consistency in Shakespeare's judgment of love's value in a world so easily susceptible to evil.

Because *Macbeth* is a play about murder and its consequences, it lends itself quite naturally to clear-cut moral judgments. *Antony and Cleopatra,* however, is about love, a presence, to paraphrase sonnet 116, whose light provides guidance through a wicked world but whose true worth remains mysterious and therefore under-appreciated. As dramatic material, love is far more complex, morally and emotionally, than an act of murder. After *Lear*'s brilliant examination of love and forgiveness, of reason's limitations and the need to mitigate its judgments with a sensitivity to those visceral feelings connecting family and community, the application of simple moral distinctions will miss much of this play's rich complexity, in particular, the nature and value of Cleopatra's love. As always, that complexity is examined through the play's multiplicity of viewpoints, divided roughly between the citizens of Rome and Egypt.

Though Shakespeare lifts some of North's descriptive passages almost verbatim, he largely resists the generally accepted view that Cleopatra corrupted Antony's Roman nobility. That view of her, however, is voiced by Demetrius, one of Antony's Roman attendants, at the very beginning of the play. As the two lovers cavort in the background, he speaks to another Roman:

> Nay, but this dotage of our general's
> O'erflows the measure. Those his goodly eyes,
> That o'er the files and musters of the war

> Have glow'd like plated Mars, now bend, now turn
> The office and devotion of their view
> Upon a tawny front; his captain's heart...
> Reneges all temper,
> And is become the bellows and the fan
> To cool a gipsy's lust.... Look where they come!
> Take but good note, and you shall see in him
> The triple pillar of the world transform'd
> Into a strumpet's fool. (1.1.1-13)

The displeasure expressed is not so much moral as it is an acknowledgment that Cleopatra has distracted Antony from his administrative and military duties. While Demetrius condemns the influence Cleopatra's sexual availability has on Antony, the remainder of the play explores the validity of this Roman view. His view should not be seen, therefore, as simply a statement of fact but more as an assertion to be verified. What, in fact, is Cleopatra's true nature? Having created female characters like Gertrude, Lady Macbeth, Goneril and Regan, Shakespeare clearly did not over-idealize or romanticize women. But he also created strong, positive female characters like Rosalind in *As You Like It*, Olivia and Viola in *Twelfth Night*, Desdemona in *Othello*, and Cordelia in *Lear*, all of whom know more about love than the men who profess their devotion and commitment.

Antony and Cleopatra answers this implied question about the Egyptian queen in several different ways. Besides these opening lines, the play provides additional perspectives on Cleopatra. She is viewed from the vantage of various Romans, from Antony's perspective, and from Cleopatra's own viewpoint. As a result of these different perspectives, a complex view of this legendary woman emerges, making the truth of Cleopatra's identity the play's central concern. But Shakespeare also verifies her identity and her significance by devoting the last act almost entirely to her, a dazzling theatrical finale. While Antony's decline and death are certainly pitiful, his dramatic role is really to demonstrate what effect she has on him, and so he disappears from view at the end of the fourth act. What remains after he is gone is the truth about the Egyptian queen's heart, and it is this final vision of feminine constancy that Shakespeare wants us to remember.

    That is not to say that Antony is irrelevant. The play provides sufficient justification for the love and admiration Cleopatra expresses for him. When Fulvia's rebellion and death compel Antony's return to Rome to deny any part in her misadventure, he patiently explains his actions to a suspicious Caesar. Quite magnanimously during that exchange, Antony never tries to use his age or his military experience to intimidate the much younger man. In fact, Antony freely admits that his Egyptian distractions have caused him to neglect his imperial duties. In another scene where Antony is not present, Caesar himself admires his rival's courage and self-discipline in the face of military hardship. And when, after Antony's final, inglorious defeat, his honest and loyal friend, Enobarbus, leaves him to join Caesar, Antony very generously sends the deserter's treasures after him. All of this shows Antony to be able, noble, generous, and, eventually, loving toward Cleopatra. With echoes from the New Testament, his destiny is a tragic paradox already familiar from Lear's story: he has to lose what's important, in this case, his imperial and military identity, before he can fully appreciate Cleopatra's value. His journey from that original ignorance to understanding demonstrates her effect on him. He always feels that magic in her presence but it isn't until he's on the verge of losing it that he appreciates what being near her, being part of her, has meant to him. Since this magic cannot be explained or defined, the final act belongs to her so that what Antony came to appreciate about the Egyptian queen is clear for all to see.

    Throughout Shakespeare's plays, the difficulty of seeing what is true about life has been a consistent motif. All too often, characters mistake the obvious as truth only to discover how blind they have been to deeper realities. As Heilman noted in the *Lear* chapter, such blindness has many causes: the opaqueness of the world, desire's ability to distort judgment, and the inaccuracies resulting from people's assumptions among them. To all the Romans who have seen Cleopatra, her sensuality, her reputation for an almost irresistible sexuality, are the most obvious facts. While this is what they see when she is near, her sexuality also embodies a force that, in many ways, stands in opposition to much of what Rome represents. Compared to the Roman preoccupations with empire, war, and death, Cleopatra is life force incarnate. Abundance and prosperity surround her, emanate from her. Having returned to Rome with Antony, Enobarbus describes life in Cleopatra's court and Antony's first, very dramatic meeting with the queen:

> Maec. Eight wild-boars roasted whole at a breakfast, and but twelve persons there; is this true?
>
> Eno. This was but as a fly by an eagle; we had much more monstrous matter of feast, which worthily deserv'd noting.
>
> Maec. She's a most triumphant lady, if report be square to her.
>
> Eno. When she first met Mark Antony, she purs'd up his Heart upon the river of Cydnus. . . .
> The barge she sat in, like a burnish'd throne,
> Burnt on the water. The poop was beaten gold,
> Purple the sails, and so perfumed that
> The winds were love-sick with them; the oars were silver
> Which to the tune of flutes kept stroke, and made
> The water . . .
> As amorous of their strokes. For her own person,
> It beggar'd all description: she did lie
> In her pavilion—cloth of gold, of tissue—
> O'er picturing that Venus where we see
> The fancy outwork nature. (2.2.179-201)

The Spartan-like Romans are fascinated by the seductive sensuality of the Egyptian queen and the sumptuous excesses of her court. Subtly modifying that first impression of the gypsy strumpet, Cleopatra's magic has even managed to invade Rome. Like Venus, the goddess of love, sex, beauty, and fertility, Cleopatra's magnetic feminine nature has seduced the Roman imagination. Her extravagant banquets, her fabulous wealth, her feminine beauty, her dramatic entrances, but most of all her sensual, sexual allure confirm her ability to command male attention. The very waves of the River Cydnus fall in love with her. The soldiers and generals listening to Enobarbus's description are enraptured by this report of Cleopatra's charms, though mere words cannot possibly match her actual presence. Even from faraway Alexandria, she can fire the imagination of men hardened by war and self-discipline. Though all of them disapprove of her effect on her distracted Roman lover, Agrippa cannot help but exclaim "O, rare for Antony!" For some critics, it must be said, Cleopatra's impact on others has less to do with feminine magic than with a penchant for self-dramatization. If this were true, however, the eventual betrayal of her emotional commitment to Antony would be necessary confirmation. Such a betrayal never comes.

If this kind of magic is an Egyptian trait, no one is so moved to describe Octavia, Caesar's sister, who is used to patch up the quarrel between her brother and Antony. Quickly following this enchanting description of Cleopatra, Maecenas expresses the hope that Octavia, betrothed now to Antony, will cool his desire for his Egyptian paramour:

> If beauty, wisdom, modesty, can settle
> The heart of Antony, Octavia is
> A blessed lottery to him. (2.2.240-242)

Though there's admiration here for this woman's virtues, there is no magic, nothing that compels attention or fires the imagination. The comparison is meant to point to something unique and special about the Egyptian queen. Ever the good Roman wife, Octavia proves her virtues to her new husband, but she eventually falls victim to the rivalry between spouse and brother. When Caesar informs her that Antony has returned to Egypt to be with Cleopatra, she can only exclaim, "Ay me, most wretched, That have my heart parted betwixt two friends That do afflict each other" (3.6.77-79)! Possessing no magic, Octavia can only function as a political expediency. While Caesar seems to love her, he is not above using her for the good of the empire, even though he is fully aware of Antony's Egyptian inclinations. Used by her own brother, Octavia does her duty, and in her compliant, pleasant, completely asexual demeanor, she is Cleopatra's complete opposite. Dutiful, devoted, loyal, even loving, there is much to admire in Octavia, but she will never ignite anyone's imagination the way Cleopatra can.

The frankly sexual relationship between Antony and Cleopatra certainly distinguishes this play from the far more innocent *Romeo and Juliet,* a play about desire rather than its fulfillment. But that innocence quickly dissipates in subsequent plays where sexual misconduct is linked to the bestial aspects of human behavior. Hamlet, obsessed with his mother's sexual union with the murderer Claudius, associates her with the disease that infects Denmark. Othello's love for the innocent Desdemona is transformed into jealous hatred by Iago's lurid whisperings. In terms brimming with disgust, the mad Lear associates female sexuality with the cruel ingratitude of his daughters, Goneril and Regan. Throughout these later plays, this sexual nausea reveals as much about the characters who exhibit it as it does about the object of their disgust.

Here, though, there's something qualitatively different about the treatment Cleopatra's sexual appeal receives, for, while she is really all about commitment, it is only the Romans who talk about her sensual and sexual nature. In her "salad days," she admits, she allowed herself to be carried to Julius Caesar in a mattress, but she is older now and she has Antony in her life. The problem is no longer with her sexuality but with reductive Roman assumptions about women and love. We have seen this reductive attitude before in Mercutio, in Touchstone, even in Hamlet. It is the sickness Iago passes on to Othello. As a Roman, Antony is not immune to this same emotional and moral hypocrisy. Because of that ignorance, he completely undervalues Cleopatra's true worth, he forges a doomed alliance with Caesar, he returns to Egypt for the wrong reasons, and he betrays the hard-won trust of his soldiers by expecting Cleopatra to fight alongside him in the Roman fashion, ignoring how vulnerable her love has made him to her whims and fears.

Besides the erotic allusions early in the play, Cleopatra's sexual nature figures in other ways. It is part of her past connection to Rome, for Julius Caesar, the father of this play's Octavius Caesar, had a child with her, which the Romans in this play view with flippant condescension. Listening to Enobarbus describe Cleopatra's grand first encounter with Antony, Agrippa is reminded of her affair with Julius Caesar. "Royal wench!" he begins, "She made great Caesar lay his sword to bed; He ploughed her, and she cropp'd" (2.2.227ff). Egyptian fecundity is present even in this condescending quip. Because of her colorful past, the Romans feel comfortable speaking of her in this juvenile, prurient manner. For them, she is defined by her previous sexual indiscretions, which, like Antony, limits their understanding of who she is now. Consequently, that past sexual behavior has also become part of her present. It defines her even for Antony. With typical Roman aplomb, the newly married Antony decides to return to Egypt because, as he says privately, "I 'th 'East my pleasure lies." At this point in his relationship with Cleopatra, his attraction doesn't go any deeper than the physical. What he fails to comprehend, though, is that Cleopatra understands that her sexuality is the one way she can communicate love to a man who is only capable of appreciating its physical expression. That much they share in common right now. Her trust he will eventually understand something more than that is why she alone owns the play's final act.

But the agricultural allusions in the memory of great Caesar plowing Cleopatra so she would crop also suggest that Cleopatra's sexuality, her physical desire for the man she loves, aligns her with nature's purpose. This notion is not unique to *Antony and Cleopatra*. Lady Macbeth tries to violate this principle with her "unsex me" speech. Many of the comedies and the late romances, like *The Tempest*, associate love with lavish feasts and bounteous nature. Here in *Antony and Cleopatra*, the Egyptian queen's dominion, the very land she presides over, partakes of Cleopatra's fertility. After Antony manages to patch up his first quarrel with Caesar, he shares some of his observations about life in Egypt with his Roman companions:

> Thus do they, sir; they take the flow o' th' Nile,
> By certain scales i' th' pyramid; they know,
> By th' height, the lowness, or the mean, if dearth
> Or foison follow. The higher Nilus swells,
> The more it promises; as it ebbs, the seedsman,
> Upon the slime and ooze scatters his grain,
> And shortly comes the harvest. (2.7.17-23)

As we have seen before, when Duncan observes the swallow's procreant cradles near Macbeth's castle, the fertility and abundance of nature reflect the moral framework of a divinely created world that, Biblically, is under man's dominion and that reflects God's desire to provide. Egypt, a land where new life emerges out of the mud and slime of the Nile, personifies the life-giving force of its queen. The play's many allusions to nature's abundant and fertile goodness, therefore, confirm the virtue of the sexuality associated with her. Love and sex are part of nature's creative force, and the lovers desire for union is what, metaphorically, separates Egypt from Rome, an empire built on rapacious conquest.

Unlike Egypt, a land of cyclical fertility, Rome is associated with war and military discipline. The contrast between a seemingly ascetic Rome and sensual Egypt is, of course, deliberate. Virtue and moral rectitude appear to reside in Rome; weak, self-indulgent sensuality, at least from the Roman point of view, dominates Egypt. Caesar, recalling Antony's exploits, cannot help but admire his rival's incredible perseverance in the face of war's hardships. "When thou once Was beaten from Modena," he muses:

> . . . at thy heel
> Did famine follow, whom thou fought'st against
> . . . with patience more
> Than savages could suffer. Thou didst drink
> The stale of horses and the gilded puddle
> Which beasts would cough at; thy palate then did deign
> The roughest berry on the rudest hedge . . . On the Alps
> It is reported thou didst eat strange flesh
> Which some did die to look on. . . . . and all this
> Was borne so like a soldier, that thy cheek
> So much as lank'd not. (1.5.56-71)

In contrast to the abundant life of Egypt, self-denial in the face of impoverishment is what built the Roman Empire and therefore what the Romans value. Before he met Cleopatra, this was Antony's identity. This masculine determination is why the play often associates him with Hercules, the demi-god of legendary strength and endurance. The contrast with the luxurious beds of Egypt, where Antony now finds his pleasure, suggests that he is at a crossroad where self-denial and desire point in different directions.

Circumstances eventually force Antony to choose between them. The choice is reminiscent of Hal's dilemma in

1Henry4 where the young prince must choose between the frivolous and self-indulgent play of Fat Jack Falstaff, stuffed with sack and capons, and the taxing duties of the throne. For Hal, a young man looking to prove his worth, it is relatively easy to forgo the temptations that Falstaff represents. He understands that duty and self-control are what the English throne needs after his father took the crown from Richard. Circumstances are much different between Rome and Egypt, however. First, unlike Falstaff, Cleopatra will prove to be much more than the self-indulgent sensualist who exists to tempt Antony into a depraved indifference to anything besides pleasure. And unlike Hal, Antony has already proven his value to Rome. But his relationship with Cleopatra promises wholly different emotions and commitments that challenge him to develop unrealized aspects of his identity. Standing at the crossroad, Antony must decide either to continue thinking, acting, speaking in the role he's always known or to embrace an entirely different mode of being.

Making that decision occupies most of *Antony and Cleopatra*'s events, and everything depends on Antony's ability to evaluate Cleopatra accurately. For a Roman steeped in the ways of war and unfamiliar with liaisons based on love rather than political expediency, such discernment does not come easily. At first, Antony is ignorant of the emotional bond that has formed out of his physical relationship with Cleopatra. Though he believes returning to Egypt after the disastrous marriage to Octavia is only for his "pleasure," it is obvious that physical union has created far deeper though little understood emotional bonds. Revealing more truth about him than he realizes, the reference to pleasure trivializes what actually draws him back to Egypt. Though he does not yet possess the vocabulary to define it more precisely, he is drawn to whatever is so captivating, so irresistible about Cleopatra's magic. The very different characterizations of Octavia and Cleopatra are meant to emphasize the magical allure of the Egyptian, and wherever the power of that force is not recognized, as it isn't in Rome, the fullness of life is no longer available. People and events continue, but it is an existence without life as it was meant to be. Although he cannot resist the power of this life force, Antony's trivialization of sex as mere pleasure reveals his ignorance of love's magic.

Whether or not Antony understands the strength of the bond that ties him to Cleopatra, she has placed considerable hope in the resilience of their connection, for she continuously tests those bonds in an effort to make them more secure, to encourage him to choose her. Right from the start, it is clear she wants something more from her relationship with Antony than he does. Their first appearance on stage begins with some playful banter. She asks him a question that should resonate after *Lear*:

> Cleo: If it be love indeed, tell me how much?
> Ant: There's beggary in the love that can be reckon'd.
> Cleo. I'll set a bourn how far to be belov'd.
> Ant. Then must thou needs find out new heaven, new earth. (1.1.14-17)

In the afterglow, love is huge and boundless. But this good-humored playfulness is quickly undermined by a troubling insecurity hiding in Cleopatra's thoughts. Well-schooled in the ways of men who too easily exaggerate professions of love to take what they want, Cleopatra—unlike Lear—does not accept Antony's words at face value. Her playful repartee quickly turns petulant when she recalls his infidelity to Fulvia, his Roman wife. "Why should I think you can be mine, and true... Who have been false to Fulvia?" she asks indignantly. That betrayal threatens her desire for his loyalty to her, and the conversation becomes tense. Envious of Fulvia's status as Antony's wife, Cleopatra's jealousy acknowledges a harsh truth: Antony has loyalties elsewhere.

But when news of Fulvia's rebellion sparks Antony's determination to return to Rome, she relents with touching vulnerability. Afraid she might be losing him, her words reveal both helplessness and the depth of her emotional confusion:

> Ant. I'll leave you, lady.
> Cleo. Courteous lord, one word:
> Sir, you and I must part, but that's not it;
> Sir, you and I have lov'd, but there's not it.
> That you know well. Something it is I would---
> O, my oblivion is a very Antony,
> And I am all forgotten. (1.3.86-92)

Unable to complete her thoughts coherently, she tries several times to express her fear and sorrow at their parting.

But to Antony, the melodramatic reference to his absence as her oblivion sounds emotionally manipulative, and his Roman determination is replaced by exasperation. "But that your royalty Holds idleness your subject," he replies, "I should take you for idleness itself." Egyptian idleness, according to Antony, allows time for love, but when the more important business of empire beckons, love must be put aside. While this position is understandable, his impatience with her turns it into a harsh, unwarranted, personal rebuke. Trying to put any bruised feelings aside, she begins with a reminder of her investment in their relationship but quickly moves on to an apology that is both intimate and dignified:

> 'Tis sweating labor
> To bear such idleness so near the heart
> As Cleopatra this. But, sir, forgive me,
> Since my becomings kill me when they do not
> Eye well to you. Your honor calls you hence,
> Therefore be deaf to all my unpitied folly,
> And all the gods go with you! (1.3.93-99)

With the kind of tempered fortitude reminiscent of Viola's patience with Orsino in *Twelfth Night*, Cleopatra rejects his assertion that she is the queen of all idleness by reminding him that it is difficult work to bear the weight of an emotionally uncaring Roman so near her heart. Her sexual metaphor neatly highlights the irony of a physical union that masks the labor required to overcome his emotional distance. Very aware of his preoccupation with his own pleasure, she is anything but idle. Though it isn't on the grand scale of empires, Cleopatra's work is to bring Antony to a deeper appreciation of her love.

In her precarious emotional situation, therefore, she cares very much about his perception of her, and so she regains emotional balance and finds the strength to wish him well. She recognizes that her self-concern is secondary to the honor he values, so go he must. This is the Egyptian form of Antony's much-admired fortitude and generosity. In the face of his rebuke, she accepts his determination to leave with uncommon grace. Though her emotional turmoil is evident, it is hard to see this as anything less than the sacrificial love exhibited by other Shakespearean women in other plays. Even if Antony is at first blind to her worth, her words not only validate what is in Cleopatra's heart but also demonstrate the emotional strength that will eventually transform his as well.

Additional confirmation of her love for Antony comes in several subsequent scenes, leaving no doubt that her devotion to him is genuine. Before she hears of the marriage to Octavia, she implores her servant to bring the sleeping potion, mandragora, so she might "sleep out this great gap of time My Antony is away" (1.4.4-5). Since he's already in Rome, there is no artifice at all in her longing to be with him again. Even when she learns of the marriage, she works to recover her equanimity. At first, her ire falls upon the hapless messenger, whom she strikes. But remorse quickly sets in. Eager to size up her competition, she is now desperate to learn all she can about Octavia's appearance, which the trembling messenger describes with great tact. Encouraged by this artful information, Cleopatra concludes that "all may be well enough." She is undeterred. To weaker personalities, the second Roman marriage might seem an insurmountable challenge, but, like the earlier Juliet, the strength of her love waivers only momentarily. Though Antony has yet to exhibit any similar loyalty to their relationship, hers remains steadfast no matter the circumstances, the North Star to his wandering heart.

    Cleopatra certainly has her faults. She can be melodramatic when it suits her, as her jealous outburst over Fulvia shows. Her fears sometimes get the best of her, as they do when she flees the two naval battles that turn the tide against Antony. And she is not above faking her death in an ill-conceived effort to assuage Antony's rage. Yet, at this moment, she faces this very difficult test of her fidelity in a way that proves the persistence of her love. By doing so, ironically, she shows herself to be a better Roman than the Romans.

    While loyalty might seem a very Roman value, much of what happens in the empire's capital reveals the hollowness of their professed reverence for honor, nobility, and virtue. There is a sense in this play that, after the assassination of Julius Caesar, Rome has changed, and not entirely for the better. Now, Antony, Lepidus, and Octavius Caesar, the son of Julius, share the empire's governmental and military responsibilities. Of these three triumvirs, Octavius is considerably younger than the other two, but he wears his authority well. During the conversation where Antony explains his dalliance in Egypt while a wife and a brother rebel against the empire, Antony is always on the defensive, protecting himself from Caesar's dogged accusations.

    But Caesar's confidence is not the only quality that distinguishes him from Antony, a man who is generous, who is self-disciplined in war, and who, perhaps because of his age, shows no signs of the imperial ambition that drives Caesar. In this world, a man's character has little to do with his worldly fortunes. According to a soothsayer Antony encounters before the nuptials to Octavia, Caesar is simply favored by luck and good fortune. "If thou dost play with him at any game," the oracle says, "Thou art sure to lose." And when Antony asks him whose fortunes shall rise, the soothsayer's answer is unequivocal: "Caesar's." Acknowledging the truth of this prophecy, Antony is now motivated to return to Egypt, to escape the luckier Caesar, despite his promise to marry Caesar's sister. Defying all logic and political common sense, the decision is evidence of the powerful hold that Cleopatra's magic has on this Roman.

Despite his rational and pragmatic nature, however, Caesar is not entirely without his own virtues. He not only admires Antony's military accomplishments but also expresses what seems to be a genuine love for his sister. With considerable foresight, he carefully warns Antony before the marriage:

> You take from me a great part of myself;
> Use me well in't. Sister, prove such a wife
> As my thoughts make thee. . . .Most noble Antony,
> Let not the piece of virtue which is set
> Betwixt us, as the cement of our love
> To keep it builded, be the ram to batter
> The fortress of it; for better might we
> Have lov'd without this means, if on both parts
> This be not cherish'd. (3.2.24-32)

Caesar is very transparent about his reasons for this marriage and the potential danger that it represents. But his view of it, as it has been for all the Romans, is entirely pragmatic. While the marriage is intended to "cement" the love and respect between the two men, trusting Antony to revere and cherish his sister, this "piece of virtue," is a risk for all involved.

In matters politic, Caesar proves to be a much better tactician. Far more than Antony, he understands what is at stake in this marriage. Being a Roman, he views the purpose of this marriage almost entirely in rational and political terms. Unlike the emotional forces at work in Antony's relationship with Cleopatra, love has nothing to do with this very Roman arrangement. Octavia simply has a duty "to prove such a wife" as Caesar needs her to be. It is possible to see this as a cynical ploy to trap Antony in a relationship that cannot last and that will therefore provide Caesar with the excuse he needs to eliminate all potential challengers to his ambition. But Antony never expresses any imperial ambitions. It seems more thematically plausible, therefore, that Caesar's very pragmatic view of marriage aligns with what other Romans have said about love, which, as their comments about Cleopatra show, is largely utilitarian. No one in Rome, Caesar included, comprehends the kind of magic and power embodied in a woman like Cleopatra. They may recognize it, as their recollection of the Egyptian queen in her barge indicates, but they don't understand or appreciate it. Of all the Romans, Antony alone responds deeply to her love. Though he doesn't understand why at first, his actions show that, somehow, at this time of his life, he values it more than he values what Rome has to offer. Where Caesar cunningly uses power to realize his ambitions, that pragmatic realism limits his understanding of the heart. Antony is different. His generous, magnanimous spirit distinguishes him from all the other Romans. And because of this generosity, he possesses an openness to the full possibility of life that allow him to respond to Cleopatra.

From the Roman perspective, however, Antony has wasted precious time in sensual idleness. With a certain smug, moral superiority, they blame Cleopatra for this dotage, this decline. Pompey, who has raised a naval force to threaten the triumvirs, hears that Antony has returned to Rome. The news surprises him and he offers a mock prayer:

> But all the charms of love,
> Salt Cleopatra, soften thy wan'd lip!
> Let witchcraft join with beauty, lust with both,
> Tie up the libertine in a field of feasts,
> Keep his brain fuming; epicurean cooks
> Sharpen with cloyless sauce his appetite.... (1.5.20-25)

As Pompey's food imagery suggests, Antony is in Egypt feeding his appetites while true Romans are busily working to shape the world. But underneath the rational, virtuous-seeming surface of Rome lurks considerable moral dishonesty too, as Pompey's actions against the empire suggest. Though his desire is for power rather than love, he too is feeding an appetite. In plays like *Othello* and *Lear,* evil blossoms where misunderstood or unacknowledged desires transform reason's virtues into rationalizations. If Egyptian sexuality tempts Antony toward love, the Roman temptation is clearly power.

To commemorate the truce as well as the impending marriage, the triumvirs and their friends hold a celebration where wine flows freely. Even the normally cautious Caesar partakes. Quietly at the party's fringe, though, Menas whispers to Pompey that he has an opportunity to assassinate the others and seize sole control of the empire. Having just reconciled with the triumvirs, though, Pompey resists the temptation. Rather than condemning this amoral proposition, Pompey weakly mutters that, had the assassinations occurred without informing him, he would have been able to claim plausible deniability. Because power and dominance trump moral integrity, Roman virtue is largely a sham. Frustrated by such indecision, Menas disavows any further loyalty to Pompey. "For this, I'll never follow thy pall'd fortunes more. Who seeks, and will not take when once 'tis offer'd, Shall never find it more" (2.7.81ff).

Proof of that hypocrisy comes quickly. Unlike Pompey, Caesar does not hesitate to act when a similar opportunity is presented to him. For daring to raise a navy to challenge the Triumvir, Pompey is eliminated, and, with total power within his grasp, the third triumvir, Lepidus, is clearly next. Antony remains with Octavia long enough to witness the beginning of this effort to consolidate power. Offended by Caesar's behavior, he voices his complaint to his new wife:

> Nay, nay, Octavia, not only that---
> That were excusable. . . . but he hath wag'd
> New wars 'gainst Pompey; made his will, and read it
> To public ear;
> Spoke scantly of me; when perforce he could not
> But pay me terms of honor. . . . (3.4.1-7)

Caesar's political realism offends Antony's sense of honor, though he himself provides several examples of marital and emotional disloyalty. Even virtuous-seeming Roman women are subjects of a similar moral equivocation. In contrast to the self-assurance of a woman like Cleopatra, Octavia's reply to Antony is passive and perplexed. "Husband win, win brother. . . no midway 'twixt these extremes at all." In a marriage based on duty rather than love, she is unable to stand firmly with Antony, so even though he sends her to plead his case to Caesar, he follows his heart back to Egypt where he will "raise the preparation of a war." Both men have now made their fateful choice. But the circumstances that led them to this point reveal the hypocrisy of the Roman allegiance to honor and virtue.

This Rome, then, is a pale shadow of that city's former golden age. Instead, virtuous-sounding men speak of honor as they wage war against admired elders and leave dutiful and innocent wives in the name of pleasure. Temptation is rejected, not for any valid reason, but because it has the wrong optics. With a strange little scene, the play argues that Pompey and Caesar's rationalized calculation of self-interest has infected every level of Roman society. In it, an obscure Roman lieutenant refuses to take military action because it might make him look too ambitious in the eyes of his superiors. "Better to leave undone," he begins, "than by our deed Acquire too high a fame when him we serve's away." He goes on to cite the example of one of Sossius's lieutenants whose "quick accumulation of renown, which he achiev'd by th 'minute, lost his favor" (3.1.16-20). Inaction, the argument goes, will be more acceptable than any action that might offend an ambitious and easily jealous superior. The moral rot evident in the resolution of Pompey's rebellion and Caesar's ambition is prevalent throughout the empire. From top to bottom, Roman values have been corrupted by various human weaknesses, and that corruption begins to make what Egypt offers considerably more attractive.

Because a more politically cunning Pompey could have easily agreed to Menas's assassination proposal, military skill or even political cunning alone cannot explain Caesar's decision to seize power, though he certainly has both. His moment has simply arrived. As the Egyptian sorcerer had foreseen, Caesar was fortunate that Menas spoke to a man who cared more for his public reputation than for power. Nevertheless, though Pompey's temptation goes nowhere, the brush with treachery prepares us for the Machiavellian tactics that the young Caesar employs. Pompey hesitates and is lost. Caesar isn't the kind of man to make the same mistake. As soon as he learns that Antony has betrayed his sister, Caesar begins to secure all remaining imperial power for himself. After he eliminates Pompey and Lepidus, he then prepares to move on Antony, who is now in Egypt. Despite his admiration and respect for Antony's military experience, Caesar uses the dishonor shown to his sister to rationalize what he desires most: the power to rule a vast empire without complications or interference. Their respective fates now sealed, both men have made their choice.

Antony, who has been associated with the demi-god, Hercules, throughout the play, engages Caesar in two separate naval battles, even though his soldiers warn him that his advantage is on land. Encouraged by Cleopatra, he ignores the warning, only to suffer humiliating defeat after leaving the fray prematurely to follow the queen's fleeing ships. By allowing love to influence a military decision, Antony is defeated by those very same emotions. One of Antony's soldiers tries to warn his superior of his tactically foolish choice to fight at sea, which Cleopatra prefers. "We are women's men," he laments, and so a woman must now console a defeated Antony:

> Cleo. O my lord, my lord,
> Forgive my fearful sails! I little thought
> You would have followed.
> Ant. Egypt, thou knew'st too well
> My heart was to thy rudder tied by th' strings,
> And thou shouldst tow me after. O'er my spirit
> Thy full supremacy thou knew'st and that
> Thy beck might from the bidding of the gods
> Command me.
> Cleo. O, my pardon! (3.11.54-62)

Unfortunately, this is precisely what Cleopatra didn't know about Antony until this moment, and the realization renders her all but speechless. In a moment of joy mixed with profound sorrow, she can only ask for his forgiveness. Antony's deteriorating fortunes are clear when, following this defeat, he dares great Caesar to single combat. It is an empty, pathetic challenge that eventually leads the very loyal Enobarbus to desert the general he loves too much and whose decline he cannot bear to witness. The paradox, of course, is that Antony's defeat finally reveals how deeply her love is now rooted in his heart. Out of this enormous loss of worldly power and status comes much personal gain.

As soon as he has declared his love, however, it is put to the test, for Caesar sends an emissary to entice Cleopatra to leave Antony. Pretending to be receptive to the idea, Cleopatra entertains the messenger, who is about to kiss her hand when Antony reappears and completely misinterprets her intentions. He is irate, has the messenger whipped, and then sends the man back to Caesar before turning to Cleopatra in a cold fury that gives way quickly to self-pity:

> Ant. You were half blasted ere I knew you, ha?
> Have I my pillow left unpress'd in Rome,

>   Forborne the getting of a lawful race,
>   And by a gem of women, to be abus'd
>   By one that looks on feeders?
>   . . . .
> Cleo.   Have you done yet?
> Ant.   Alack, our terrene moon
>   Is now eclips'd, and it portends alone
>   The fall of Antony.
> Cleo.   I must stay his time.
> Ant.   To flatter Caesar, would you mingle eyes
>   With one that ties his points?
> Cleo.   Not know me yet?
> Ant.   Cold-hearted toward me?
> Cleo.   Ah, dear, if it be so,
>   From my cold heart let heaven engender hail,
>   And poison it in the source, and the first stone
>   Drop in my neck; as it determines, so
>   Dissolve my life! (3.13.153-162)

There is no pretense, no provocative play-acting for attention here. Her denial of any indifference toward him is absolute and total. Undaunted by his fury, the constancy of Cleopatra's love is unmistakable in that simple, direct question "Not know me yet?" Finally responding to her authenticity, Antony is encouraged enough to regroup and fight his second and this time decisive battle with Caesar. But not before Cleopatra tenderly helps Antony put on his armor, a dramatization of a favorite Renaissance icon of Venus similarly helping Mars. Soon after, Enobarbus hears music underground, which he interprets as the spirit of Hercules abandoning Antony. Though the fading Herculean music signals that Antony's martial and imperial decline is well underway, the visual reference to Mars and Venus indicates that his devotion now belongs to a different Roman deity. Venus has superseded Mars. The transformation of his identity is all but complete.

The second and final battle with Caesar ends like the first. This time, though, afraid of Antony's anger, Cleopatra sends word from her pyramid that she has died, which redoubles Antony's sense of loss and provokes him to fall on his own sword. But he botches the suicide only to learn that the queen is still alive. The time for anger having passed, he asks to be brought to the pyramid where he can speak his final words to her. There, she draws him up in a symbolic act of elevation where they exchange their last thoughts. He very generously assumes all blame. Full of remorse and sorrow, she is confronted by the limitations of her love:

> Ant. Not Caesar's valor hath o'erthrown Antony,
> But Antony's hath triump'd on itself.
> Cleo. So it should be, that none but Antony
> Should conquer Antony, but woe 'tis so!
> Ant. I am dying, Egypt, dying; only
> I here importune death awhile, until
> Of many thousand kisses the poor last
> I lay upon thy lips.
> Cleo. . . . But come, come, Antony---
> Help me, my women--- we must draw thee up. . . .
> Ant. O, quick, or I am gone.
> Cleo. Here's sport indeed! How heavy weighs my lord!
> Our strength is all gone into heaviness,
> That makes the weight. . . .Die when thou hast liv'd,
> Quicken with kissing. Had my lips that power,
> Thus would I wear them out. (4.15.14-39)

As in the sepulcher with Romeo and Juliet, death begins to be associated with love. This second allusion to Antony's weight recalls that earlier sexual reference when he was about to leave for Rome, as does her use of the word "sport." But the earlier irony has now been replaced by a deep pathos, for the joy of bearing his weight is intermixed with desperation and sorrow. Any blame or anger notably absent, his thoughts turn to her welfare as he implores her to befriend Caesar after he's gone. "Of Caesar seek your honor, with your safety," he instructs, to which she replies, "My resolution and my hands I'll trust,

None about Caesar." Though she is already resolute for death, his passing elicits a moving tribute to the man she has long loved with all her heart:

> Noblest of men, woo't die?
> Hast thou no care of me? Shall I abide
> In this dull world, which in thy absence is
> No better than a sty? O, see, my women;
>   [Antony dies.]
> The crown o' th' earth doth melt. My lord!
> O, wither'd is the garland of the war,
> The soldier's pole is fall'n. Young boys and girls
> Are level now with men; the odds is gone,
> And there is nothing left remarkable
> Beneath the visiting moon [faints.] (4.14.59-68)

Throughout, Cleopatra's desire for Antony's love has been constant. She has worked, to use her word, to bring him to a realization of that truth. If sex and pleasure were the only vocabulary of love he understood, she would fearlessly use that to help him see more, and she returns to that theme here because it has been their common ground. But to her, he was far more than the physical aspects of love, and she pays homage, as she should, to his incomparable nobility. A bit later, in magnificent, almost dreamy poetry, her admiration for Antony is all but overwhelming:

> His legs bestrid the ocean, his rear'd arm
> Crested the world, his voice was propertied
> As all the tuned spheres. . . .
> But when he meant to quail and shake the orb,
> He was as rattling thunder. For his bounty,
> There was no winter in't; an autumn it was
> That grew the more by reaping. . . .In his livery
> Walk'd crowns and crownets; realms and islands were
> As plates dropp'd from his pocket. (5.2.82-92)

This is clearly Cleopatra expressing what she admired about Antony, but it is easy to miss the remarkable within the familiar. She knows that Antony could very easily have been, like Caesar is now, the ruler of the known world. Despite his defeat on the water at Actium, he was a better soldier on land than his rival, but he sacrificed all that was possible for her, and he did so because he lacked the bold and cunning opportunism of this Caesar, who should remind us of another opportunist, Henry Bolingbroke of *1Henry4*. In Caesar's case, he was willing to risk his sister in a marriage to a man whose heart was obviously elsewhere. What part of that decision was sincere and what part was calculated to purposely fail for Caesar's advantage? Cunning is not an attribute Shakespeare respected, as Iago should remind us. No, what Cleopatra admires about Antony is his generosity, his carelessness about things of this world, those "realms and islands" that dropped from his pocket in exchange for something of real value. That matters to her, greatly. The awe and gratitude for what Antony was willing to give up for her are unmistakable.

The play begins with two very different views of the Egyptian queen. Which of those is true has been answered and will receive further confirmation by her death. Her love, which the very limited Roman imagination mistook for something shallow and small, is anything but. As she claimed early on, she alone would set the boundaries for love, and those boundaries far exceed the ordinary, exceedingly shallow version that occupies Roman imaginations. The play's final act, almost entirely given over to her, is a tribute to the magic and the mystery of the kind of devotion that lovingly envisions a giant bestriding seas and continents, shedding the wealth of empires in careless generosity from his pockets.

After Antony's death, Cleopatra is engaged in a psychological war with Caesar over her fate. Though at first she declares her intention to follow Antony, she pretends to be convinced by Caesar's assurances of a safe and dignified future. Getting final confirmation that he really intends to parade her through the streets of Rome where, as she imagines it, "I shall see some squeaking Cleopatra boy my greatness I' the posture of a whore" (5.2.219ff), she declares, "I am again for Cydnus to meet Mark Antony." Ready, that is, to re-enact their first, very dramatic encounter as she sailed seductively in colorful barges toward the man she would come to love. Deserving of an extensive and close reading, the death that follows is at once magnificently dramatic and weighty with tragic paradox.

Just as death awaited Duncan inside a castle adorned with procreant cradles, emblems of Egyptian fertility and abundance also frame Cleopatra's demise. In rhythm with the Nile, Egypt accepts that decay and death are inseparable from life, and as Hamlet said, the readiness is all. When the "rural fellow" enters with his basket of figs hiding the poisonous asps, she calmly observes that "he brings me liberty." Because death now represents deliverance from a world without her beloved, her determination is absolute:

> ... I have nothing
> Of woman in me; now from head to foot
> I am marble-constant; now the fleeting moon
> No planet is of mine. (5.2.238-241)

As she faces her final moments, Cleopatra steels herself by denying feminine weakness and embracing the marble determination of Rome, sentiments that echo Lady Macbeth's "unsex me" speech. But the sentiment originates from a desire for love, not cruelty. Although she has already proven that her constancy to Antony is more Roman than Egyptian, she cannot undo the essential, feminine quality that makes her Cleopatra, again reminiscent of Lady Macbeth's inability to do what she asked of her husband. Like a good wife, Cleopatra wants to look her best when she meets Antony in the hereafter. Having dressed in her "best attire," she continues her journey to meet her lover again:

> Give me my robe, put on my crown, I have
> Immortal longings in me.... Methinks I hear
> Antony call; I see him rouse himself
> To praise my noble act. I hear him mock
> The luck of Caesar.... Husband, I come!
> Now to that name my courage prove my title!
> I am fire and air; my other elements
> I give to baser life. (5.2.280-290)

Of the four elements known to Renaissance science, earth and water are the lower two, fire and air belong to the heavens. Hearing the voice of her lover, Cleopatra is now joyously determined for the latter. Whatever else has been said by other Romans, be they characters of this play or simply those who judge her by overly simple moral dichotomies, this is magnificent, emotional poetry, full of longing for union with the beloved. It is the first and only time she calls Antony husband, implicitly gaining the concomitant title for herself that she earns by courageously letting go of "baser life" and giving herself over to "fire and air." When her maidservant, Iras, falls, mortally poisoned by the aspic on Cleopatra's lips, the queen cannot resist one final sexual allusion. It is an essential part of who she is with Antony. Looking at Iras, she notes:

> If thou and nature can so gently part,
> The stroke of death is as a lover's pinch,
> Which hurts and is desired. (5.2.294-296)

Worried that Iras will reach Antony first, Cleopatra is moved to take the final, fatal step into fire and air:

> This proves me base.
> If she first meet the curled Antony,
> He'll make demand of her, and spend that kiss

>   Which is my heaven to have. Come, thou mortal wretch
>   [to the asp, which she applies to her breast]
>   With thy sharp teeth this knot intrinsicate
>   Of life at once untie. Poor venomous fool. . . .
>   O, couldst thou speak,
>   That I might hear thee call great Caesar ass
>   Unpolicied.
> Char. O eastern star!
> Cleo.   Peace! Peace!
>   Dost thou not see my baby at my breast,
>   That sucks the nurse asleep?
> Char.   O, break! O, break!
> Cleo. As sweet as balm, as soft as air, as gentle---
>   O Antony! (5.2.300-313)

If Antony is now husband through this death, Cleopatra simultaneously becomes wife and mother both. It is difficult to witness this and not feel that she has triumphed, not only over Caesar, that "ass unpolicied," but over death itself. Yes, she probably has, as Caesar points out when he sees her lifeless body, "pursu'd conclusions infinite of easy ways to die." But her "immortal longings" have magically transformed any fear of death she might have had into something that mimics wedded bliss. What was little more than rhetorical flourish in *Romeo and Juliet* is much more explicit in his last tragedy. It's as if Shakespeare wants us to fully understand what was significant about Juliet's decision in that tomb. Once again, we witness another remarkable woman passing fearlessly through death into a love perfected from simple lust of the flesh into something truly noble, splendid, and transcendent.

Not all critics are so sanguine about the implications of these deaths. In a very thoughtful essay, John Danby writes:

> The Roman condemnation of the lovers is obviously inadequate. The sentimental reaction in their favor is equally mistaken. There is no so-called "love-romanticism" in the

play. The flesh has its glory and passion, its witchery. Love in *Antony and Cleopatra* is both of these. The love of Antony and Cleopatra, however, is not asserted as a "final value." The whole tenor of the play, in fact, moves in an opposite direction. Egypt is the Egypt of the Biblical glosses: exile from the spirit, thralldom to the flesh-pots, diminution of human kindness. To go further still in sentimentality and claim that there is a "redemption" motif in Antony and Cleopatra's love is an even more violent error. . . . The fourth and fifth acts of *Antony and Cleopatra* are not epiphanies. They are the ends moved to by that process whereby things rot themselves with motion. . . . Shakespeare may have his plays in which "redemption" is a theme (and I think he has), but *Antony and Cleopatra* is not one of them. (424)

To see Shakespeare's Cleopatra and her land as the Biblical Egypt that enslaved the Israelites contradicts every positive female character preceding her. Her refusal to abandon Antony even after his Roman marriage is no different from their constancy. The fertility of Duncan's Scotland is this Egypt's fertile Nile mud. And when death becomes a transcendent reunion with her beloved, she aligns herself with Juliet, Ophelia, Desdemona, and Cordelia. To experience *Antony and Cleopatra*'s final scenes is not to be caught between redemption or condemnation. Nor, despite her memorable entrance when Antony first arrived in Egypt, is it particularly satisfying to read this as Cleopatra's final, grand performance. At the pyramid, she has no audience to speak of, she is completely focused on her lover rather than herself, and mere histrionics moments before death is quite implausible. What Shakespeare is offering here is far more sublime than any of this. Cleopatra's final dream of union with Antony began with Juliet's search for a drop of poison on Romeo's lips. But where that play's metaphor of death as an eager paramour is highly rhetorical and artificial, here the audience is invited to share imaginatively in the powerfully dramatic experience of feminine love that endures to "the edge of doom," a phrase taken from Shakespeare's great definition of love, sonnet 116.

Shakespeare absorbed Ovid's lessons on the dual power of the erotic in profound ways, its ability to debase human potential as well as its ability to transform what's merely mortal into something of eternal beauty. Cleopatra's final words are Shakespeare's homage to that second aspect of love, and, as such, he takes us far beyond moral simplification into the spiritual. Hamlet's question about what follows after a person shuffles off this mortal coil is ultimately unanswerable, but Cleopatra's final moments are a glorious celebration of a love that transcends, and, as such, it is a glimpse, however dim and limited, into a love that is divine, belonging to fire and air rather than earth and water. Rome admired Antony for his stoic acceptance of the hardships of military campaigns, his willingness to drink water contaminated with horse urine. But this is a perspective that is pragmatic and earthbound. Cleopatra's final moments are a reminder of how limited that perspective is.

Danby's moralism is far more simplistic than Shakespeare's, for Cleopatra really has no one to redeem. Caesar, who lives to incorporate the P*ax Romana*, has no interest in redemption, and there is no one of any stature who hasn't already been corrupted by Roman hypocrisy. Caesar implements the kind of *realpolitik* so familiar in our modern era, but it's good to recognize that, like many of Shakespeare's vice figures, he breaks his vow to take what rightfully belongs to others. We have seen what judgment is passed on Bolingbroke in *1Henry 4*; on Falstaff, who robs the pilgrims at Gadshill; on Sir Toby and on Iago, who both pilfer the purses of those who suffer under the illusion that they're among friends; on Lear's eldest daughters who lie to obtain a share of his kingdom. If such self-interest is the seed that sprouts into evil, it's equally important to recall the central metaphor of plays like *The Merchant* where generosity is the monetary equivalent of the mercy and forgiveness necessary for love, and that here, in this play, Antony's generosity contrasts sharply with Caesar's lack of that virtue.

Rather than being redemptive, Cleopatra's final scene shows her irresistible, life-giving, endlessly abundant love overcoming the world's intractable evil of death. As horrible and permanent as death certainly is, it cannot overcome Cleopatra's feminine conviction of her right to be Antony's wife, his lover, the mother of his children. The quote from Berlin's *The Secret Cause* spoke of tragedy's ability to confront life's essential mysteries. Though different from Lear's tragedy, the last scene of *Antony and Cleopatra* confronts us with the amazing and profound mystery of that kind of love: What is its origin? Why do some people feel it so deeply and others not? And, ultimately, what is its value for those who do respond to its magic? As the great 116th sonnet has it, love somehow guides life down certain paths, but ultimately its full emotional, moral, and spiritual value can never really be comprehended by the very limited capacity of the human mind. As the Romans do, the mystery of love can certainly be reduced to sex, but the merely physical can never adequately explain the selfless devotion of an Edgar, a Cordelia, or the magnificent constancy of a Cleopatra.

Resolving the mystery of Cleopatra isn't as simple as saying that Rome is evil and Egypt is good. To achieve what Caesar does requires the cunning and sometimes ruthless application of power. While good men like Antony pay a price for that, the many years of peace that followed Caesar's actions are not without value. But such ruthless exercise of power raises the question whether what Caesar achieves is capable of enriching his life in the same way that Antony and Cleopatra enrich theirs. Similar to Hal in *1Henry4*, Caesar sacrifices something quite precious at the personal level to achieve something grand but entirely worldly. In contrast, Antony and Cleopatra are forced by political circumstances to sacrifice something worldly but end up gaining something personal and immensely valuable. It is possible to argue that neither choice is better than the other, but *Antony and Cleopatra* demonstrates that only one choice can save and ennoble the heart. Caesar triumphs but his political skills leave little room for genuine love. Somehow, Caesar's choice diminishes the person. Because the choice, unfortunately, is stark, no one, not even the all-conquering Caesar, can have them both.

The foundations of this drama are basic Christian concepts about love and human nature, which must eventually confront the choice between things of this world and those of the spirit. This was not the original design of creation, which began in a fertile garden that freely provided the first Adam with nature's full, indivisible bounty, including complete union, body and soul, with a loving mate and with his fully visible creator. This was the intention until sin destroyed that Eden, and the Creator sent man out into the world to work by the sweat of his brow. Ever since, the necessity of work distracts men from the women who love them. For women like Cleopatra who were born with a deeply embedded need for love, such devotion becomes part of their identity. Though men often fail to understand this, something within their nature cannot help but respond. This miracle, this magic, is what Shakespeare celebrates with his Egyptian queen. Embodied though that love is in fallible human beings, it has the power to transform lives. Its steadfast and patient persistence, its conviction that human weakness and misunderstandings must be forgiven, are dim but significant reflections of the perfect love that, according to the stories that Shakespeare knew well, designed the world. Such love is the spark of divine fire that women like Cleopatra possess, and because of it, they are able to hold their men close to their hearts, even through and beyond death itself. This is the mystery that Antony and Cleopatra's tragic story demonstrates. What the two of them have is far different from what Caesar achieves, but Shakespeare makes it very clear why the final act of this play does not belong to him.

Shakespeare's final group of plays, collectively known as romances, take a step back from tragedy. Though they address similar themes and issues, they reflect changing theatrical tastes, deliberately creating a context that is less realistic and much closer to folklore or fairy tale. Ever the adapter and experimenter, Shakespeare meets audience expectations without sacrificing any of his hard-won convictions about love and human life. Perhaps the best of his final plays, *The Tempest* is an example of this great author's life-long effort to use art to educate and enlighten his audience about the value and meaning of human being.

The Tempest

The quality that perhaps best defines what makes Shakespeare and his art exceptional is his willingness to engage with rather than avoid complexity and to do so without the slightest hint of intellectual superiority or condescension. The consistent assumption is that the complexity is as interesting to others as it is to him. To his credit, Harold Bloom recognizes this ability in Shakespeare's many memorable characterizations. In *The Invention of the Human*, Bloom pays homage to the unique vitality of Shakespeare's characters who breathe life into a stage presence composed primarily of gesture and language. Ever observant himself, Shakespeare acknowledges such vitality is a consequence of the strange alchemy available to the dramatist from the interaction of actor and audience imaginations, the power to give "airy nothing" a "local habitation and a name."

But Shakespeare's complexity isn't limited to just character. Preceding chapters have demonstrated a similar engagement with the moral complexity of desire and love, with distinctions between good and evil, with the relevance of Christian belief for a life enriched with meaning and purpose beyond the stifling limitations of selfish self-absorption. Because the life that interested Shakespeare was complex rather than simple, fascinating rather than dull, life itself was filled with unmistakable magic, a metaphor he used in multiple ways. In *A Midsummer Night's Dream*, the magic in Puck's fairy dust represents desire's power to overcome reluctance or self-doubt enabling love to evolve from possibility into reality. In *Othello,* the magic in Desdemona's lost handkerchief is the very fragile presence of romance and respect in a marriage under attack from Iago's pruient verbal assault, a form of linguistic evil opposed to the kind of love able to recognize value despite difference.

In *The Tempest*, however, the concept of magic has multiple facets that, diamond-like, flash brilliance in different directions. No longer just a useful but peripheral association, magic becomes *The Tempest's* working metaphor and deserves careful consideration because, despite the metaphor's connection to previous work, the theatrical experience of it seems very different. For some, that difference is a detectable element of the biographical. Prospero, for example, is an elderly magician who uses his powers to redeem three men who had participated in a conspiracy to wrong both him and his young daughter, Miranda. He does so by orchestrating events much as a theater director would manage a play. And when Prospero relinquishes his magic in the last scenes, some critics see this as Shakespeare's farewell to his career, a supposition given additional credence by the fact *The Tempest* was his last major solo work.

While few reliable records have been found to document Shakespeare's final years, *The Tempest* was certainly written as he approached retirement. He had purchased one of the finest Stratford homes, New Place, in 1597, and retired there sometime between 1610 and 1613, the year his theater, The Globe, accidentally burned to the ground. As he composed *The Tempest* sometime between 1610 and 1611, his retirement from these incessant professional demands was likely on his mind. Already wealthy and respected by his peers, he would have been about forty-six years old at the time. For many, an unmistakable note of nostalgia can be heard in *The Tempest*. The magic only available through theater was coming to an end.

But that very personal decision was only part of what Shakespeare was dealing with. Other historical factors also contribute to *The Tempest*'s bravura combination of realism with magic and miracle as well. His chosen profession had come under siege from two directions. The frontal assault was launched by the Puritan elect while the rear action was taken by Ben Jonson, busily shaping theatrical tastes to suit artistic gifts very different from Shakespeare's.

Like Elizabeth, James enjoyed and gladly supported the theater, sponsoring Shakespeare's company with notable largesse. But James also had to contend with the growing cultural and political influence of the Puritans who grew increasingly uncomfortable with London theaters. Though their initial aim was to remove the last remnants of Catholicism from the Anglican Church, their purifications eventually confronted every aspect of English culture. With uncompromising zeal, the Puritans viewed any religious accommodation as a subordination of principles to convenience, and they used the pulpit, the pamphlet, and the politician to attack any religious, political, or cultural activity that violated their beliefs. Viewed as dens of rowdy, sometimes licentious behavior, London's theaters were considered idolatrous diversions from productive work and spiritual devotions. Such uncompromising positions fueled an intense dislike of the theaters, and they longed for the day when all of them would finally be closed.

Such passionate opposition eventually had a chilling effect on attendance, the driving force behind the intense creative effort that made Elizabethan theaters so successful. Anticipating what now seemed inevitable, James Burbage, one of the co-owners of Shakespeare's Globe, refurbished London's Blackfriar's Theater for smaller, indoor productions. At first used primarily during the winter, it attracted a wealthier, better-educated clientele who brought with them different theatrical expectations. Influenced by the classically trained Ben Jonson, who authored the First Folio's dedication to Shakespeare, this audience preferred Jonson's witty, satirical comedy or his elaborate masques featuring light-hearted, frivolous spectacles in an idealized pastoral location. Heavy with song and dance, these plays featured easily digestible fare designed to delight rather than instruct. With strengthening Puritan opposition to the theaters and changing audience expectations, Shakespeare probably knew the choice was either adapt or retire. The late romances suggest he was willing for a time to adapt.

For the far more accomplished Shakespeare, the competition was now Jonson whose elaborate sets were designed by the famous architect, Inigo Jones. Artistic standards as well as audience expectations for the masque were established by their collaboration. Endlessly inventive, however, Shakespeare produced a play not only satisfying these new expectations but transforming the frothy, Jonsonian masque into a profound statement about the proper foundation of political authority. And in what amounts to an implicit critique of Jonson's extravagant but intellectually empty spectacles, *The Tempest* effectively argues art's purpose is not just to entertain but to assist in the reformation of those, both onstage and in the audience, still susceptible to correction. But the rivalry involved more than the staging and content of a masque. Jonson was willing to acknowledge Shakespeare's natural talent and popularity but thought his rival's works ignored the standards set by the Latin and Greek models taught at university. As if to prove his adaptability, Shakespeare carefully constructs *The Tempest* to follow the unities of action, time, and place, artificial criteria that mattered so much to Jonson. Even at his age, with his achievements, it's as if Shakespeare were trying to show his relevance in a theatrical world already moving in an entirely new direction. Four hundred years later, ironically, *The Tempest* remains one of his most popular plays while Jonson's masques, for all their flashy spectacle, have long been forgotten.

The Tempest's unique effect has one additional cause beyond an impending retirement, Puritan zealotry, and Jonson's masques. It was influenced by the many books and pamphlets about the Americas that had begun circulating throughout London. These electrified the English imagination with visions of a pristine, unblemished society, untouched by the sins of a supposedly civilized culture. Among the most notable were William Strachey's *A True Reportory of the Wreck and Redemption of Sir Thomas Gates*, Silvester Jourdain's *A Discovery in the Bermudas*, and Montaigne's *The Cannibals*, all of which, in some ways and for a variety of purposes, idealized the land and the peoples of the new world. Montaigne's essay, in fact, which romanticized the inhabitants of these far-off lands to satirize the moral hypocrisy of European society, is the source for Gonzalo's naïve utopian vision as the corrupt Italian nobles, shipwrecked by the play's storm, survey their new home. Aware of mankind's inherently sinful nature, *The Tempest* carefully qualifies the pamphlet writers' assumptions about the primal innocence of the new world's inhabitants. Shakespeare understood that no one, either in Europe or the New World, lived outside the truth of what *Genesis* describes as mankind's fall from virtue and a shared need for divine mercy. Never very comfortable with satire, he neither idealized nor condemned England's Christian culture but offered a reminder of the universality of sin and the necessity of repentance, forgiveness, and redemption. Those in authority were no exception.

Not surprisingly, *The Tempest* is old wine in new skin. Though Shakespeare's Henriad is an essential part of its pedigree, every preceding literary effort was preparation for this unique island with its stern disciplinarian whose magical powers are employed to reform his enemies. Despite its fairytale quality, Prospero's story, like Prince Hal's, is a serious play about the personal qualities necessary for the responsible exercise of power and authority. All along, Shakespeare recognized the moral and emotional similarities between Ovid's stories about desire degrading human potential and Seneca's concern about anger undermining self-control and civilized behavior. Seneca's work influences the early *Titus Andronicus*, provides the background feud in *Romeo and Juliet*, inspires the action of *Hamlet*, explains an

Othello willing to murder Desdemona, and, as it turns out, is the energy pushing *The Tempest* toward its resolution. Like the other late romances, *Cymbeline* and *The Winter's Tale*, *The Tempest* confronts the painful consequences of anger that imprison both perpetrator and victim until both are released by an act of generous mercy. While the masque-like presentation may be new, the thematic concerns remain vintage Shakespeare.

A theme common to these romance plays is release from bondage. The second of them, *The Winter's Tale*, in fact, reimagines Ovid's story of the sculptor, Pygmalion, who creates a statue of a woman so beautiful he falls in love and brings her to life with a kiss. But *The Winter's Tale* recasts Ovid's fable by incorporating a false accusation of infidelity only resolved when a prodigal child's return inspires a husband's repentance. The couple's sixteen years of separation ends when the accused wife reappears as a statue reanimated by the husband's belated remorse. Thus, a classical fable of love's restorative power is neatly integrated with Christian ideas of repentance for jealous anger redeemed through forgiveness.

With these late romances, then, those earlier, prevalent themes of desire and revenge reappear with an emphasis on mercy and release from sin. Portia's great speech on mercy certainly applies here, but also reminiscent of Prince Hal's progress toward the throne, *The Tempest* argues personal virtues are the prerequisite for Prospero's return to an authority where decisions are carefully evaluated within the context of death and divine judgment. The self-discipline and mercy Prospero learns to exercise on his island are preparation for a return to civil authority where his renewed respect for justice honors a just and merciful Creator.

Because of the play's nebulously remote, magical environment, it is easy to misread *The Tempest* as simple folklore. The play functions quite well at that level, too. Formerly Duke of Milan but now a castaway magician inhabiting a remote island with his daughter Miranda, Prospero is at the very center of the play's events. The two exiles have languished on this unnamed island with Caliban, a savage, and Ariel, a spirit who implements Prospero's magic. As the play opens, a storm ravages a ship carrying several Italian noblemen on their way home from the wedding of the King of Naples's daughter. Prospero initiated this tempest to punish Naples and Prospero's brother, Antonio, who collaborated to dethrone and exile Prospero's entire family. Though Prospero's art keeps both vessel and passengers safe, everyone aboard the foundering ship comes to believe they've been shipwrecked. Explaining this history to his daughter, Prospero admits that his preoccupation with magic led to the negligence of his governmental duties and to his brother's opportunistic decision to take Milan's authority for himself, something he couldn't have done without the tacit approval of his fellow passenger, Alonso, King of Naples. All three men, therefore, have played some part in the origins of these current circumstances. As the travelers make their way ashore, Alonso believes his son, Ferdinand, has drowned. In reality, they are only separated. The king's brother, Sebastian, blames him for bringing them so far from home. Very quickly, these shipwrecked noblemen divide into two morally distinguishable camps. Though no discernible advantage could possibly be gained, Prospero's brother, Antonio, and Alonso's brother, Sebastian, set out to murder the king of Naples, whose love for his lost son eventually delivers the shipwrecked party from their unwilling detention.

But what is Prospero's intention for these men? Unlike the magic that hides Bottom's deformity from the ardent Titania in *A Midsummer Night's Dream*, Prospero's power has no connection to the random intrusions of erotic love. Instead, his magic is exercised intentionally to educate, correct, and sometimes punish as he occasionally does to a recalcitrant Caliban. Whether his aim for the shipwrecked nobles is retribution or something more benign, consequently, isn't clear until he explicitly renounces revenge near the end of the play. The reason for his renunciation is carefully worked out in two parallel murder plots, one ominous, the other absurdly comic. Mimicking the planned murder of Naples, two drunken sailors from the ship collaborate with Caliban to kill Prospero. Macbeth's ambition is the proper paradigm here since all the conspirators, like the Scottish warrior, imagine some benefit to a morally reprehensible act. Rather than power, however, what they seek is the freedom to do as they please, an undisciplined posture that should preclude any access to a power capable of cruel abuse. Though Prospero seems different, he himself could not resist a pre-exile dalliance with magic that, because it promised unlimited power, now represents a temptation to unlimited retribution.

    Much like the punishing downpour Lear endures on the heath, the storm referenced in this play's title suggests the turmoil sin engenders can also encourage moral and spiritual growth. Imprisoned on the island with his daughter, Prospero needs relief from an exile for which he was at least partly responsible. Except for the innocent Ferdinand and Miranda, who are victimized by other men's sins, every other character is somehow confined by the consequences of their own transgressions. Clearly at the cusp where revenge is within his grasp, Prospero is faced either with satisfying his anger or finding a way toward redemption and reintegration into society. Since executing his enemies won't end his exile nor achieve either of those goals, bringing those three men of sin to an appreciation of their own evil is the only logical way forward. Salvation does not come easily, however. It only happens because Prospero is moved by Ariel's pity for the sad plight of the Italians trapped on the island by the storm. Much in the spirit of Portia's speech on mercy, *The Tempest,* demonstrates how mercy, like love, is a form of generosity that frees both the forgiver and the forgiven. In the end,

Prospero comes to understand this is the only magic that truly matters.

Prospero's magic, therefore, comes with multiple implications. From one perspective, the desire for and acquisition of this power was illicit, a sin punished by exile from authority in Milan. From another perspective, it is the tool, much like Shakespeare's art, by which Prospero redeems both his brother and himself. From still another, more Ovidian perspective, magic is a power bringing those innocent lovers, Ferdinand and Miranda, together. And finally, it is a force, much like divine grace, that fosters marital and civic unity among disparate people tempted to rule their lives as they please but willing to submit to authority nevertheless. At various times during the play, any one of these meanings may be operative. But there is one additional perspective: though nobody accepts Prospero's magic as factually real, *The Tempest* creates a theatrical environment where an audience's willing suspension of disbelief becomes one more version of magic Shakespeare deliberately invokes. All of these forms of magic contribute to the experience of life as miracle.

Power's potential for abuse was previously noted in both *Lear* and *Macbeth*, and it is once again a concern in *The Tempest*. The good-natured Gonzalo, who is described in the play's list of characters as "an honest old councilor," envisions a society where any ambition for dominance and control are no longer necessary. His utopian vision is cynically mocked by Sebastian and Antonio, the amoral brothers of Alonso and Prospero respectively:

> Gon. Had I plantation of this isle, my lord—
> Ant. He'd sow't with nettle-seed.
> Seb.   Or docks, or mallows.
> Gon. And were the king on't, what would I do?
> Seb. 'Scape being drunk, for want of wine.
> Gon. I' th' commonwealth, I would, by contraries,
>   Execute all things; for no kind of traffic
>   Would I admit; no name of magistrate;

	Letters should not be known; riches, poverty,
	And use of service, none; contract, succession,
	Bourn, bound of land, tilth, vineyard, none;
	No use of metal, corn, or wine, or oil;
	No occupation, all men idle, all;
	And women too but innocent and pure;
	No sovereignty—
Seb.	Yet he would be king on't.
Ant.	The latter end of his commonwealth forgets the beginning.
Gon.	All things in common nature should produce Without sweat or endeavor; treason, felony, Sword, pike, knife, gun, or need of any engine, Would I not have; but nature should bring forth, Of its own kind, all foison, all abundance, To feed my innocent people.
Seb.	No marrying 'mong his subjects?
Ant.	None, man, all idle—whores and knaves.
Gon.	I would with such perfection govern, sir, T' excel the golden age. (2.1.144-168)

Gonzalo's idyllic society would "excel the golden age" of Hesiod, which, very much like the Biblical Eden, described a time of innocence and plenty. If Gonzalo ruled there, culture, labor, laws, military preparedness—in short, everything that constitutes civilization– would be unnecessary because the nature Gonzalo perceives is prodigiously abundant and good. Honest and well-meaning, Gonzalo's vision of what might be reflects an assumption about the world and man's essential, perfectible nature. That naiveté, however, makes him vulnerable to the two cynical brothers, who see the world quite differently. Because Sebastian and Antonio are themselves so easily swayed by the dark desires of their hearts, they find the old man's dream unrealistic and foolish. "How lush and lusty the grass looks!" Gonzalo remarks about his current surroundings. "The ground indeed is tawny," responds Antonio. Two very different men, two very different views of the world. Where Gonzalo's world is green with promise, theirs is tawny, dry, and arid, good only for nettles, whores, and knaves.

Unfortunately, Gonzalo's idyllic vision is rendered untenable by the harsh realities of the world. Men like Sebastian and Antonio are precisely what make the innocence of Gonzalo's Eden an impossibility. As sympathetic as the old man is, his vision is a verbal dream that fails to account for the dark hearts of his companions who, like Iago, refuse to acknowledge any value in goodness. The reality of such cynicism comes when Ariel bewitches everyone except these two amoral brothers, who immediately begin to hatch their nefarious murder plot. The prospect of taking the throne of Naples and forging an alliance for their mutual benefit proves too tempting to resist. Even pangs of conscience are forsaken. Though Antonio had heartlessly cast Prospero and his daughter adrift at sea, Sebastian worries that his companion might be too troubled by his conscience to assist in the murder. "But, for your conscience?" he asks cautiously. "I feel not this deity in my bosom," replies Antonio, a man whose previous sins, like Macbeth, have inured him to this one as well.

Though comic in tone, the play's interrelated plots serve as a commentary of authority's nature as it attempts to maintain social order, which, the play argues, is impossible without personal commitments to moral principles by leaders as well as citizens. *The Tempest* begins, in fact, with the ship's crew struggling to control the storm-ravaged vessel while the terrified noblemen foolishly try to assert their wills upon the sailors. "What cares these roarers," the boatswain chastises, "for the name of king? To cabin! Silence! Trouble us not." In moments of crisis, competence matters far more than titular authority, a problem extensively addressed in the Henriad. Here, the question is posed several ways. It is visible in Gonzalo's reverie about the Golden Age where he dreams of being king in a civilization that needs no king. And the murder plots originate from the temptation to exercise power unrestrained by anything except personal desires. But in the background is another instance: an ambitious brother once forced Prospero, distracted from his duties by an interest in occult powers, to abdicate the seat of Milan's authority. All three stories have something to say about the proper foundation for civic rule, an unfortunate necessity in a world inhabited by the likes of Antonio and Sebastian.

    Shakespeare's opinion seems to have been that civil order fails whenever self-interest supersedes respect for established boundaries between subjects and rulers. In fact, in multiple plays self-interest insidiously corrupts civil order from both directions: citizens who mistake freedom for license, as the Caliban faction does, or rulers who use authority to satisfy personal needs, as demonstrated by Richard II, Bolingbroke, Claudius, and others. As Duke of Milan, Prospero failed to understand how his desire for magical powers filled a personal need at the expense of his public responsibilities, a sin for which both he and his daughter Miranda are paying a heavy price. But unlike Bolingbroke, who wanted to excise his guilt with a crusade that never took place, Prospero succeeds in using his unusual gifts to rectify and redeem.

    On Prospero's island, then, the sin of self-indulgence is pervasive. Such decadence is, the play argues through the character of Caliban, an inescapable aspect of human nature. An aboriginal primitive, Caliban believes he has a legitimate claim to rule the island. The offspring of Sycorax, the witch who ensconced Ariel in a tree for some unnamed transgression, Caliban had once roamed the island unhindered, surviving off the fruit of the land, much like the natives described in those idealized accounts of the New World. When the deposed Duke and his daughter arrive, he willingly shares his knowledge of the island, something that Prospero repays by trying to teach him the basics of civilization.

But that initial trust is broken when Caliban attempts to rape Miranda and propagate "[t]his isle with Calibans" (1.2.351). Mentioned only in passing, the unschooled brute's inclination to satisfy desire without regard for others contradicts Gonzalo's assumption that natural man is basically well-intentioned. As a rebellion against accepted norms, the attempted rape exemplifies the same self-indulgence seen to varying degrees in the other characters, none of whom consistently exercises sufficient self-discipline to harness desire, listen to the inner voice of conscience, or reason out the proper course of action.

Like Sebastian and Antonio, Caliban craves the freedom to do as he pleases, to take what he wants when he wants it. A version of Falstaff without the endearing wit, he behaves as if the island is there for his pleasure. In his first appearance, he is cursing Prospero for making him work. He remembers a time before Prospero's arrival when he was free to do as he pleased. Then he was a king unto himself. But with Prospero's arrival and dominion over the island, his state has changed dramatically. Despising the discipline imposed by Prospero, he laments the loss of his freedom. Now, he begins:

> I must eat my dinner.
> This island's mine by Sycorax my mother,
> Which thou tak'st from me. When thou cam'st first,
> Thou. . . made much of me. . . , wouldst give me
> Water with berries in't. . . .and then I lov'd thee. . . .
> Curs'd be I that did so! . . . .
> For I am all the subjects that you have,
> Which first was mine own king . . . . (1.2.330-342)

Like Prospero, Caliban has also been deposed, but he lost authority over the island and its bounty because his base desire threatened Miranda's virtue, which a good father is duty-bound to protect and encourage. The issue, *The Tempest* argues, really isn't between freedom and enslavement but between license and an orderly society built on respect, duty, and love. Motivated by anything other than such virtues, the effort to take matters in hand, to be "mine own king," does little more than create an illusion of freedom that dissipates as soon as others violate boundaries to feed their needs. The same dynamic Bolingbroke unleashes when he deposes Richard.

    The absurdity of thinking otherwise is mocked by events in the subplot. Because of the attempted rape, Prospero tries to teach Caliban some discipline by assigning menial tasks, but he chafes at the unpleasant work. After the storm, the wild native of the island encounters the drunken butler, Stephano, and the jester, Trinculo, who share a cask of wine with the credulous islander. Because the effects of the liquor strike him as magical, he foolishly assumes those who bring it must be gods with the power to release him from Prospero's bondage.

Cal.	[Aside] These be fine things, and if they be not sprites. That's a brave god, and bears a celestial liquor. I will kneel to him.
Ste.	Swear by this bottle how thou cam'st hither—I escap'd upon a butt of sack which the sailors heav'd o'erboard—by this bottle, which I made of the bark of a tree with mine own hands since I was cast ashore.
Cal.	I'll swear upon that bottle to be thy true subject, for the liquor is not earthly. . . .
Trin.	O Stephano, hast any more of this?
Ste.	The whole butt, man. My cellar is in a rock by the sea-side. . . . How now, moon-calf? How does thine ague?
Cal.	Hast thou not dropp'd from heaven?
Ste.	Out o' th' moon, I do assure thee. . . .
Cal.	I have seen thee in her, and I do adore thee. . . . I'll show thee every fertile inch o' th' island; And I will kiss thy foot. I prithee, be my god.

(2.2.116-149)

Happily exchanging servitude to Prospero to become the "true subject" of a drunken butler and a clown, Caliban seizes this opportunity to escape from his daily drudgery, enlisting his newfound friends in a plot to murder his erstwhile master. When the three of them concur, he joyously exits the stage, singing:

> 'Ban, 'Ban, Ca-Caliban
> Has a new master, get a new man,
> Freedom, high-day!
> High-day, freedom! Freedom, high-day, freedom!
> (2.2.184-186)

Never aware those menial chores are his master's way of instilling some useful self-discipline, Caliban, much like Othello, exchanges true magic for the liquid magic of two drunken fools. As recalcitrant, natural man, Caliban cannot fathom the spiritual and moral truth that everyone must be a servant of some master, what the theologian Paul Tillich called a person's ultimate concern. For some, like Sebastian and Antonio, it is the lust for power. For others, like Ferdinand and Miranda, it is union with a loving other. For Caliban, it is those demi-gods in charge of a butt of wine. And, for Prospero, it was the magical authority found in book, robe, and staff. For each of these characters, the choice is not between freedom and servitude but between worthy and unworthy masters. As the play's initial storm shows, the conviction that man controls his own fate, that, being his "own king," he can do whatever he chooses, is a dangerous illusion created by pride and a wrongfully conceived notion of freedom.

The Tempest, of course, offers an alternative definition of freedom. A far more reliable servant than Caliban, Ariel also longs for his freedom. When the willing sprite first appears on stage, he is assisting Prospero with the storm, the ship, and all the onboard passengers. Having accounted for all of these, he reminds Prospero of a promise:

> Ariel: Let me remember thee what thou hast promis'd
> Which is not yet perform'd me.
> Pros: How now? Moody?
> What is't thou canst demand?
> Ariel: My liberty. (1.2.243-245)

Ariel's history is somewhat different from Caliban's. Both arrived on the island with the witch, Sycorax, but where the amoral Caliban roamed free, the witch imprisoned Ariel in a pine tree for failing to carry out some of her distasteful commands. Unlike Caliban, who remains in foolish bondage to his ridiculous gods, Ariel makes a moral judgment about which master is worthy of his loyalty, and he carries out every task assigned to him until self-discipline and duty become habitual. Patiently serving until release has been earned, he is moving toward the freedom he longs for. His task is to assist Prospero's effort to reform any of the ship's passengers open to repentance. As the story progresses, theirs becomes a relationship where both master and disciple understand self-discipline is the path to durable freedom: freedom from conflict, from restless anxiety, from fear, from sin and the consequent guilt. Ruled by the nearly irresistible impulse to do what pleases, the natural man Caliban resists the paradoxical but very Christian notion freedom just might be a product of disciplined service.

Shakespeare's adaptation of Ovid's Pygmalion story in both *The Winter's Tale* and *The Tempest* illuminates this paradoxical conception of freedom, a central concern of both stories. Moved by the spirit's pity for the suffering Europeans, Prospero releases Ariel from any further servitude. Through the magic of love and desire, Ferdinand and Miranda are freed from isolation into romance. Every shipwrecked passenger is freed from the island by the reconciliation of

Prospero and Alonso. But Prospero's imprisonment ends as a result of a qualitatively different but still related kind of magic, one less earth-bound and more spiritual. As the play's events unfold, the old man's exile only ends when he chooses to forgive his enemies, an act of generous mercy that earns his return to the dukedom he lost to an ambitious brother. Blessed with an authority to orchestrate his return to Milan, he too must repay the debt incurred when that power came to him. Prospero and Sycorax, who once punished Ariel, are both purveyors of magic, but the choice of mercy rather than revenge aligns only one of them with the unnamed author of all magic.

As always in Shakespeare, love is an especially precious form of magic. Spellbound by romance, Miranda and Ferdinand unknowingly begin the process of universal expiation. Though the young man is keenly aware of being shipwrecked and confined to this desert island, she is only vaguely aware of her own need for liberation, a precious gift the young man brings to her. Having fallen in love, they prove worthy of this relationship by accepting the same moral and spiritual obligations as disciples owe their masters and citizens to their authorities. As *The Merchant*'s lottery implies, the Christian principle of dying to self, that willing excision of self-indulgence, is the proper basis for harmonious relationships. Having learned this lesson through the hard experience of exile, Prospero takes great pains to convey this truth to the starry-eyed couple, brought together under the aegis of his special powers.

The suspicion this romance is part of Prospero's larger plan increases as he intervenes to ensure the proper outcome. He addresses Ferdinand, the bewitched young lover:

> Pros: Soft, sir, one word more.
> [Aside] They are both in either's pow'rs; but this swift business
> I must uneasy make, lest too light winning
> Make the prize light. (1.2.450-453)

To verify the quality of Ferdinand's devotion to his daughter, Prospero gives Ferdinand the menial task of hauling logs to their shelter, the same task previously assigned to but resented by Caliban. Prospero's island, clearly, is far different from Gonzalo's idealized society where "nature should produce without sweat or endeavor." In Prospero's world, work is a form of service, an exercise that reflects a willingness to give something from the self for the greater good of spouse, family, and society. To prove himself worthy of Miranda's love, Ferdinand needs to exhibit appropriate compliance, discipline, and the cheerful, selfless performance of responsibilities required of any husband.

Both Ferdinand and Caliban are required to work, but each accepts their tasks with completely different attitudes that measure their readiness for a place within a family and civil society. Caliban resists the drudgery, curses his master, and seizes upon the first opportunity to escape from his burdens. Ferdinand, on the other hand, understands his labor has a purpose and will be rewarded with the promised abundance that benevolent nature has embodied in Miranda. Unlike Caliban and the two amoral nobles, Sebastian and Antonio, Ferdinand is comfortable with the notion that selfless service is the role he was designed to fulfill. He is not distracted by an illusion of unrestrained freedom, which is nothing more than slavery to desire. He has chosen the worthy master. Where Gonzalo's idealized vision of society requires nothing of its inhabitants, Ferdinand's mature acceptance of Prospero's work requirement prepares him for the duties owed to a loving wife and a peaceful, orderly society.

How these two young lovers respond to Prospero's demand is indicative of a virtue that differentiates them from Caliban and the amoral nobles, Sebastian and Antonio. The lovers' innocent virtue is evident in the scene where Ferdinand and Miranda exchange vows of love to each other. He is carrying logs hither and yon; she feels compelled to provide relief:

>Fer: The very instant that I saw you, did
>My heart fly to your service, there resides,
>To make me slave to it, and for your sake
>Am I this patient log-man.
>Mir: Do you love me?
>Fer: O heaven, O earth, bear witness to this sound.
>. . .
>Beyond all limit of what else i' th' world,
>
>Do love, prize, honor you. . . .
>Wherefore weep you?
>Mir: At my own unworthiness, that dare not offer
>What I desire to give; and much less take
>What I shall die to want. . . .
>I am your wife, if you will marry me;
>If not, I'll die your maid. To be your fellow
>You may deny me, but I'll be your servant,
>Whether you will or no. (3.1.64-86)

Miranda's humble joy at the prospect of such love echoes the very same sentiments that Portia expressed when Bassanio chooses the lead casket in *The Merchant*. The same language of generosity and service is evident here: Ferdinand is her willing slave; Miranda is his unconditional servant, ready to help, with or without marriage. And though Prospero is watching this scene from afar, they are making these pledges freely. True love is impossible, Shakespeare argues over the course of his career, without this generous surrender of self to other. Love is an open-ended, generously given commitment to service, and, from that, much goodness flows.

Interestingly, the pristine innocence of these lovers illuminates Gonzalo's utopian vision of society from a different, far less cynical perspective than the one voiced earlier by Sebastian and Antonio. In his musings, Gonzalo had dreamed of the women on his island as "innocent and pure," which is surely true of both Miranda and Ferdinand. Together, they represent a kind of love that is almost otherworldly, an unblemished state of pure innocence which, in a world that contains shameless sinners, is terribly vulnerable. Like the story of Eden, they remind what should be, what could be chosen, and what has been lost to selfish willfulness. Gonzalo's utopia may be subject to worldly cynicism, but, like the story of Eden, the truth it reflects serves to condemn human sinfulness and to inspire those capable of shame and regret to do better.

Very deftly, the play presents two very different approaches to existence. One is represented by the self-interested, self-serving cynics, Antonio and Sebastian, who wear the clothing of civilized societies, know the accepted posture of the court, and speak with the right syntax and accent. But underneath, they are all Caliban, the untamed, natural man who rejects any discipline and acts only on what pleases him. Involved in schemes of murder, they serve unworthy gods and anticipate no joy. The other way of life is represented by Ferdinand and Miranda. Though one emerges from privilege and the other from want, the love they discover is sufficient to bridge any differences, and each accepts the moral and emotional discipline that lays a firm foundation for a life of sacrifice and generosity. As such, they earn the prospect of genuine love and its attendant rewards.

The consequences of either choice are made clear by the two banquet scenes that take place near the middle of the play, both of which are orchestrated by Ariel. At the end of Act III, the first banquet is presented to the shipwrecked Italian nobles, who are famished by their ordeal. Being subject to physical hunger, of course, is symbolic of their enslavement to all desires of the flesh. The lavishly furnished banquet table that appears and tantalizes them quickly vanishes, leaving their hunger unsatisfied. Speaking to Alonso and the two plotters, Ariel's message carries the same stern morality as Hal's final words to Falstaff at his royal coronation:

> You are three men of sin, whom Destiny,
> That hath to instrument this lower world
> And what is in't, the never-surfeited sea
> Hath caus'd to belch up you; and on this island
> Where man doth not inhabit—you 'mongst men
> Being most unfit to live. I have made you mad...
> But remember
> (For that's my business to you) that you three
> From Milan did supplant good Prospero,
> Expos'd unto the sea (which hath requit it)
> Him and his innocent child; for which foul deed
> The pow'rs, delaying (not forgetting) have
> Incens'd the seas and shores—yea, all the
>   creatures,
> Against your peace. Thee of thy son, Alonso,
> They have bereft; and do pronounce by me
> Ling'ring perdition... shall step by step attend
> You and your ways...
> Which here... is nothing but heart's sorrow
> And a clear life ensuing. (3.3.53-82)

These "three men of sin" are called to remember what they did to Prospero and Miranda. The vanishing banquet symbolically reenacts their callousness, which took away everything that had at one time sustained the exiled duke and his daughter. For supporting the coup that abandoned a father and his innocent daughter to dire uncertainty, the king, Alonso, must now endure a similar loss of a child. Separation, sorrow, and perdition are the wages earned by a heart closed to the tender mercies only Gonzalo was brave enough to extend as exile threatened. Before repentance is possible, sin must be exposed and remembered. Symbolically, a banquet that vanishes before hunger is satisfied indicates that none of nature's sustaining bounty will ever be available to them unless they change. The "Destiny that... instrument[s] this lower world" rejects them, belches them up onto this remote island to present them with the opportunity to acknowledge and repent. As it did for Lear, a tempest has come to shake complacent and morally lazy men out of selfishness and self-delusion. But the chastisement also contains a message of hope. There is a benevolent purpose, an over-arching plan within nature that works toward their redemption if they are open to it.

Because both Prospero and Alonso are capable of unconditional love for their children, the promised redemption is available to them. Where evil separates and divides, love holds spouses, families, communities, and nations together. The necessary prerequisite is a heart open to feelings so basic that, as Cordelia admitted, they cannot be heaved into the mouth. It is Alonso's love for his son that enables his repentance. He is salvageable. Sebastian and Antonio, who never express anything like that tenderness toward anyone, remain recalcitrant and unredeemable. Like the wicked daughters in *King Lear*, their cynicism blinds them to the possibility of goodness, of forgiveness, of redemption, of an Eden lost to sin but promised and secured by a lifetime of service. Like Caliban, Sebastian and Antonio lack any awareness of a choice that might benefit them far more than the self-indulgent path they've chosen. Enslaved to self, they remain ostracized, emotionally, morally, and spiritually if not physically, from a civil society that will always regard them with suspicion. Like Caliban, Sebastian and Antonio have made their fool their god. They are trapped inside their sinful natures.

But the first banquet with its bitter aftertaste is soon followed by a contrasting second. The next one for Ferdinand and Miranda is a sweet celebration of their innocent love, which they've preserved by cooperating with Prospero's hard-earned wisdom. Because they have persisted in that obedience, they are provided with all the bounty of nature. Their banquet suggests that all manner of sustenance, physical, emotional, and spiritual, is available to them precisely because of their desire to serve the other over the self. But that kind of emotional and spiritual control is hard work, a constant struggle against any desire that threatens to subvert that selfless attitude. Instilling that spiritual vigilance is the reason for the work that Prospero obligated Ferdinand to do, and it trained both young lovers about the necessity of self-discipline. Because of their generous, selfless spirit, however, the hard work of self-discipline actually becomes a source of joy.

Though the second banquet functions as Prospero's blessing on the pair, he is fully aware that desire can always overpower whatever restrains man's behavior, so he insists that Ferdinand must continue to exercise self-control by abstaining from physical intimacy until the lovers are officially married. Ferdinand's willing consent to this stands in sharp contrast to Caliban's attempted rape of Miranda. Self-control, which is the obedient submission to a higher good, is a choice that leads somewhere far different from the destination that awaits those who only serve themselves. After the fall, Eden is no longer available. The Sebastian's and Antonio's of the world will always be present in the post-Edenic garden, but the utopian dream, the Edenic memory, reminds man of what he might eventually become if he chooses to follow the worthy master.

For most of the play, it isn't entirely clear what Prospero's intent is for the three men of sin, whether he intends to punish or reform them. Yet it is precisely sin's persistence in a fallen world that requires something further from the victims of that sin. If the victims are to escape the allure of sin themselves, they must turn away from the evil of revenge and embrace forgiveness, the turning of the other cheek. In *Hamlet* and other plays, Shakespeare examined the personal and social consequences of revenge. Those consequences were unacceptable to both providence and mankind. The only tenable alternative available in a world where everyone is imperfect and fallible is forgiveness, a foundational principle of the New Testament as well as the Lord's Prayer. Grievously hurt by a brother's betrayal, by a forced removal from power, by the callous exile to the sea and an uncertain fate, Prospero possesses the power to crush his enemies completely but chooses otherwise. Moved by Ariel's pity for the suffering aristocrats of Naples and Milan, Prospero makes a decision:

> Though with their high wrongs I am strook to the quick,
> Yet, with my nobler reason, 'gainst my fury
> Do I take part. The rarer action is
> In virtue than in vengeance. They being penitent,
> The sole drift of my purpose doth extend
> Not a frown further. (5.1.25-30)

Completely different from power, which can enforce someone's will on another, forgiveness makes a demand on the injured party. Similar to the self-discipline that Prospero asked of Caliban and Ferdinand, forgiveness demands that the aggrieved relinquish any desire to personally punish the wrongdoer. Faced with a choice between revenge or mercy, Prospero's decision enacts the same truth he has instilled in others: that the self-discipline holding selfish desires in check promotes God's design for a fallen world, that obedience to that principle makes all of nature's abundant provisions available.

Prospero himself has to undergo his own tempest before he understood this lesson fully, and even now, at this crucial moment, it takes an act of will. His decision demonstrates that he has acquired the self-discipline missing from his tenure as Duke of Milan, for, as Prospero explains to Miranda, his brother, Antonio, was able to seize his title and authority because of his obsession with magic:

> My brother and thy uncle, call'd Antonio...

> He whom next thyself
> Of all the world I lov'd, and to him put
> The manage of my state... being so reputed
> In dignity, and for the liberal arts
> Without parallel; those being my study,
> The government I cast upon my brother,
> And to my state grew stranger, being transported
> And rapt in secret studies. (1.2.66-77)

Just as Caliban chooses the wrong master when he follows his two foolish gods, Prospero had at one time allowed his fascination with magic to distract him from his duties. Magic had become his master. As he admits to Miranda, by "neglecting worldly ends," he "awak'd an evil nature" in Antonio that blossomed into mutiny and their forced removal from Milan. Those "secret studies" weren't in themselves problematic, for the secret arts he learned during those hours now enable Prospero to reform Alonso and regain his civil authority in Milan. What made his obsession with magic problematic is that he allowed it to become more important than his responsibilities. In effect, Prospero lost his dukedom, suffered exile to a remote and desolate island, and endangered his daughter because he made the same mistake that Caliban does. It is partly for this reason that Prospero now refers to his magical powers as this "vile art." Like anything of this world, it has the power to tempt man away from his assigned purpose. Vigilance and discipline are necessary to avoid such ultimately foolish distractions.

In the final scene, all of the unresolved issues are settled. For his faithful service, Ariel earns his freedom, and even Caliban recognizes a needs to be "wise hereafter," to "seek for grace," because he has been "a thrice-double ass . . . to take this drunkard for a god, and worship this dull fool." Most importantly, however, Prospero and Alonso are reconciled through the love of Ferdinand and Miranda, who greets these "three men of sin" with the naiveté of the innocent. "O wonder!" she exclaims with joyful excitement. "How beauteous mankind is! O brave new world, that has such people in't!" For the moment, forgiveness has indeed created a brave new world. Touched by the miracle that he has experienced, Alonso returns the stolen dukedom to Prospero and asks him to "pardon me my wrongs" (5.1.119).

But this calm, unfortunately, cannot last. Those devious brothers, Sebastian and Antonio, remain silent throughout the reconciliations except to observe that "the devil speaks in" Prospero who quietly threatens to reveal their thwarted plan to murder Alonso. Despite benefitting from the general rescue, the ironic misreading of the old magician shows both men remain trapped in their sinful nature, blind to both goodness and joy. Unchanged, their resilient evil makes Gonzalo's utopia an impossibility. As preparations to leave the island begin, everyone else has been relieved of their most immediate concerns except the play's two unhappy cynics.

The Tempest's final mystery is why Prospero disposes of his magic, which was instrumental in bringing about not only young love but repentance and reconciliation. Despite its obvious power to control people and events, however, Prospero decides to leave his magic behind:

> Graves at my command
> Have wak'd their sleepers, op'd, and let 'em forth
> By my so potent art. But this rough magic
> I here abjure; and when I have requir'd
> Some heavenly music (which even now I do)
> To work mine end upon their senses that
> This airy charm is for, I'll break my staff,
> Bury it certain fathoms in the earth,
> And deeper than did ever plummet sound
> I'll drown my book. (5.1.48-57)

What makes Prospero's magic "rough" is precisely its unlimited power, the temptation to use it merely to satisfy personal pique. Portia's speech on mercy sheds light on

Prospero's surprising decision, for she reminds her audience that those privileged with authority need to maintain a moral and spiritual connection with their Maker. "Earthly power," she reminds us, "doth . . .show likest God's When mercy seasons justice." Human judgment requires the discipline to subsume the merely personal before mercy can reflect what God generously shows His people. Prospero's magic is a "vile art" because it contains the possibility of violating this divine standard set for authority. Having been tempted to avenge his unjust exile, Prospero understands why he must reject the alluring power of his magic.

Though Prospero resists the temptations of unchecked power, his magic is primarily used to educate and enlighten rather than to harm. Prospero can be strict and demanding, but, with the benevolent authority of a caring father, he seeks to instill the spirit of self-sacrifice and discipline enabling his willing students to maintain their allegiance to good rather than to evil. As Ms. Colie writes in *Shakespeare's Living Art*:

> This, then, is Prospero's "art": to heighten nature's effects so that the miraculous achievement of human kindness, human solidarity, and human gentleness may be seen for the rarity it is: the patient, gifted work of self-civilizing men and women, who, on the one hand, pull themselves out of a bestial life and, on the other, resist the moral temptations omnipresent in the complexity of any society and civilization. (291)

The similarities between Prospero's magic and Shakespeare's art make it entirely appropriate to recall Shakespeare's cultural and personal circumstance: an aging man about to retire from a theater under attack by sometimes legalistic and judgmental moralists. The possible termination of what he loved, of everything he had accomplished, might well have raised questions about the purpose of his professional life. If so, he needn't have worried, especially because, four hundred years and counting, his art encourages his followers to examine and debate what distinguishes the merely erotic from love, what's good from what's evil, what's truly human from the bestial.

The island where *The Tempest* takes place is a magical setting where the difference between good and evil can easily be discerned, where true and innocent love prevails, where lives can be transformed for the better, where forgiveness engenders reconciliation. It is a pastoral, idyllic setting whose unreality we willingly but only momentarily accept as real. Like Prospero, we know it cannot last beyond the two hours or so that actors practice their art, their magic, onstage. Like Prospero, we must leave the magic behind and return to our real lives, drab and ordinary as those might be. But it is precisely there that our choices matter most. As he draws the action to its proper conclusion, Prospero is completely transparent about this:

> Our revels now are ended. These our actors
> (As I foretold you) were all spirits, and
> Are melted into air, thin air. . . . the gorgeous palaces,
> The solemn temples, the great globe itself,
> Yea, all which it inherit, shall dissolve,
> And like the insubstantial pageant faded,
> Leave not a rack behind. We are such stuff
> As dreams are made on; and our little life
> Is rounded with a sleep. (4.1.148-158)

The passage refers to all three levels of our experience of *The Tempest*: the magical island, capable of transforming Alonso; the play that the audience has just witnessed; and, of course, everyone's encounter with this world, with its "insubstantial pageants." All are "rounded with a sleep." Death and the grave will bring all of that to an end. The question is, what have we learned? How will that change our lives? While it still matters, will we move away from what makes us susceptible to evil and toward what's good?

Prospero returns to the "real" world of Milan, without the magic, where "every third thought shall be [his] grave."

The inevitability of that final sleep will serve to keep him focused on what matters, what's far more real than what uncivil natural man values, the flashy garments blowing in the breeze. Concluding a very insightful essay on *The Tempest*, Northrop Frye deserves the final word:

> In the Epilogue Prospero tells us that he has used up all his magic, and the rest is up to us. We then hear him pleading for release, in a tone echoing the Lord's Prayer and going far beyond any conventional appeal for applause. How are we to release him? In many tales of the *Tempest* type, the island sinks back into the sea when the magic leaves. But we, going out of the theater, perhaps have it in our pockets. . . ; perhaps our children can sow the seeds. . . and bring forth again the island that the world has been searching for since the dawn of history, the island that is both nature and human society restored to their original form, where there is no sovereignty and yet where all of us are kings. (*On Shakespeare*, 186)

Prospero's island is not quite Eden, but that's precisely why the ability to distinguish between good and evil matters greatly, and in this realm, the magic of Shakespeare's art has a real and valid purpose.

The Rarer Action

•◆•◆•◆•◆•◆•

The rarer action is in virtue than in vengeance.
(Prospero, 5.1.27-28)

So, after reviewing these eleven plays, how should Shakespeare be remembered? Most readers will likely come away with two impressions: first, how artfully he presented deeply felt moral truths to his fellow countrymen and, second, a sense of what the man himself might have been like. As mentioned in the introduction, Jonson, the man who penned the dedicatory poem for the First Folio, claimed that the plays bore the image of the artist who wrote them. They reflect, that is, what the man believed and probably how he bore himself in the world. That his fellow actors saw fit to undertake the arduous and financially risky proposition of publishing his works is a strong indication of the affection they held for him.

Perhaps the basis for that regard is too obvious to be stated, but a recent biography by Stephen Greenblatt, the Harvard professor who articulated New Historicism's foundational principles mentioned briefly in the first chapter, draws a very different conclusion. Though he also spends considerable time looking at religious influences that might have affected Shakespeare's plays, Greenblatt argues that the tensions between Catholic and Protestant were of more consequence than orthodox beliefs. Unlike Thomas Campion, a Catholic who refused to denounce his religious convictions and who paid for that with his life, Greenblatt's Shakespeare is a morally timid individual unable to live out any of his core values. Citing evidence that Shakespeare's father might have had Catholic leanings, he suggests that William likely absorbed that sentiment but suppressed it while working with a theater company financially supported by an aggressively Anglican aristocracy. Moreover, from Shakespeare's migration to London soon after marrying Anne Hathaway, Greenblatt extrapolates an estrangement resulting from his homosexual inclinations. Because of this ingrained hypocrisy, he suggests, Shakespeare's retirement in Stratford had to have been devoid of any recognizable faith and love. He concludes:

> Shakespeare began his life with questions about his faith, his love, and his social role. He had never found anything equivalent to the faith on which some of his contemporaries had staked their lives. If he had once been drawn toward such a commitment, he had turned away from it many years before. To be sure, he had infused his theatrical vision with the vital remnants of that faith, but he never lost sight of the unreality of the stage and never pretended that his literary visions could simply substitute for the beliefs that led Campion to his death. And though he may have had brief glimpses of bliss, he had never found or could never realize the love of which he wrote and dreamed so powerfully. (*Will in the World* 388)

For Greenblatt, Shakespeare's clandestine Catholicism, his suppressed homosexuality, his exodus to London to escape a marriage he didn't want, inevitably lead to an emotionally and sexually unhappy life. Given New Historicism's bias against those old, dead, white men for their supposedly unsavory views of race, sexuality, and individual liberty, a miserable and gloomy portrait was almost certainly predictable. Whatever disagreements a person might have with Bloom's critique of Shakespeare's plays, he was arguing vigorously against New Historicism's excesses and is to be commended for his deep appreciation of Shakespeare's contribution to Western culture.

But the problem with this biography isn't just a lack of appreciation for thirty-six literary artifacts. What easily gets lost in Greenblatt's interesting social commentary is the paucity of evidence that actually applies to the subject of the biography. The carefully selected cultural history and the person under scrutiny are only connected by a leap of faith. Do we have any evidence of Shakespeare's Catholicism or homosexuality? Since the few records specifically about Shakespeare's life have to do with baptisms, weddings, land contracts, and legal proceedings, it is virtually impossible to know anything about his private life, let alone whether he knew anything about bliss. If this speculative biography about Shakespeare's supposed homosexuality is meant to support the denigration of the West's literary icons, then it is equally plausible that Rosalind, Cordelia, and Cleopatra exist because Shakespeare valued and enjoyed the company of steadfastly loving women, that his views on sin and redemption were deeply Christian rather than simply Catholic or Protestant.

So, again, how should we remember this man? What basis do we have for projecting what he may have been like? Shakespeare's peers show us the way, for Greenblatt's gloomy conclusion is contradicted by Jonson's claim that these moving, sometimes glorious plays accurately reflect who the author was and what he was like. This from a man who worked with and knew Shakespeare personally. When Jonson wrote his poem, Shakespeare had been dead for almost seven years, so his admirer had little reason to flatter. In fact, anecdotal evidence indicates that Shakespeare was not only loving and forgiving but the cause of those virtues in others, to paraphrase that great wit, Falstaff. His professional relationship with his fellow actors and with Jonson makes the point.

Despite his education and a comic predisposition, Jonson had a reputation for a choleric temper. Early in his career, he quarreled with a man by the name of Gabriel Spenser, one of the actors in Shakespeare's theater company. Their disagreement ended sordidly when Jonson killed his antagonist in a duel. Though a legal loophole allowed Jonson to avoid execution, he could not escape other consequences altogether. Phillip Henslowe, one of the founding members of Shakespeare's company, was greatly dismayed by Spenser's death. In a letter to a friend, he complained that he had "lost one of my company, which hurteth me greatly; that is Gabriel, for he is slain in Hogsdon Fields by the hands of Benjamin Jonson, bricklayer" (Wells 134). The reference to Jonson as a lowly bricklayer reflects Henslowe's displeasure with the rival playwright's actions. As a result of that unfortunate death, the managers of the Globe Theater refused to perform Jonson's next comedy, *Every Man In His Humour*. But Shakespeare, also one of the founding members of the company, read the manuscript and intervened on Jonson's behalf. Not only was the play performed at the Globe, but Shakespeare apparently acted one of the significant parts. This gesture resurrected Jonson's stage reputation, and he and Shakespeare became relatively good friends as a result. They disagreed on many aspects of the theater, but from that time on Jonson never forgot the kindness Shakespeare had shown him.

In the fall of 1623, however, almost thirty years after this incident, Jonson had an opportunity to repay Shakespeare's compassion. A remarkable literary event was about to occur, the publication of Shakespeare's collected plays. Two men who had partnered with him at the Globe Theater, John Hemmings and Henry Condell, had been working since their colleague's passing to preserve his plays. All three men had been business partners, good friends as well as fellow actors. Their friendship was so solid, in fact, that John and Henry helped care for William's fatherless children after his death. Though it isn't known for sure if Condell had been with Shakespeare from the start of their theatrical careers, Hemmings not only had been but had also witnessed the writing and production of each play. Because of his intimate knowledge of the plays and of their author, he was the perfect choice to oversee such an important and arduous task as a collected edition. Without their familiarity with the plays and the author himself, confidence in the canon would be much weaker.

The First Folio project was something of a financial gamble, however, because the physically larger folio editions were generally more expensive than the average Elizabethan would be willing to pay. Moreover, it was unusual, almost presumptuous, to package theatrical works as literature. But Hemmings and Condell clearly understood the cultural value of what they were dealing with. To lend the Folio the proper caché, therefore, they dedicated it to William Herbert, Earl of Pembroke, who had long been a major sponsor of Shakespeare's theater company. This too was somewhat presumptuous, for, normally, only poets dedicated their volumes to an important aristocrat. Unlike petty dramatists, poets considered their works to be literary art and used such dedications to win the patronage of wealthy nobles willing to pay to see their names in print. But Hemmings and Condell took one additional step to ensure the success of their effort: they asked Jonson to write a commemorative verse for the Folio's cover pages. Because of Shakespeare's earlier kindness, Jonson's poem of some eighty lines was warm and full of genuine admiration. Shakespeare's work, he wrote, is far superior to that of those renowned English poets, Chaucer and Spenser. He even equates Shakespeare with the great Greek playwrights, Aeschylus, Euripides, Sophocles for tragedy, and Aristophanes, Terence, and Plautus for comedy. From a man well-educated in both Greek and Latin literature, this was high praise indeed.

The First Folio, then, represents the remarkable devotion of three men to a friend's life and art, and Western culture owes them a debt of gratitude for that vision and persistence. What is worth speculating about is why Jonson, Hemmings, and Condell would participate in such a financially risky and culturally presumptuous undertaking if not for the love and respect they felt for both the plays and the man who wrote them.

Because we have no documents that are clearly in his own hand other than the plays, Shakespeare the man will always remain something of an enigma, and the only reliable documentation we have of him is what Hemmings and Condell edited into the First Folio. What we see in these plays is what we can reasonably determine about the man: extraordinary talent, a marvelous facility with language, an ability to view people objectively and with minimal personal prejudice, a consistent sense of fairness and balance, an awareness of the universality of sin and suffering, a keen understanding of what genuine love demands and what it promises, and a deeply felt conviction of God's presence, His love and mercy, in human endeavors. In light of such enduring truths, whether he was gay or Catholic seems either improbable, irrelevant, or both.

In the end, Shakespeare's enduring appeal rests upon his relationship with his audience, which contrasts sharply with his friend and rival, Jonson, who could be quite prickly about the public reception his plays received. Somewhat peeved by Shakespeare's success despite his ignorance of classical standards, Jonson tried to educate his audience about the necessary rules of dramatic structure. In his short but illuminating book on Shakespearean comedy, *A Natural Perspective*, Northrop Frye describes with sly irony Jonson's defense of the very convoluted and long-forgotten comedy, *The Magnetic Lady*:

> There is something very disarming in the way that Jonson, both here and in the entr'actes to his next play, *The Magnetic Lady*, attempts to instruct us in the art of liking Jonson. He would call our attention particularly to the extraordinary skill with which the play has been constructed. Is not his protasis logically and clearly laid out in the first act, his epitasis developed from it with equal clarity and logic, his fourth act a catastasis or cleverly disguised recognition scene, where the recognitions are false clues, and his fifth act a brilliantly resolved catastrophe, where all is made clear? (15)

Though it was most likely counter-productive, Jonson, it seems, was not above haranguing his audience about their ignorance of rhetorical and dramatic standards. Not surprisingly, Jonson's haughty marketing strategy never burnished his reputation as brightly as Shakespeare's selfless attention to theatrical success. Never one to slavishly follow any rule except what worked on stage, Shakespeare's first objective was to please his audience. As much businessman as playwright and actor, he understood that his job was not to insult his audience but to motivate them to return to his theater for more. In the end, his lack of a university education actually helped him avoid any obsessive adherence to rules, academic or otherwise. After *Titus*, his short experiment with Senecan tragedy, what he did possess and what he learned to trust was an uncanny ability to please his audience, to give them plays they not only enjoyed but plays that also enlightened.

Above all, Shakespeare was a master storyteller. As the very dramatic opening scene of *Hamlet* indicates, he knew how to capture an audience's attention. He absorbed and experimented with both comic and tragic conventions, using only those that made theatrical sense, discarding those, like Seneca's grotesquely bloody spectacles, that didn't. He intuitively understood dramatic rhythm and pacing; he understood that tension could be built in successive waves only to be relieved in the final scenes. That awareness of rhythm and pacing made him fearlessly unrestrained about mingling genres, much to the dismay of his less imaginative rivals and critics. *Lear*, for example, intermixes the comic fool with the deeply tragic experience of his royal master. And there is a shade of tragic pathos in Malvolio's comic imprisonment in a symbolically darkened cell. Comfortably foregoing any pretense of realism in his late romances, he blithely incorporates supernatural spirits and magic into a story that functions quite well as fairytale, as serious drama, or as an elegant combination of both. Throughout his career, Shakespeare's attention to the art of storytelling is what immediately captivates an audience and brings it willingly and happily into the dramatic worlds he created for the stage.

Based on existing attendance records, Londoners were quite willing to spend a penny or two to set aside their daily cares and watch two hours of make-believe transpire on stage. Shakespeare was very aware of the inherent power in this ability to create imaginary worlds, some realistic, as in the histories, some not, as in the romances. He was also fully aware that his audiences were, in some sense, participants in the plays because of their imaginative involvement. And he was grateful for their attention, often thanking them at the end of his plays. Alone on stage, the magician Prospero provides a representative epilogue for his play, *The Tempest:*

> Let me not,
> Since I have my dukedom got,
> And pardon'd the deceiver, dwell
> In this bare island by your spell,
> But release me from my bands
> With the help of your good hands.
> Gentle breath of yours my sails
> Must fill, or else my project fails,
> Which was to please.   Now I want
> Spirits to enforce, art to enchant,
> And my ending is despair,
> Unless I be reliev'd by prayer,
> Which pierces so, that it assaults
> Mercy itself, and frees all faults,
> As you from crimes would pardon'd be,
> Let your indulgence set me free. (Epilogue 5-20)

With faint echoes of the Lord's Prayer, this charming appeal for a minute or two of enthusiastic applause to indicate their willingness to forgive the play's faults and dispel the illusion also deftly manages to allude to the play's themes of mercy and freedom. Unlike Jonson's grumpy antagonism, Shakespeare cultivated this symbiotic relationship with his audience, a posture that reflects a gentle and humble spirit appreciative of their patronage and their attention. It is undoubtedly that spirit that endeared him not only to his audience but also to his co-workers who were instrumental in bringing that First Folio to publication.

Clearly, though, there was much more to Shakespeare's popularity than good public relations and intriguing stories. It is fair to say that Shakespeare's popularity among his fellow Londoners rested in large part on a bedrock of shared ideas, values, and assumptions presented with deliberate attention to dramatic and artistic detail. As the close readings in the previous chapters have indicated, this consummate artist usually constructed parallel dramatic structures to encourage comparisons between characters. Such comparisons develop a variety of themes that acquire further nuance through an intricate web of imagery.

How much of Shakespeare's structural and thematic complexity could his Elizabethan audience actually appreciate, though? Does such close analysis read more into the plays than the average Elizabethan would ever find? To assume they could not distinguish between good and bad drama is not borne out by historical evidence. As Alfred Harbage notes in *Shakespeare's Audience:*

> There is no need to magnify the individual [Elizabethan] spectator. All that Shakespeare had to offer was immediately apparent to him no more than it is to us. He was willing to accept on the average much less than Shakespeare offered. But he preferred Shakespeare. . . . He found in these plays room for his soul at its widest dimension. He preferred too much to too little. He could grasp some things, touch others, and sense the presence of more. (160)

The Elizabethans experienced Shakespearean drama, then, exactly as audiences do today, which is to say with a pleasure that is not diminished by an awareness that these plays contain a richness sensed in performance but only understood through a careful reading of the text.

The pleasure derived from these plays has manifold causes and strikes different people in different ways, but what shines through most clearly to nearly everyone, even today, are those shared values. Precisely because Shakespeare lacked a university education, he shared an affinity with his audience that eluded Jonson. As Harbage mentions elsewhere, the greater portion of his audience was composed of the working classes of London, people who had acquired an education similar to Shakespeare's own (82). As a result, author and audience worked with a set of common assumptions and beliefs. As Frye astutely observes:

> It is consistent with Shakespeare's perfect objectivity that he should show no signs of wanting to improve his audience's tastes, or to address the more instructed members of it with a particular intimacy. His chief motive in writing, apparently, was to make money, which is the best motive for writing yet discovered, as it creates exactly the right blend of detachment and concern. He seems to start out with an almost empathic relation to his audience: their assumptions about patriotism and sovereignty, their clichés about Frenchmen and Jews, their notions of what constitutes a joke, seem to be acceptable to him as dramatic postulates. (*A Natural* 38)

This set of shared opinions and values, including religious values, it should be noted, removes any incentive to preach or educate, to insert authorial statements where they aren't needed. With no incentive to preach, characters are free to speak for themselves. Withholding any judgment and allowing characters to exhibit unique personalities through their language is what Frye means by Shakespeare's "perfect objectivity." Where Jonson craved attention and accolades, the egoless Shakespeare disappears behind his story, allowing his characters to come alive for themselves. As a dramatic tool, this verisimilitude takes advantage of the normal desire to understand what people are really like behind their public faces. It is why, even today, readers delve into the motives of these characters and seek to understand why they do what they do.

To some extent, then, Bloom is right to extol Shakespeare's ability to create uniquely vital characters. While each is given a voice suitable to their thematic purpose, their individuality evokes genuine emotional responses, just as real people do. Falstaff's playfulness, Hamlet's inquisitive intelligence, and Lear's justifiable outrage at being grievously wronged inspire genuine feelings of delight, awe, and sympathy. They speak in ways and about topics that seem significant, yet also absolutely true to life. But, as we have seen, acknowledging that is not sufficient. It may very well be reasonable to prefer Falstaff to Hotspur, Hamlet to Polonius, Lear to Gloucester, but the implicit invitation to contrast characters includes an invitation to recognize their similarities as well: to see how both Falstaff and Hotspur dilute the real meaning of honor; to recognize how both Hamlet and Polonius misread what they observe; to recognize that the mad Lear and the blind Gloucester have both been victimized by opportunistic and selfish children. Though uniquely individual within their dramatic context, each of these main characters is meant to be evaluated and judged by their similarities to and differences from other characters. While vitality of characterization is certainly noteworthy, it was one tool among many Shakespeare used to enhance his story, to draw his audience into the play's action, and to validate what they knew was right and good.

But life-like characterizations were not the only means by which he acquired the involvement of his audience. Another means by which Shakespeare deliberately met the assumptions and expectations of his audience was his reliance on dramatic convention. This was particularly true of his comedies and late romances, both of which lend themselves to plot patterns and character types. Comic confusions of identity are initiated by disguised twins or the displacement of court aristocrats onto a remote island where what once seemed normal suddenly appears to be completely abnormal. Regardless of their origins in classical comedy, these conventions were recognizable artistic patterns to his audience. The development of Shakespearean tragedy, however, was a bit different.

Perhaps fortunately, there were no widely accepted conventions for tragedy. The only well-known pattern for tragic action was Seneca, and while Shakespeare tried that formula once, he quickly saw its limitations and moved on. Beginning with Thomas Sackville's, *Gorboduc*, first performed in 1561, three years before Shakespeare was born, the Elizabethan fascination with their own history eventually generated an alternative pattern for Shakespeare's tragedies. As Normand Berlin writes, Sackville's play about the Duke of Buckingham:

> . . .confronts the important question of tragic responsibility in a way that directly anticipates later Elizabethan tragedy. . . . Sackville fuses the ideas of Fortune, individual responsibility, and God's justice; he makes [the protagonist] responsible for his own actions which cause him to become a slave of Fortune and which lead to his fall and death. At the same time, Sackville surrounds this fusion with an air of mystery (the constant use of the question), emphasizes the idea of mutability, and propels the narrative by means of the revenge theme. . . . In this tragical narrative, therefore, Sackville brought to Elizabethan tragedy one approach to the complexity of tragic responsibility – a tragic character who errs but is sympathetic. . . . (*Thomas Sackville* 121)

Because this tragic pattern of great men who err and fall from fortune's favor was played out many times throughout English history, it evolved quite naturally from Shakespeare's experiments in the history genre. The story of the self-involved royal protagonist of *Richard II* proved to be a very workable tragic pattern, one that provided depth and richness to human suffering. After the delightful experiment of *Romeo and Juliet*, which effortlessly turns a comic pattern into a courtly love tragedy, the capacity for ruthlessly honest self-examination became the gateway to the great tragedies of *Hamlet*, *Macbeth*, *Lear*, and, yes, Cleopatra, a woman who knew what she wanted and was willing to wait patiently, like the Viola of *Twelfth Night*, for her man to understand who she really was.

One final and very significant difference between Jonson and Shakespeare, one that may very well explain the difference between their reputations four hundred years later, is Shakespeare's willingness to experiment with different genres. For all his immense talent, Jonson was primarily a comic or satiric dramatist only. Unlike Shakespeare, he never had the inclination or the natural talent to produce anything vastly different in kind. But Shakespeare's forays into different genres like history, comedy, tragedy, and romance forced him to confront commonly experienced human problems from different perspectives, in different moods, with different types of language. By doing so, these different perspectives cross-pollinated each other, and the result is often a more fully-rounded understanding of character and issues. Even common comic types like Shylock or Malvolio are given some very human qualities that soften their hard edges. It is this comprehensiveness, as some critics term it, that separates Shakespeare from his contemporaries. By way of contrast, Jonson adhered to a theory of comedy that was based on the four humours, roughly equivalent to accepted Elizabethan psychological categories. Funny as these comic types could be, they were two-dimensional characterizations and could never be confused with the very human vitality of Juliet's nurse or the Falstaff of *1 Henry 4*.

Along with his sensitivity to the common assumptions of his audience, then, Shakespeare's very thoughtful and intelligent experimentation with different genres served to enrich all his plays. Not only do his characters gain unique and very human qualities as a result, but the themes explored in each play, whether comedy or tragedy, have an intellectual depth that continues to attract critical attention four centuries later. This is not to say that his ideas are in any way *avant garde* for his time or ours. Far from it, in fact. Instead, they are commonplace, a worldview shared with a solidly Christian audience. Rather than Bloom's anachronistic nihilism, the ideas promulgated in Shakespeare's plays reflect the ancient and enduring truths of the Bible that were familiar to every church-going Elizabethan. If Richard II's failure to fulfill his royal duties led to the loss of his crown, his self-indulgent nature was easily recognized by the audience who shared the same sin in less significant ways. All are punished for their complicity, declares the prince at the end of *Romeo and Juliet*. The ancient wisdom of the Bible requires the moral humility that can recognize the essential commonalities of human existence, including the pervasiveness of sin, the need for forgiveness, the hunger for union with another that reflects the very nature of the divine.

All of these factors differentiate Shakespeare from the other playwrights of his era, including the best of his rivals, Marlowe and Jonson. Marlowe, possibly an atheist, died young and wrote only one or two plays that maintain any interest today. Except for an occasional academic production of his *Doctor Faustus*, his works are rarely performed on stage anymore. Because Jonson's comedies and satires reveal the kind of wit and invention that still resonates with modern audiences, his works have enjoyed a somewhat better fate. But neither of these authors exhibits the depth, richness, or wisdom that is so evident in Shakespeare, almost from the beginning of his career. There are many explanations for this, as this chapter has argued, but central to all of them is a humility that is completely aware of our necessary dependence on divine grace. On this, Northrop Frye deserves the last word:

> What Shakespeare has that Jonson neither has nor wants is the sense of nature as comprising not merely an order but a power, at once supernatural and connatural, expressed most eloquently in the dance and controlled either by benevolent human magic or by divine will. Prospero in particular may appropriately be said to make nature afraid, as he treats nature, including the spirits of the elements, much as Petruchio [in *The Taming of the Shrew*] treats Katharina. . . .[In] the myth of nature in Shakespeare. . .the emphasis is thrown, not on the visible rational order that obeys, but on the mysterious personal force that commands. As a somewhat bewildered Theseus remarks [in *A Midsummer Night's Dream*], after the world represented by his authority is turned upside down by the fairies in the forest:
>
>> Such tricks hath strong imagination,
>> That, if it would but apprehend some joy,
>> It comprehends some bringer of that joy.
>> (*A Natural* 71)

Shakespeare's view of nature, including human nature, is not theological in any ordinary or obvious sense. For him, the attributes of the "bringer of joy" seem to remain largely mysterious, what Hamlet, paraphrasing the gospel of Matthew, refers to as that "special providence in the fall of a sparrow." Anything more than that eludes the fallible human eye, and there is not much sense in peering through the gray fog of this world to try to catch a better glimpse of the eternal. That will come in due time.

What can be known, what can be valued and cherished, is the evidence of the divine working within the world of human experience. This is the very premise of the Bible itself, which teaches that such evidence is all around. And that conviction is the source of Shakespeare's contagious admiration for all the miracles, both small and large, evident in our world. We need only think of Cordelia, without whom Lear would never be more than an angry old man raging at the ingratitude of his wicked daughters. Or of Juliet, without whom Romeo would indeed be little more than "fortune's fool." Or of the innocent and ever-faithful Desdemona, murdered by an uncomprehending husband who has been duped by the devil incarnate. Or, finally, of the magnificent Cleopatra, whose love for Antony transforms her last moments on earth into divine fire and air. None of this has anything to do with feminism, either, for, given Goneril and Regan, given Lady Macbeth or Gertrude, it is not really about the social, political, or financial stature of women. It is, however, about the spark of the divine visible through the loving relationship some men have with some women, both of whom must first be blessed with a heart habitually vulnerable to the world and therefore to each other. This, to use Frye's terminology, is the force in nature that, despite evil and human folly, brings two lovers together. It is the force that reconciles parents with children. It excises the evil of Macbeth and restores social order and peace. This is the evidence that can be seen and acknowledged for what it reveals as well as what it cannot. In God's design for the world, human love is meant to reflect divine love. It is the divinely provided instrument we can use to glimpse His nature. While none of this provides an escape from suffering or death, human imagination can, as Theseus attests, apprehend through such things both the joy and the cause of joy.

  If Shakespeare's assumption about women in love could never be mistaken for modern feminism, neither should it be mistaken as strictly religious either. It seems especially noteworthy that his final tribute to this kind of love, *Antony and Cleopatra*, is set in the pagan environs of ancient Rome and Egypt, decades before that historic birth in Bethlehem. Shakespeare certainly had been exposed to the sectarian struggles between Catholics and Protestants and the horrors perpetrated in the name of "the one true" religion. The distinction he establishes in that play between the worldly and pragmatic Romans, who see love as sexual attraction employed in the service of political expediency, and the feminine luxury of Egypt suggests that the particular manifestation of the divine within the human knows no bounds, pays no attention whatsoever to the preconceived and limited notions of the religious. As the Bible stipulates, that force mentioned by Frye has been at work in human affairs from the very first moment of creation. Though it is an integral part of experience, it ultimately defies human comprehension. Other than a recognition that this is our experiential connection to the divine, the origin and manifestations of that love remain a mystery. What, we may rightly ask, can fully explain Juliet's feud-and-grave-defying connection to Romeo? Or Cordelia's sacrificial bond to the father who had so cruelly rejected her? Or Cleopatra's immortal longing to be Antony's wife, a mother to his children? These things defy the simplistic reductions of an Iago or even the well-meaning Enobarbus, friend to Antony. By its unshakeable constancy, genuine love defines how we must act in the world, yet its miraculous presence will forever remain essentially mysterious.

  The various influences that coalesced to make love the primary concern of Shakespeare's art are part of that mystery. Ideas from Ovid, courtly love conventions, and his Christian faith made that possible at the very time that theaters were flourishing in London and a young man from Stratford looked for work. All of this very well might not have happened, and we would have been the poorer for that cultural void. Each of these three influences played a part in the way he presented the experience of love on stage, but it was his Christian faith that gave his presentations the kind of moral depth and richness that made his greatest plays possible. At the very heart of those plays, Shakespeare demonstrates his conviction that our human nature involves us in intractable sin and, as a consequence, necessitates forgiveness. Only through such acts of loving generosity do we confirm our connection to the divine.

Assuredly, there are significant differences between contemporary democracies and Shakespeare's political and cultural environment. Elizabethan culture had not yet developed a mature regard for human rights. In certain respects, it was far less tolerant than modern Western societies. And even though it was stoutly Christian in its beliefs, it was not uniformly better at implementing those beliefs than our own. Perhaps it was precisely because of that gap between intention and act that Shakespeare used his art to demonstrate the difference between good and evil and to call his audience to the rarer action.

Works Cited

Bate, Jonathan. *How the Classics Made Shakespeare.* Princeton UP, 2019.

---,*Shakespeare and Ovid*, Oxford UP, 2001.

Berlin, Normand. *The Secret Cause: A Discussion of Tragedy.* U of Massachusetts P, 1981.

---,*Thomas Sackville.* Twayne Publishers, Inc.,1974.

Bindoff, S.T. *Tudor England.* Penguin Books, 1950.

Bloom, Harold. *Shakespeare: The Invention of the Human.* Riverhead Books, 1998.

Brooks, Cleanth. "The Naked Babe and the Cloak of Manliness." *Modern Shakespearean Criticism: Essays on Style, Dramaturgy, and the Major Plays,* edited by Alvin B. Kernan, Harcourt Brace Jovanovich, Inc., 1970, pp.385-403.

Brown, John Russell. *Shakespeare and His Comedies.* Methuen & Co. LTD, 1957.

Chute, Marchette. *Shakespeare of London.* E.P. Dutton Co., Inc, 1949.

Colie, Rosalie L. *Shakespeare's Living Art.* Princeton UP, 1974.

Cunningham, Dolora G. "Macbeth: The Tragedy of the Hardened Heart." *Approaches to Macbeth*, edited by Jay L. Halio, Wadsworth Publishing Company, Inc., 1966, pp. 70-80.

Danby, John. "Antony and Cleopatra: A Shakespearean Adjustment." *Modern Shakespearean Criticism: Essays on Style, Dramaturgy, and the*

Major Plays, edited by Alvin B. Kernan, Harcourt Brace Jovanovich, Inc., 1970, pp.407-426.

Ellis, Havelock, ed. *Christopher Marlow: Five Plays.* Hill and Wang, 1956.

Frye, Northrop. *Anatomy of Criticism: Four Essays.* Princeton UP, 1968.

---,*A Natural Perspective: The Development of Shakespearean Comedy and Romance.* Harcourt, Brace, And World, Inc.,1965.

Greenblatt, Stephen. *Will in the World: How Shakespeare Became Shakespeare.* W.W. Norton & Company,2004.

Harbage, Alfred. *As They Liked It: A Study of Shakespeare's Moral Artistry.* U of Pennsylvania P, 1947.

---,*Shakespeare's Audience.* Columbia UP, 1941.

Heilman, Robert Bechtold. *This Great Stage: Image and Structure in King Lear.* U of Washington P, 1967.

---, *Magic in the Web.* U of Kentucky P, 1956.

Highet, Gilbert. *The Classical Tradition: Greek and Roman Influences on Western Literature.* Oxford UP, 1949.

Hubler, Edward. "The Economy of the Closed Heart." *Shakespeare: Modern Essays in Criticism,* edited by Leonard F. Dean, Oxford UP, 1967, pp. 467-476.

Karim-Cooper, Farah. The Great White Bard. Viking, 2023.

Kernan, Alvin B. "The Henriad: Shakespeare's Major History Play." *Modern Shakespearean Criticism: Essays on Style, Dramaturgy, and the Major Plays,* edited by Alvin B. Kernan, Harcourt Brace Jovanovich, Inc., 1970, pp.245-275.

Levin, Harry. *The Question of Hamlet.* Oxford UP, 1959.

Lewis, C.S. *The Allegory of Love: A Study in Medieval Tradition.* Oxford UP, 1967.

Loomba, Ania. *Shakespeare, Race, and Colonialism.* Oxford UP, 2002.

Rabkin, Norman. *Shakespeare and the Common Understanding.* The Free Press, 1967.

Rose, Mark. *Shakespearean Design.* Belknap Press of Harvard University, 1972.

Spencer, Theodore. *Shakespeare and the Nature of Man.* Collier Books, 1966.

Tillyard, E.M.W. *The Elizabethan World Picture.* Random House, 1941.

Wells, Stanley. *Shakespeare and Co.* Pantheon Books, 2006.

The New Jerusalem Bible. General editor, Henry Wansbrough, Doubleday, 1985.

The Riverside Shakespeare. General editor, G. Blakemore Evans, et. al., Houghton Mifflin Company, 1997.

www.ingramcontent.com/pod-product-compliance
Lightning Source LLC
Chambersburg PA
CBHW071229070526
44583CB00017B/2103